DIAMOND
A BIOGRAPHY

DIAMOND
A BIOGRAPHY

ALAN GROSSMAN, BILL TRUMAN, AND ROY OKI YAMANAKA

CONTEMPORARY
BOOKS, INC.
CHICAGO ▪ NEW YORK

Library of Congress Cataloging-in-Publication Data

Grossman, Alan.
　Diamond, a biography.

　1. Diamond, Neil.　2. Singers—United States—
Biography.　I. Truman, Bill.　II. Yamanaka, Roy Oki.
III. Title.
ML420.D54G7　　1987　　784.5'0092'4 [B]　　86-29260
ISBN 0-8092-4825-5

Published by Contemporary Books, Inc.
180 North Michigan Avenue, Chicago, Illinois 60601
Manufactured in the United States of America
Library of Congress Catalog Card Number: 86-29260
International Standard Book Number: 0-8092-4825-5

Published simultaneously in Canada by Beaverbooks, Ltd.
195 Allstate Parkway, Valleywood Business Park
Markham, Ontario L3R 4T8 Canada

Perseverance

Contents

Acknowledgments

The authors would like to thank the following publications and media sources for their help, whether or not they appear in this book: ABC-TV, ABC Radio Network, Associated Press, BBC Radio Network, *Billboard*, CBS-TV, *Chicago Tribune*, *Dick Clark's Music Magazine*, Cleveland *Plain Dealer*, *Cleveland Press*, *Detroit Free Press*, "Entertainment Tonight"/"This Week," *Family Weekly*, *Hit Parader*, *Hollywood Reporter*, *Indianapolis News*, KIIS Radio, KNX-FM Radio, *Ladies Home Journal*, Los Angeles *Herald-Examiner*, *Los Angeles Times*, *Marquee*, *Melody Maker*, NBC-TV, *Newsweek*, New York *Daily News*, *New York Times*, "Night Rock News," *Orange County Register*, *Phoenix Gazette*, *Playboy*, "PM Magazine," RKO Radio Network, *Rolling Stone/US*, *San Diego Union*, *Seattle Times*, *Seventeen*, *Showtime*, *Song Hits*, *St. Louis Globe-Democrat*, *St. Louis Post-Dispatch*, *Teen*, Time/Life Publications, United Press International, *USA Today*, *Variety*, *Washington Post*, WNBC Radio, and *Woman's Day*.

We want to thank the people at the University of Southern California whose support and encouragement made this book possible, especially Robert Conot, Lee Dye, Denton Z. Holland, and A. J. Langguth.

Finally, we are grateful for the support given us by family and friends, our agent Michael J. Hamilburg, and the special few who stuck by us through it all. Thanks, Bach.

The radio at the other end of the pool suddenly sent a shock wave of sound crashing through the hazy barrier surrounding my mind. It was a tinny and dissipated version of "Brother Love's Travelling Salvation Show," but it brought me back to the unpleasant reality that I had been avoiding: I had to go to work. Specifically, I had to go and turn out a piece on Neil Diamond, and if that sounds easy . . . let me tell you—it isn't.

It would be easy if I just copped out and printed the hour-long rap I had with him a while back, and though that interview was interesting, it never got down to the basic question of "who is Neil Diamond and why is he worth writing about in depth?" But to be perfectly honest, I still don't know who Neil Diamond is.

—Allan Rinde, *Hit Parader*, February 1971

Introduction: Solitary Man

Sixteen years and many hit records after Rinde made his attempt to explain who Neil Diamond is, the answer still remains a mystery. Interviewers posing personal questions to Diamond in countless publications from *Rolling Stone* to *LIFE*, the *Los Angeles Times*, and the scholarly *Current Biography*, have only come up with meager details about the man.

To call Diamond a private person is an understatement. He is proud and protective of his family and his ability to live a relatively normal life in his time away from work. Since the 1970s, he has been described as the anonymous superstar.

He rarely grants interviews, declining all but a few in recent years. Diamond is so guarded and self-conscious that little of what escapes can be considered revealing. It is common for him to set standards for questioning beforehand. Even Barbara Walters was unable to glean much new information from him.

1

His low public profile provides few gossip items. He is a self-avowed family man whose sixteen-year second marriage grows increasingly stronger from his need to participate in "everyday" life. Away from his music, he finds pleasure in riding motorcycles, playing chess, and taking his sons to video arcades and Los Angeles Lakers basketball games.

At the same time, this moody and quiet superstar has racked up dozens of hit singles and albums and broken concert attendance records around the world with his sensitive but brooding voice and a songwriting sensibility ranging from the brightest celebration to total despair.

"I Am . . . I Said," "Love on the Rocks," "You Don't Bring Me Flowers," "Solitary Man," "Longfellow Serenade," "September Morn'," "Holly Holy," "Play Me," "Cracklin' Rosie," "Heartlight," "Sweet Caroline," "Beautiful Noise," "Cherry, Cherry," "I Thank the Lord for the Night Time," "America," "Song Sung Blue," and many more. Everybody knows at least one.

Since 1966, Diamond has been one of American pop's most consistent successes. His early music for Bang Records was relatively straightforward rock, with a certain introspection that suggested a bridge between the appeal of an Elvis Presley and that of a Paul Simon.

His 1968–72 period with MCA's Uni label produced the bulk of his most famous songs and showed a change to a more mature sound, emphasizing ballads with full orchestration. The move established him as the performer whose music attracted audiences older than that of the rock generation.

Following his signing with Columbia Records in 1973, Diamond began almost exclusively to create traditionally styled pop music. In doing so, he completed his move up to the virtually untouchable plateau of "musical institution." His album releases were pre-sold hits, even through a four-year hiatus from concert touring (1972–76).

When Diamond's 1980 acting debut in *The Jazz Singer*

failed to win much critical praise or noteworthy box office success, critics believed that he had passed his peak and lost the young audiences. However, the soundtrack was a major triumph, and Diamond's subsequent American and European minitours continued to show his ability to draw substantial crowds. His June 1983 seven-night sell-out of the Forum in Los Angeles has yet to be equalled—not even by the Jacksons' much-heralded 1984 "Victory Tour."

Critical reaction to Diamond's music may be gauged roughly by age groups. Writers who identify closest with the era before or during his ascent to fame in the mid-1970s tend to like him. Most who began careers during the mid-1970s or later—after he had essentially given up rock for middle-of-the-road pop—consider him a mere antique. He is now past his twentieth anniversary year as a successful entertainer, and still there is no consensus as to what, if any, influence he has had on music.

Diamond's songs are beset by the conflict that forever divides critics and fans: the difference between artistry and entertainment. The rift has arisen over whether Diamond's music is simply slick entertainment or sincere artistic endeavor.

Because Diamond's main vogue as a timely songwriter came in the early 1970s, his work is judged by the "intellectual/relevant/innovative" standards that have characterized the post-1960s. Looking to enhance his stature among serious songwriters, he has undertaken ambitious projects more artistic than commercial. These works, including his soundtrack for *Jonathan Livingston Seagull* and acting debut in *The Jazz Singer*, have consistently received less acclaim than his more commercial works.

Diamond is an anomaly. His musical roots are closer to the period of pop music prior to rock & roll. He grew up listening to singing cowboys and Latin dance bands. As Diamond told the *Los Angeles Times*: "I'm like the Will Rogers of pop. There isn't a musical form I've heard that

I haven't liked. . . . Rock & roll was never substantial enough for me to devote my life to it. Music is substantial enough for me to devote my life to it."

Details of his life and early musical development have become lost and have been replaced by a standard, often error-filled biography which ignores the many questions which have grown out of the Diamond legend. Long-standing myths tend to substitute for any in-depth discussion of Diamond's thoughts, character, personality, or development.

Diamond is uncomfortable talking about himself, and his memory is sometimes hazy. His explanations vary from time to time and thus are often contradictory. He is equally inconsistent in his attitudes. He has gone on record as saying that he never wanted to be a singer and that he always wanted to be a singer. Since there is no evidence of deep, dark secrets in his past, this can only be attributed to an honest insecurity.

His character includes a faith in his talent in spite of an insecurity about his self-worth, a definite strain of activism displayed in his political alignments, and a reluctance to identify with modern musical trends. There is a certain protective shell about him, developed through a lonely childhood, a frustrating adolescence, some encounters with disagreeable business interests, a failed first marriage, and a general distaste for public relations.

In answering the question of who Neil Diamond really is, he often says he reveals himself most through his songs. He has declined to authorize this biography, stating he was too young and had far too much to accomplish before a biography was warranted.

The purpose of this book, then, is to put the proverbial pieces together and present another view of this man, who remains an enigma even as a devoted following is ready to place him among the greatest of all musical talents.

I wouldn't trust anything you didn't hear yourself on tape that came out of his mouth, as far as what's been written about him. I mean, not anything.

—Herb Cohen
Interview with the authors, December 1983

1
Brooklyn Roads
(1941–1958)

Neil Diamond's early history is sketchy, due in part to his reluctance to discuss it at length, and also because his recollections sometimes deviate from fact. As an example, four years were subtracted from his age in interviews during his early career—whether by his or his publicists' choice—to improve on his "youth appeal."

Neil Leslie Diamond was born January 24, 1941, to Akeeba and Rose Diamond, first-generation Americans of Polish-Russian ancestry. The Diamonds were poor shopkeepers who struggled to make ends meet. Neil slept in a dresser drawer for the first six months of his life because his parents couldn't afford a crib.

The Brooklyn-born singer has always had a soft spot in his heart for the infamous borough, and has drawn upon its inspiration for a sizeable portion of his songwriting catalog; his most recent work about the area is 1984's "Brooklyn on a Saturday Night."

"Brooklyn is not the easiest place in the world to grow up in, although I would not change that experience for anything," he would recall in 1971.

"I had my own dreams, like everybody has, and New York was a good place to have those kind of dreams because it was a very exciting city. We were always exposed to life—the raw ends of it were always near you. Ambulances going by, police, people, and children. It was there—all of life within a few blocks." He named the elements that make up the essence of New York: "The drama, the intensity, the loneliness, and the power." When asked by *Playboy* in 1980 why so many celebrities came out of Brooklyn, he replied, "We were indoors a lot. The weather wasn't so good. It's not as though we were on surfboards all day."

The Diamonds moved from apartment to apartment throughout Brooklyn as his father attempted to establish a successful dry goods (clothes and sewing supplies) business. Often during his first three years, Neil and his younger brother Harvey (born in 1943) were left in the care of their Orthodox Jewish grandparents who had been the first family members to settle in America. The first language taught to Neil and Harvey was Yiddish.

When Akeeba entered the Army in 1944, Rose, Neil, and Harvey accompanied him to Cheyenne, Wyoming, where he was stationed. Although Neil was only five when his family moved back to Brooklyn in 1946, he retained memories of the period—the mountains, the prairies, the western clothes, and the country music.

For quite a while afterward, Neil had just as many aspirations toward cowpunching and singing to a faithful horse as any boy his age. He idolized the cowboys of the silver screen and the songs they sang. His memories of Cheyenne heavily influenced him long after he'd hung up his cap pistols.

This brush with country music started his lifelong love of singing. Such an influence would logically lead him to folk music and eventually to material close to the rock & roll style. Listening to his music from the 1968–70 period points out that the western influences are still apparent in his most orchestrated works.

From his first day in grade school to his graduation from Lincoln High School in 1958, he attended nine different Brooklyn public schools. "Making and keeping friends was difficult under those circumstances, and I was, for the most part, an outsider in each new school," he said in a Uni Records press release.

Though a bright child, he consistently performed below expectations in class. He found it difficult to apply himself to his studies and had a genuine interest in only a few subjects, particularly science. Compared to the more scholarly Harvey and a cousin who was the smartest kid in his school, Neil had to live down being the black sheep of the family.

An introvert, he became very sensitive about himself— his big nose, bigger ears, gangly limbs, and nervous mannerisms. The feelings grew worse during the many times he found himself alone. He took to inventing imaginary companions—one of which returned to life in his pivotal 1967 song, "Shilo." The ingrained feelings of loneliness stayed with him as he grew older. Not until his teenage years did he really become comfortable with talking to his peers.

Diamond told *Seventeen* magazine in 1973 that his "perpetual outsider status gave me a lonely, solitary existence. Because of our financial situation, my mother worked, and I would come home from school to an empty house. That left a deep impression."

This is not to say that the family life was always unhappy. The Diamonds were a fairly close clan. Akeeba and Rose remained happily married until Akeeba's death in 1985, and despite the frustrating business failures, there was never a lack of food on the table. Neil's closest friend during their high school and college years, Herb Cohen, remembered: "They were very close. That [song] 'Brooklyn Roads' was a true story. He used to wait up for his father. I used to eat at his parents' house a lot. They were always very close."

But gaps developed between the family members as

they shared few common interests. His younger brother Harvey was deeply interested in electronics and gadgetry, whereas Neil leaned towards biology. As Neil told *Seventeen*, "Although we're friends now, we didn't have a close relationship as children; we were traveling in separate orbits around the same sun."

By adolescence they were closing the gap: "When I was fourteen, he built me a pair of sunglasses with windshield wipers. Once he gave me a crib sheet in the shape of a scroll inside a wristwatch. When you turned the stem, it gave you the answers. . . . I never had enough nerve to use it."

He told *People* magazine, "My brother could do or make anything mechanical. I had to lock my microscopes and guitars in the closet because he was always tearing them down and rebuilding them."

Diamond's father was usually busy at work, while his mother worked at odd jobs to supplement the family income. Though he remained close to his grandparents, he may have found it difficult to identify with their conservative Old World ways.

Given the choice, Neil would have preferred the chance to spend more time with his father. He has always described Akeeba as the family member he felt was his closest kindred spirit. "My father was a hippie in his head," Neil says. "He never made much money . . . just paid the bills. But he was happy . . . he found success in what he had. He treasured his independence and hoarded his freedom. We both have a strong need to be free of people . . . to run our lives our way."

Although he eventually worked for his father at the dry goods business, Neil wasn't really interested in the shop. Diamond remembered in a 1976 Australian interview with Michael Schildberger that he preferred looking at the outside world through the front window to waiting on customers. This prompted his father to tell him, "Neil, I want you always to remember this. Keep your eye on the doughnut and not on the hole."

His family had always been conscious of show business to a certain degree. Diamond has said that his maternal grandfather was one of those people who'd pick up an instrument and learn to play it in a week. Even more impressive was his paternal grandfather: "He was known as the greatest double-talk artist in New York. He'd give dissertations in clubs in English and Yiddish."

Akeeba was far from shy: "My father was an amateur theater buff. Let anyone announce they were putting on an amateur show any place, and he'd drop his tape measure and run to offer his services."

Neil might have been an introverted child in school, but he did sing and lip-sync to records (an act he'd picked up from his father) at family gatherings. The family was only too glad to indulge him in this interest. His public singing began at the age of three when Akeeba entered him in a children's singing contest. Neil won the grand prize—twenty-five cents—by mouthing selections from *The Marriage of Figaro* as it was played in the background. He eventually entered a few talent shows in elementary school but never won again.

Ironically, in one of these losses he was booed off the stage while imitating the original "jazz singer," Al Jolson. "I swore I'd come back and do it right someday," he said, following his signing to a second remake of the first talking film.

Music always played a large role in the Diamond household. Akeeba and Rose were avid ballroom-dance enthusiasts, to the degree that they used to crash wedding receptions just for the chance to dance.

The diverse family record collection exposed Neil to many different kinds of music. Along with big band hits of the 1930s and 1940s, Diamond grew up listening to the works of the era's legendary songwriters sung by equally famous popular vocalists, assorted classical titles, and traditional Yiddish material.

"In my father's shop, the radio was always on a Top Forty station . . . [my parents also] took me to ballrooms where I listened to the great dance bands like Tito Rodriguez and Tito Puente.''

Significantly, Diamond was unlike others of his musical generation in that he was not solely motivated as a performer by the coming of rock & roll. He had already been acquainted with at least three generations of music before Bill Haley and the Comets' "Rock Around the Clock." The first records he ever owned himself were early-1950s albums by the Weavers.

In 1980 he admitted to Robert Hilburn of the *Los Angeles Times* that Elvis Presley was not a major influence on him, "not so much as the Everly Brothers were. . . . Elvis was so very stylized and so unique, but the Everly Brothers made records that everybody could sing with, and everybody, even in Brooklyn, wanted to be the Everly Brothers. There were duets all over the place; people singing Everly Brothers music. So I think they— more than any of those early rock stars—affected me.''

At the age of ten, Neil was singing just such folk-country tunes to a neighborhood girl while pushing her on the swing. He spent hot summer nights on the front stoop singing under the moonlight.

The story circulates that he later formed an a cappella group with a few friends he had managed to make upon moving to a new neighborhood; and that they sang for change on streetcorners under the name the Memphis Backstreet Boys. Legends persist that this small taste of performing success, along with feelings of supposed alienation, may have led him to run away from home at fifteen to allegedly join a touring folk group in Kansas City called the Roadrunners.

Both of these episodes are thought to have been invented by some overzealous publicity people. Yet, they still turn up in various reference sources and seem contradictory to the general impression that Neil's teen years were spent almost entirely at home with his family. According to Herb Cohen, "They'd have died if he ran away. He might have dreamt about it, sure . . . but he never mentioned it." In any event, there is no evidence of Diamond as a paid entertainer prior to 1960.

Of the homes the family made in Brooklyn, the one where they lived the longest was the south-side flat "two floors above the butcher" described in Diamond's 1968 song, "Brooklyn Roads." Neil began working with Akeeba in the dry goods store, strengthening their father-son relationship and easing Neil's need for imaginary friends. But all too soon, a new set of growing pains emerged from a burgeoning adolescence which would partly be expressed on the neighborhood streets.

The last particularly dramatic aspect of his pre-adolescent years was his brief involvement with the street gangs which hung out in the notoriously tough areas around Coney Island. He explained to Schildberger in the 1976 Australian interview that most boys found it hard not to be in a gang. "We lived in a number of sections of Brooklyn that were poor. When you have poor kids running around with not very much to do, they tend to get into all kinds of trouble."

Although it may have been hard for him to express himself socially, "it was easy to settle things with my hands. I didn't have to look for trouble. There were always fights in Brooklyn. I was reliving all those Van Johnson war movies I used to go to."

Diamond told Schildberger that in one gang, he carried the weapons since the older boys figured him to be too small to fight. Neil quipped, "It was much quicker to duck than to punch."

Neil's experience as a juvenile delinquent ended when he was shot during a gang rumble. Although his wound was not severe, it was enough to set him straight for good.

In an effort to channel his frustrations in a constructive way, he began to read more, and he developed a particular fondness for Cyrano de Bergerac.

"Why Cyrano? First of all, because he was a misfit. He had this enormously long nose that just went on forever. . . . I was about fourteen or fifteen, and I was kind of an awkward kid, and so Cyrano certainly became someone I could identify with. The second reason: he was a great swordsman . . . and there was always a great deal of poetry and romance in swordsmanship. Later on, I started to study sabre fencing, and I know I did that because of Cyrano. And the third reason: that Cyrano was a poet. He wrote these beautiful poems to a woman whom he loved but could never have. I always ached for Cyrano because there he was, writing this stuff, and she never knew who it was from," he told the audience at his 1976 Sydney Sports Arena concert.

Fencing proved to be a terrific way to vent his aggressiveness. He now had an outlet for any violent tendency he might have, but the age-old teenage boy's lament—namely, how to get girls to notice—was another problem. "Only other fencers go to fencing matches," he said.

So Neil took another inspiration from de Bergerac and set about composing minor verse. Songwriting per se was far from his mind. "I started very practically. . . . Instead of talking to girls directly, I used to write them poems asking for dates or whatever. It worked! In fact, some of the other kids used my poems, and I became kind of a hit poet."

Neil claims little artistic merit for his early work: "The high school rhymes were dumb and simple, but for a kid who had never done anything well, it was a whole new thing."

The songwriting spark finally came in the summer of 1956, when the fifteen-year-old Diamond went to Surprise Lake Camp in upstate New York. Folksinger Pete Seeger, formerly of the Weavers and one of the most well-known left-wing voices of the Eisenhower era, appeared as an assembly guest to speak to the kids about his music and play a few tunes. For the occasion, a few of the campers performed an original song for Seeger.

Oddly enough, it was not Seeger's words or performance that changed Diamond, but the campers' song. It was then and there that he began to believe that perhaps he too could write—if not necessarily perform—his own songs.

Soon, he got his hands on his first guitar—a nine-dollar second-hand item. Depending on what story sounds best, it was either a sixteenth birthday gift from his parents or an installment-plan purchase that he paid off at the rate of a dollar a week. He began taking lessons but lost interest in them quickly—he did not yet have the discipline to devote himself to the technical aspects of playing. The lessons stopped after he had learned enough to write his first song.

Neil has since explained why he quit. "I wanted to play from the heart, and this they could never teach me." He did later admit that "[the lessons] were good in that they forced me to rely on melody and rhythm and the dramatic sense, as opposed to technical things."

(Actually, in 1966, Diamond said that he had taken piano lessons at age fourteen to please his parents: "I took lessons for a month, much longer than the guitar. I gave up the lessons when I felt I had achieved the virtuosity necessary for my career. And then I took up the comb and tissue paper. . . .")

His first song, written on the day he learned his first chord progression, was called "Hear Them Bells." It was little more than a tune with rhyming words, but it was a song. Diamond knew that he had at last found a means of expression.

"It had a melody, and a beginning, and an ending, and it rhymed. It was even pretty in places. The song had some value only to me, and I made a point of remembering, was how he described "Hear Them Bells." . . .

"That day I wrote my first song, it was like learning to talk. I was so excited at finding a way of expressing myself that I didn't want to just talk. I started screaming at the top of my lungs. I wrote four or five songs a day, all very consistent, all terrible."

In no time at all, Neil took to improving his writing through constant practice. "I wrote on anything I could find—envelopes, the back of receipts, paper bags. There was never enough paper in the beginning," Diamond said in his Uni Records biography.

His writing became a pastime with priority over anything else. "I used to sit in class and write songs while my teachers thought I was taking notes. You know what happened? I passed all my courses but one. I flunked music!"

How serious was Neil's ambition to be famous? Though he enjoyed playing and singing, at this time he did not believe he could make it as a performer—it seemed too fantastic. Songwriting was different—a person could be successful even if he remained faceless. Shyness was not as big a factor as was some hopeful sense of practicality on Diamond's part.

Originally, his parents were tolerant of his new passion, even when he suggested he might try pitching some of his songs to the Tin Pan Alley industry. "The family was pretty good about my songwriting. Songwriting was considered a kind of respectable thing. It wasn't all that unusual," he said.

But their patience was not absolute. Rose and Akeeba wanted something better for their son than they had, and even though they respected his talent, they wanted to be sure he knew what he wanted to do with his life. Diamond told Leeza Gibbons of the syndicated television show "Entertainment This Week" in 1986 that his parents arranged a meeting between himself and a respected (and prosperous) family friend.

"When I was about sixteen or seventeen, I didn't really know what I wanted to do and what I was interested in," Neil recalled. "So my dad asked a friend of his who was a very successful businessman to come and talk to me, and really get to the bottom of it. . . . I started to get angry with him because he was grilling me, and I said, 'I want to be a rock star.' It was the first time that ever came out of my mouth. I was a little bit shocked . . . but I had to stand up for it. And he looked at me like I was crazy and

I kind of felt a little crazy, but it felt good to say it."

Diamond had already started high school at Brooklyn's Erasmus Hall and sang in the mixed chorus with Barbra Streisand, although his only recollection of her at the time involved a crush she had on the choral director. The experience of singing Handel's *Messiah* with this choir at Christmas moved him to cry afterward and later inspired him to write "Childsong" for "The African Trilogy."

But before Neil entered his senior year, Akeeba was forced to relocate his business closer to Coney Island. The Diamonds moved from that flat above the butcher, near the corner of Church Avenue and Flatbush Street, to a house on West End Avenue in the Brighton Beach section of Brooklyn. With the move came the inevitable change of schools.

Neil began attending Lincoln High School in his junior year. Figuring he would probably not be changing schools again, he finally found the motivation to overcome his shyness. His father had graduated from Lincoln and had belonged to five extracurricular clubs, and Neil, trying to emulate his father, decided to match that and plunged wholeheartedly into after-school activities. Although he remained excluded from the high school cliques, he nevertheless settled in and overcame much of his social awkwardness.

Among Neil's five choices for his extra time were the science club, the mixed chorus, and the varsity fencing team. Cohen was Lincoln's team captain when he and Neil met near the opening of the 1957–58 season. "The first time we saw him *en garde* . . . we said, 'You're on the team.' He really had a terrific lunge," Cohen said.

Cohen explained that the year before Neil joined the Lincoln fencing team, the squad had won some divisional championships but had lost most of their best swordsmen to graduation. Although Neil was good with the bowl-shaped épée, the lack of players guaranteed him an immediate spot on the team. Herb remembers having to sometimes compete with both of the other two fencing

weapons—the straight-bladed foil and the curved sabre—
during tournaments because of the lack of teammates.
Neil eventually had to learn the sabre, and did quite well
with it.

Sports were fine as recreation, but parents of Lincoln
High athletes insisted that their boys concentrate on
academics. As Herb recalled, "It was very important to be
a good student." Feeling the outside pressure, Lincoln
downplayed athletics in favor of grades. As a result, the
school paid little attention to the fencing team, even after
its success.

"We didn't have much support from the school," Herb
said. "We didn't have any real coach—I was [really] the
coach, just like the captains before me. We didn't have a
faculty advisor because we didn't want somebody who
didn't know about fencing. Our uniforms were home-
made. We made pants, we made gloves—all of it home-
made stuff except the swords and the masks. We had all
kinds of strange outfits, and the other teams, like our
arch-rival Stuyvesant, were all beautifully outfitted with
nice socks from their schools and everything." Seeing
how important "this fencing stuff" was to Neil and Herb,
the Cohens and the Diamonds helped make their sons'
fencing apparel.

Meanwhile, Neil's need to write and express himself
through music continued to grow. One night not long
before his seventeenth birthday, Neil came downstairs to
the living room where his mother and father were sitting.
He perched himself on the battered brown couch and
played his just-completed song, "Blue Destiny." His father
was properly, if reservedly, impressed. Rose didn't say a
word at first, but tears rolled down her cheeks.

Neil realized for the first time that his music was
touching someone, as it had affected him. He felt vindicated at last, and resolved that night to become a serious
songwriter. Although Diamond never recorded "Blue
Destiny," he did feel strongly enough about it to include
the song in *The Neil Diamond Collection* songbook.

Deeply encouraged by his newly found acceptance, Neil was nevertheless still wary of the risky songwriting profession. He sensed his parents' uneasiness regarding his abandoning pre-med studies in favor of it. Thus, he continued to study medicine.

A strong bond developed between Diamond and Cohen, and Herb became privy to Neil's life. Interestingly, Cohen didn't really consider Diamond shy at all when he met him, although he agrees that Neil was not the average high school kid. "There was something different going on in him that didn't come out [except in his music], which I discovered when . . . all of a sudden, he bought a guitar totally out of the blue. He never mentioned how he got interested in it to me. All I know is he bought a book and was learning to play it by himself, so he could teach himself how to write."

A few other kids from Lincoln were also interested in music to the point of trying to turn professional. Most ended their careers in Brooklyn night clubs and bars, but Neil Sedaka, who was one year ahead of Neil and Herb, had graduated into stardom. He was signed to RCA Records and by December 1958 already had a Top Twenty hit with "The Diary." Herb remembered that Sedaka's success (and others' attempts at it) inspired Diamond. "Neil said, 'If these guys can make money at it, I can,' and that's how he started.

"He was very good right from the beginning. I always felt Neil understood the psychology of the people in our social environment . . . the romantic problems, the pressures of a teenager. It is true that for me, there was something inside of him that never really came out in conversation."

Neil and Herb usually stuck together, independent of any social clique. Sometimes other fencers would join them, but it was usually just the two of them.

But Neil's ease with girls had improved to the point where he could afford to be decidedly cocky about the situation; he no longer felt he had to write rhymes. When asked if Neil might have asked anyone else to marry him prior to meeting his future first wife, Cohen claimed no knowledge of anything of the sort but added, "That's very possible, knowing him. He had an uncle that he told me about, whom he admired a lot at that time, who always had a couple of girls. He said that he would talk about girls and stuff; and his uncle told him, 'Say whatever you have to say to them to get them to do whatever you want.' So, I don't know. . . ."

Cohen recounts one particular instance concerning romance that illustrated the closeness of Neil and Herb's friendship. "I had met someone. I fell in love with her, and she didn't care too much for me. I really was nuts about her, so I got a picture of her. One day after the summer, when I was telling Neil all of my problems—he knew all about them anyway—he saw the picture, and he just picked it up and tore it up! I said, Neil! What're you doing? He said, 'Herbie . . . she sits on the pot and shits just like everybody else!' That was the way he was. Very, very spontaneous. Always was. That statement represented Neil's view of life."

Throughout high school (and college, for that matter), Neil was lucky to scrape by with a "C" in most of his classes. He spent a lot of time talking his way out of various predicaments with his teachers. "He was a terrible student," remembers Cohen. "He was incredible. He didn't study at all. I would yell to him, Neil! What're you going to do? You got a plan or something? He'd say, 'I don't know . . . don't worry about it. . . . when I get there, I'll think of something.' He would tell the teacher some story. . . . That's the way he was."

Because Neil only really cared about fencing and writing lyrics, there was some doubt about whether he could find a college to accept him in a pre-med program with his scholastic record and financial situation. He was saved when Lincoln's varsity fencing team won the New York City public school championship in 1958, and his prowess with the épée attracted New York University's

famed fencing coach, Hugo Castello. But after seeing
Diamond's grades, Castello only agreed to a fencing
scholarship at Cohen's insistence. Cohen was heavily
recruited, and he pointed out to Castello the advantage of
keeping part of a city championship team together.

Attending college was Neil's chance to pursue his dual
objectives of pre-med and music until he was sure of
which path to take. Needless to say, Neil Leslie Diamond
never got to put "M.D." after his name.

The growing fortune of a man is to be born to some pursuit which finds him employment and happiness, whether it be to make baskets, or broad-swords, or canals, or statues, or songs.

—Ralph Waldo Emerson

2
Surviving the Life (1958–1964)

Finding the need to earn some extra money the summer before entering New York University, Neil and Herb took jobs as busboys at the Fun Crest resort in the Catskills Mountains. (The Catskills resorts have long been nicknamed "the Borscht Belt" for the Jewish comedians and entertainers who gained their start there, including Mel Brooks and Woody Allen.)

Neil and Herb worked days in the restaurant and worked at summer romance by night. In New York, they had often bet each other which one could get a pretty girl's telephone number first. Usually both struck out, but the other times they proved almost equally popular. One night the woman in question, Jaye Posner, a Jewish brunette from Long Island, became Neil's first truly serious romance. However, this took some time.

Cohen explained that Posner was going out with another guy named Stuart. Although Jaye took a liking to Neil, she was hesitant to break up with Stuart. It took Neil some doing to win Jaye for himself, but by the end of the summer, they were a couple. To top it off, Jaye was rooming at the Fun Crest with a girlfriend who would later marry Herb.

While working at the Fun Crest, Neil also found time to study and talk to aspiring entertainers who were playing the restaurants at night. When he told of his musical desires, he was always warned that nobody worked anywhere without an agent. He didn't know how to look for proper representation, and being naive, started asking some of the musicians if they knew of a good manager. A saxophone player heard about some young guy looking for an agent, found Neil, and promptly offered his services.

The man got Neil to sign a seven-year contract in which he would provide performing dates in return for 50 percent of Neil's income. Of course, the saxophonist didn't have many contacts outside of the booking agents at the Catskills, but Neil didn't know this and went back to New York thinking he was well on his way—both professionally and personally.

Diamond began attending New York University, but he expended most of his energy on songwriting. Although still claiming to be enthusiastic about science, Neil used his pre-med studies as a way to pacify people who asked him what he was going to do with his life. By attending college, he was also backhandedly assuring himself that he was still doing the "responsible" thing, like his brother.

Harvey had remained a good student in all the different schools he attended through all the family moves. Although he was eligible to enroll in a college with more prestige, the mechanically minded Harvey chose instead to attend a nearby trade school. Going to trade school was looked down upon in Brooklyn, but Harvey believed he could learn more by doing so. Hence the paradox that Neil, a poor student, went to college, while his smarter brother went to learn a skill.

Neil attracted more notice on the New York University fencing team, the Violets, than he had at high school.

Coach Castello, a former United States Olympic team fencing coach and a mainstay at NYU from the 1940s through the 1970s, remembered that Neil had learned the sabre so well back at Lincoln that he was used as a sabre man at NYU. "Neil was a solid athlete," Castello recalled. "We won two National College and three Intercollegiate Fencing Association championships while Neil was here, and he was third man in sabre for us. Once in two consecutive dual meets, he didn't have a touch scored against him. I think that's still a school record."

Diamond fenced for the Violets throughout college, representing the team at all championships. As good as he was, though, Castello remembered that on all away meets, Neil and his guitar were fairly inseparable when he wasn't using the sabre: "I always knew that music would eventually be his career."

Cohen recalls Neil cutting his first performing teeth by singing on the team bus and by playing at parties. Neil liked to sing his own material, including a song called "Flame," which he later reworked and had recorded by John Davidson. Herb remembers "Flame" as the first original song Neil ever played for him. By this time, Neil was already including "La Bamba" and "If I Had a Hammer," old summer camp songs, in his repertoire.

Neil was growing impatient with his saxophonist-manager after contacting him on a number of occasions only to be told of yet another opening in the Catskills. After finding out more about the entertainment business, Neil realized he was being taken advantage of and terminated the relationship.

"After a year, I realized I didn't want to spend the rest of my life working in a combo in the Catskills. I had to get out of the contract. My dad came up with the money. He drew it out of his savings—$750. That's what it took to get me out of the contract. He didn't have much. That was a lot of money for a little shopkeeper in Brooklyn. I've since repaid him."

Neil barely found time to study with his busy schedule.

Most nights he would stay up late writing and get up early
the next morning to catch the forty-five-minute subway
ride to NYU. Although he skipped some early morning
classes, missing too many would have made him lose his
scholarship. So he was in class for attendance, but instead
of taking notes, he furiously rewrote the previous night's
lyrics or composed new ones to take uptown to Tin Pan
Alley after lunch. After his usual rejection at the songwriting shops, he hurried back to campus in time for
fencing practice. Then it was time to go home and start
again.

"He was really working on his music and wasn't
working at school," Herb remembered. "I don't know
how he got as far as he did."

These trips to Tin Pan Alley were the first ones Neil
made in an effort to get his songs published. Although he
was repeatedly told his songs were too amateurish, he was
lucky in that he received advice when he asked for it. "I
thought maybe, you know, maybe somebody is going to
listen to my songs and say they're okay. I played my songs
for dark-suited gentlemen for many weeks, then a successful writer in New York—just beautiful, just as nice as can
be—said, 'Come over and play the song,' and I did. And
he gave me some encouragement and that was really the
start of it, the start of my knocking around the publishing houses with other writers."

Being a little too excited, and a little bit stubborn, he
believed he could go right back to the same agencies either
the next day or within a week with the solution. He wrote
more devotedly than ever, and used up so much class time
on his writing that he experienced the embarrassment of
failing music appreciation for the second time. Finally, he
achieved his first copyright on July 22, 1960, for a song
called "What Will I Do?"

Though he didn't realize it at the time, what Neil lacked
was a definitive sign pointing to a career in songwriting.
In his junior year, it came—with a vengeance.

Returning from fencing practice late one afternoon,

Neil was walking home from the subway stop in his neighborhood when a middle-aged man suffered a heart attack and dropped to the pavement right in front of him. Neil acted fast and tried to administer aid—artificial respiration, pulmonary resuscitation, everything someone with his schooling could have done—but it was all in vain. The man died before professional help could reach him. Terribly shaken, Neil had experienced the painful reality of medicine. "On that day," Neil remarked later, "I knew I could never be a doctor."

From then on, Diamond aimed to play it safe and get his degree in biology even though he had no intention of entering the field. This decision initiated a period of stress in his family relations that would last until he became successful with his music.

Neil's love for Jaye and his hopes that they could soon be married led him to search for a quick entrance into the music world. Despite the future problems this would cause, it was responsible for forcing him toward his final destination: a place in the music industry, which seemed almost unreachable. His days of white rats and lab coats were now numbered.

While practicing his songs, he had encountered enough opinions among his friends regarding his singing talent that he began thinking seriously about performing for the first time. After all, even if it proved only secondary to his songwriting, it couldn't hurt.

He was still uncomfortable about performing on his own and enlisted the partnership of a college friend, Jack Parker, an opera student who sang in roughly the same baritone as Neil. With practice, the two were able to harmonize fairly well. Armed with some of Diamond's earliest ballads, they set out to make a record.

The only company willing to take a chance on the duo—whose sound Neil once described as something of a Brooklyn version of the Everly Brothers—was a tiny independent master-producing firm called Shell Records. (The company's motto, "Our records are a gas," was a reference to their sister company—Gulf Records.) The label was owned by a couple of dentists and was essentially a vanity business venture.

In the spring of 1961, the act that would be billed as "Neil and Jack" on a couple of singles, made their first (and only) professional recordings. The privately contracted session gave the four songs a good technical sound, even as costs were cut with some ingenuity. The string section heard on the first single "You Are My Love at Last," was actually one violinist overdubbed more than a dozen times.

A small band was used in the studio with strings and extras added later. Of those involved, only the producer, Fred Parker, is known. Despite the low budget, the recordings were far better than most garage-band type recordings.

Two singles were released on the tiny Duel label, which was only famous during its brief history for the Ivy Three's novelty hit, "Yogi." Neither the first one, "You Are My Love at Last" b/w "What Will I Do" nor "I'm Afraid" b/w " 'Till You've Tried Love" made any money whatsoever for the duo. The first, a bombastic love song, and the other three, vaguely country-flavored tunes, are so obscure that most collectors were unaware of their existence until the late 1970s. The discs were badly distributed and promoted in their day and weren't terribly commercial-sounding in the first place. Neil and Jack were pretty much dissolved even before Diamond dropped out of school later the same year. When last heard from, Parker was teaching music in the New York City area.

Certain of his desire to marry Jaye and to make it in the music business, he inadvertently caused more stress at home. Now it was Rose who was closer to him, as it was she who was giving him the most encouragement to do what he liked best. Akeeba, concerned about his son's welfare, became more vocal in his hope that Neil would set a more normal occupational goal. He had experienced so many hardships in becoming financially stable; it was only natural for Akeeba to worry.

In addition, Akeeba was totally alienated by the sound of rock & roll. Neil later said that his father never really enjoyed nor understood his music for years.

Neil's perseverance in haunting the songwriting factories paid off toward the end of 1961 when Sunbeam Music, a small New York City publishing firm, offered him a fifty-dollar-a-week apprenticeship to write songs for other artists. It wasn't much money, but Neil was staggered at the thought of receiving any appreciation at all. Taking the gamble that the proposed sixteen-week trial period would lead to a permanent job, he left NYU just ten units short of graduation. Almost immediately afterward, he married Jaye. "I married as a child at twenty. . . . It took courage to live the way we did."

The way Neil and Jaye lived to begin with was in the Diamond home in Brooklyn. The move was almost certainly viewed with some anxiety, not only because Diamond was leaving the security of school, or because he and Jaye were marrying so young, but also because they had no money to support themselves. Marrying young may have been foolish and impulsive, but his new financial obligations forced Neil to take songwriting seriously.

Unfortunately, things started to go wrong quickly. The Sunbeam trial period ended with Neil unable to produce one salable song, and by April he was out of a job. Upon being fired, the managers offered him some fatherly advice: "Go back to school and get out of the business before you starve to death."

But Neil became more determined than ever to make it, and began roughly four years of trudging from publishing house to publishing house, attempting to succeed. By the end of 1964, five companies had shown him the door.

"I know that people do things and spend a lot of time on things to fulfill needs that they have inside of themselves. One of the needs that I had was to be accepted by people and to be respected, and I suppose that those two things were up in the forefront," Diamond said in 1971. "But I kept writing for a lot of years in the beginning because it was the only thing that I really wanted to do. I didn't really have any choice. I wanted to write, and later, I wanted to involve myself in recording, and that was all I really wanted. And so I struggled, took all kinds of jobs, and just hustled, and tried to keep myself alive for five or six years, just to be able to write.''

It might be said that Diamond's artistic sense, still mostly sympathetic to the older styles of pop music, took some time to find a niche in the era of Gerry Goffin and Carole King's "The Locomotion" (recorded by Little Eva) and Kal Mann and Dave Appell's "The Bristol Stomp" (recorded by the Dovells). But it would be hard to deny that the problem was Diamond's self-professed inability to write songs from someone else's predetermined commercial dictates.

"I found it difficult to write material for another person—to tailor it to suit someone else. I just didn't know how to do it," he said. "I went to another publisher and was hired for seventy-five dollars a week. It was still difficult for me to write the kind of material that the publisher dictated. On the other hand, I had an opportunity to sing. When you work for a publishing company, you make hundreds of demos [demonstration records] of your material. Also, working for publishers, you have continual exposure to other writers and you work with them as well as learn from them. It was a frantic existence.''

He explained, "Sell a copyright and you get a fifty- or seventy-five-dollar advance to live on. It was exciting to be in the company of other songwriters because I was in awe of them, but it was barren soil. They would tell you, 'Write a song for such-and-such a singer!' Some of those kids could really write, but I was a total failure for eight years, unable to write music to someone else's specifications.''

He further elaborated, "In a sense it was exciting for me because I didn't know anything and there was lots to learn. It was a scuffling, hand-to-mouth existence because doors are always closed to anyone new in any business. I spent about eight years knocking around, from the time I was seventeen until I was twenty-five, and learned who to know and who to avoid. I did learn a lot about songwriting and I spent a lot of time with all sorts of songwriters, from oldtimers to rhythm & blues writers.

"A publisher would tell me what ideas for the song he had and expect me to translate them for a singer with a particular style. He'd say something like: 'This singer is coming up and he wants a positive song, mostly up, with a little hook in the middle and in a certain key.' I never did well at that; in fact, I did abyssmally at it for a while, just managing to survive. I didn't start to do well until the point where I got fired for the last time. It was very frustrating."

At the song factories, Diamond found himself in situations that were not really conducive to songwriting. Most had their artists work in cramped office cubicles that were subdivided into various departments, depending on music style. Some companies had so many rooms that it seemed like the writers worked in a maze. Often they had to work while hearing others bang out songs in the next room.

As the grind continued (" 'Gloria wants an up-tempo ballad like that Patti Page thing,' the boss would say, 'and while you're at it, throw in some bongos,' "), he found little humor in his predicament. However, he did recall, "the time these two guys in the cubicle next to me kept beating out those old-fashioned Jewish tunes. Man, I knew for sure they weren't going anywhere."

The pair happened to be the songwriting team of Bock and Harnick, and the pieces they were working on became *Fiddler on the Roof*. "Actually, we never met when we were working up there. We were all signed as staff writers . . . and once or twice, just by coincidence, they would be working in the same office. I was very tempted to tell them that the type of melodies that they were doing—thinking that they were writing for recordings—were outdated and that it might be a good idea if they reconsidered. But fortunately, I didn't say anything to them."

The heyday of Tin Pan Alley had passed long before the coming of rock & roll, but the song shops were undergoing a rebirth for the first time since the end of the era of writers like Jerome Kern and Frank Loesser. Now, with the numerous teen-idol acts that were blending the youth appeal of rock with the traditional, middle-of-the-road values of straightforward pop, a new demand for "professional" songwriting material emerged. Pop singers like Dean Martin, Tony Bennett, and Patti Page would still be consistent hitmakers for another several years, but the big money was made with performers like Bobby Rydell, James Darren, and Connie Francis, who were dominating the industry. Additionally, rhythm & blues artists increasingly looked to the tune mills for material. This led to the development of the "girl group" sound and the gradual evolution of music that would later be called "soul."

The new center of activity was the Brill Building on Broadway, just north of Times Square in midtown Manhattan. Most of the more active companies were based there. The top songwriters of the period—Goffin and King, Barry Mann and Cynthia Weil, Jeff Barry and Ellie Greenwich, Neil Sedaka and Howard Greenfield, Burt Bacharach and Hal David, plus 1950s holdovers like Jerry Leiber and Mike Stoller, and Doc Pomus and Mort Shuman—all passed through the area and in the process wrote hits for the Shirelles, the Drifters, the Everly Brothers, Bobby Vee, the Chiffons, the Shangri-Las, Fabian, the various Phil Spector acts, and many more.

Into this world came Neil Diamond, and he promptly became lost. He made little impression in any of the five different companies he passed through. Time after time, he would attempt to write something that resembled the instant assembly-line pop hits of the day and would be repeatedly turned down. When someone did record one of his songs, it came to nought. Items like the Rocky Fellers' "Santa Santa"—his first composition recorded by someone else—never even touched the singles chart, and the songs he placed with hitmakers Bobby Vinton and Andy Williams were never even released in America.

"I had very few things that were even recorded. . . . Part of it was they felt there were too many words," Diamond said. "I'd spent a lot of time on lyrics, and they were looking for hooks and I didn't really understand the nature of that. The only real success I had was in being able to sell the songs in the first place to the publishers and get the advance. It was purely a matter of survival."

Neil's fortunes might have changed had he been able to form a strong linkage with the famed Don Kirshner–controlled Aldon Music, which was the most successful of the Brill-area companies. Apparently his songs were refused there, although Kirshner would later ask him for material.

But Neil's experience around the various levels of the recording business began to show. While recording his own demos, he became acquainted with producers, back-up singers, musicians, and other songwriters. One of the few close friendships he made during this time was with another struggling writer named Carl D'Errico. He wrote over a dozen copyrighted but unheard-of songs with D'Errico from 1963 to 1965. He even reportedly sang backing vocals on a record by the Echoes—a vocal group featuring Felix Cavaliere, later of the Rascals—and came close to joining them.

Diamond's next brush with professional singing came in the summer of 1962, after he was fired from Roosevelt Music when the company decided to terminate its weakest commercial writers as part of a cost-cutting house cleaning. The victims, ten in all (including the soon-to-be hitmaking team of Feldman, Goldstein, and Gottehrer), got into a bull session over their various troubles. They decided to knock off a song together just for the hell of it, and then record it the same night. The resulting tune was

"Ten Lonely Guys," a country-music parody about a flirty girl who leaves ten broken-hearted suitors in her wake. The chorus even mentioned all ten by name. Neil sang lead vocals with the other nine singing background.

All of the writers except Feldman, Goldstein, and Gottehrer were forced to adopt aliases in order to get the song published without contractual hassles. They decided to see if the demo could actually be released as it was, under the group name the Ten Lonely Guys, in hopes of gaining a novelty hit. But Feldman, Goldstein, and Gottehrer's publishers placed it with Pat Boone, whose version reached number forty-five in September 1962, and the Ten Lonely Guys version stayed unreleased until Feldman's *Sounds of Brooklyn Volume 2* compilation in 1985.

The years of failure—during which time Diamond had to cope with unfriendly and often cheap bosses, consternation from family, and an ever-decreasing self-esteem—made him defensive and withdrawn. Although he was growing professionally the hard way, by learning from his critics, he was almost as unhappy now as he had been as a child.

But now the pressures were becoming almost unbearable. His and Jaye's first daughter, Marjorie, was born in late 1962, and the family needed their own home. The three of them first took up residence in a Manhattan apartment, eventually moving to Queens. The families helped, but their patience with Neil and the songwriting business was wearing extremely thin.

Finally, in early 1963, what must have looked like the "big break" occurred. Neil's song demos had caught the attention of Tom Catalano, an artists & repertoire man at Columbia Records. Catalano, who had worked at several other record companies, was also working with Columbia's music publishing division, Blackwood Music.

Neil was surprised that his voice rather than his songs had been noticed but was perfectly willing to give performing another shot. He told Murray "the K" Kauffman in 1972: "People started saying 'You should record, your voice is not bad.' I wasn't against it because I love singing. I've been singing all my life. Who doesn't love to sing? So I got involved in the recording."

Diamond passed the audition, and even though the label was committing itself to only a one-single deal, the company's strength in the industry seemed to indicate that this was his make-or-break chance.

That spring, Neil recorded a handful of original songs for CBS with the Angels ("My Boyfriend's Back" was still in their future) on backing vocals. The song selected for the A side, "At Night," was a routine teen lament that stirred little in-company enthusiasm. The single was quickly flipped in favor of "Clown Town," an upbeat heartbreak number that recalled the concurrent sounds of Bobby Vee and Jay and the Americans.

Billboard aided the disc's release with mention in its Singles Spotlight column, which indicated some support for the record's commercial viability. Yet, the record failed to win any noticeable sales or even radio airplay. The Columbia promotional magic that had temporarily worked for Dion was not working here. Considering that Dion was pushed more toward being a pop singer while at CBS, it could be that the company, still influenced by the years of anti-rock A&R mogul Mitch Miller, wasn't quite ready for this kind of performer.

Columbia did send him out on tour to promote "Clown Town." Diamond later recalled his very first concert appearance, at a fair in Philadelphia: "I went out there, tripped on a wire, and fell flat on my face—my introduction to the stage." He did hops and some local lip-synch outings, but nothing helped. Columbia dropped him upon the presentation of his one and only royalty check for the single, for a total of twenty-three cents. He never cashed it.

The experience made Diamond much more wary of the music business. He became meticulously careful with his money and the various legalities of his chosen profession.

His marriage became more unstable. Not only were he
and Jaye too young when they married, but the combination of his commitment to songwriting, having to raise a
child, and trying to make ends meet caused resentment
between them. While Neil apparently helped out in the
dry goods store and recorded demos for other writers, Jaye
took a job.

Added to their troubles was the pressure from both
sides of the family. The way to happiness, the parents
reasoned, was for Neil to give up his crazy dreams, get a
steady job, and settle down. The problems loomed larger
than the love involved, and this was sending the relationship into a decline from which it would not recover.

Despite it all Diamond never reconsidered his career. "I
wouldn't say that I've paid my dues more than anyone
else. Yes, I went through New York, and I knocked around
the streets for several years. I was fired from five publishing companies, and my average income [from songwrit-
ing] was something like four hundred dollars a year.
That's all! That's what I did. I never thought of it as
paying my dues. There was something positive, there was
always something I loved. I woke up in the morning, and
I went out and I wanted people to hear my music. I wrote
until the wee hours of the morning because that's what I
did and I loved it. I never thought I was paying dues. I
would have done it for nothing. . . ."

This enthusiasm kept him from becoming too bitter
over the publishing house rejections. He told Robert
Hilburn in a "Midnight Special" television interview
that the rejection educated him about music and only
made him try harder. "I thought that they were right," he
said. "I thought their criticism of the songs was right, and
I was a beginner and I was just learning and it wasn't
discouraging at all. . . . I was very critical of what I was
writing, but certainly people who knew music were even
more critical in a different way. I received criticism for all
of those years, and I felt I learned a great deal from it and
it was never discouraging. It was a very, very exciting time

for me, that whole period, because I was doing what I wanted to do, I think, more than anything else."

The Beatles invaded America in January 1964, bringing a revitalization to rock music and the firm establishment once and for all of the concept of singers who wrote their own songs. Neil liked their sound and could relate to their style more than to any of the 1950s rock acts, possibly even including the Everly Brothers. He would later credit the Fab Four and Bob Dylan with "setting the writers free" from the song factories of Tin Pan Alley to record their own material and to expand their writing scope. A more mature and independent sound was emerging—something that Neil would welcome whole-heartedly.

"[Writers] were the low men on the totem pole. We were the people who were really kicked around and told what to do," he told Hilburn in that 1980 interview. "The Beatles and Bob Dylan changed that so they opened up new worlds for me and for everybody else that was struggling at the time to get their music exposed. Suddenly, I wasn't considered just a writer. So I owe the Beatles a great debt. I wouldn't be here today talking to you if it weren't for them."

The Beatles had not only put their fans and critics into a frenzy, but they started a revolution in the American popular songwriting field that began and ended careers. Some writers and singers became instantly outmoded, while the struggling writers, like Diamond, would soon get their chance.

Diamond correctly decided that he was one of those at a watershed, and unlike some others, he was willing to take that one last chance. With his family life and finances mired, Diamond decided his final opportunity would have to be away from the song factories. Reasoning that he was trying too hard to write songs for other people's tastes, he set about only writing tunes that satisfied him.

In late December 1964, Diamond rented a printer's

storage closet for thirty-five dollars a month in the
building that housed the Birdland jazz club. He converted
it into his own Broadway office, bringing in a battered
secondhand piano he picked up in a junk shop (he also
got his early guitars this way) and had a pay phone
installed. Now on his own, he would try to sell each song
individually.

"I lived in that tiny room for a year and began to write
music for myself," Diamond recalled. "No restrictions—
just what I felt, stimulated by life, love, anger—the same
things everyone feels. Music is as varied as the human
mind. That was the turning point." He later added: "It
was probably the most important year of my life."

"I began, for the first time, to write songs that I wanted
to write, that I felt, that moved me, that I cared about.
And, for the first time, I felt just the inklings of a little
blossoming of 'ooh, yes, that lyric says what I feel.' And it
became exciting again to me, and I felt that now there
was no more necessity for me to fail, that I could do what
I wanted."

He told *Melody Maker*: "I'd look down at what I'd
written and realize that I liked it for once. And I really
consider this to be the beginning of my career."

Diamond had finally reached the point of not only
loving his ability to write but also loving what he wrote;
knowing it was good. In 1977 he stated that all he had
worked for, for the eight years after "Hear Them Bells,"
had been worth it. "For the first time, my music had
something to it. I was proud of myself and the discipline
I had managed to muster up. It was a lonely but reward-
ing and wonderful time, but I must stress that even then
it wasn't something that came quickly. Like many young
people striving to create, I had spent eight or nine years in
preparation. It was just that that one year above Birdland
shaped my future and built my confidence. I knew I had
something to say."

He continued to work some hours for his father and to
cut other writers' demo records to support Jaye and

Marjorie. He allowed himself one thirty-five cent meal a day at Woolworth's. It consisted of a twenty-three-cent hoagy (submarine sandwich), a ten-cent Coke, and a two-cent piece of candy.

Within ten months, one of the songs he sent around, "Sunday and Me," was recorded and released by Jay and the Americans. It reached number eighteen and began to introduce the world to Neil Diamond.

As Diamond said when told that the song was the first time the world had heard of him: "Yeah, that was the first time I ever heard of Neil Diamond, too!"

While "Sunday and Me" climbed the charts, his future was already being mapped out by producers Jeff Barry and Ellie Greenwich. Barry and Greenwich, famous for "Do Wah Diddy," "Leader of the Pack" and coauthors with Phil Spector of most of his Wall of Sound Philles Records hits, had met Neil and were now guiding him toward a recording contract.

*. . . you may accuse the endless generations before you
for not yielding one single gene of it . . . you may
condemn an industry of plastic vendors incapable of
discovering a mold of it . . . you will envy the precious
few who are abundant with it and beat them with stones
. . . but for he endowed, is the eve of New Year, for at
midnight he shall take a tin horn and from his window
blow after the people passing by.*

—Display ad for "Solitary Man"
Billboard, April 23, 1966

3
Do It (1965-1968)

Though Neil was firmly entrenched in his songwriting
retreat above Birdland, money did not come quickly at
first. More thirty-five cent Woolworth's lunches filled his
stomach for several months. He continued to sing on
other writers' demonstration records in order to earn
money for his family and for the rent on his office.

While working on a demo in the same offices that
housed Leiber and Stoller's Red Bird Records, Neil found
he needed a female backup singer to complete the demo.
With a burst of sudden confidence he asked Ellie Greenwich, who worked at Red Bird and had an office down the
hall, to join the session, and she decided it might be fun.
She quickly became fond of Diamond's vocal talent, and
after talking to him about his own music, she was
impressed enough to introduce him to Jeff Barry, her
husband and partner.

Barry was equally excited after their first meeting and

helped Greenwich convince the skeptical Diamond that
he could be a successful singer as well as songwriter.
They urged him to become a performer again despite his
feelings about the failings of the Duel and Columbia
singles.

Diamond, Barry, and Greenwich would even write one
song together in the spring of 1965. Entitled "It's So
Strange (The Way Love Works)," the unreleased tune was
copyrighted in June but was never successfully placed.
All the while, Barry and Greenwich prodded Neil to
become a singer. "The strange thing is that I really didn't
have the hots to be a performer myself anymore. I just
wanted to get my songs heard by the right people."

He commented to the *Washington Post,* "It seemed like
it was too hard to be accepted as a performer—that was
more than I could have hoped for."

Barry and Greenwich told Neil it would take some
work. In order for them to get him a recording contract,
he would have to come up with some good songs and
learn to perform publicly. In the meantime, they would
get him a job at Red Bird as a company staff writer and
demo singer so he could support himself.

Despite the influential pull of Barry and Greenwich,
who were Red Bird's central creative talents, Diamond
was released shortly thereafter. It was not another case of
Neil's failing to please, but Red Bird's own fast-fading
commercial standing. This forced Barry and Greenwich
to strike out on their own as independent producers, and
they urged Diamond to continue his work until they
placed him somewhere else.

As he worked on the new material for himself, Jay and
the Americans' recording of "Sunday and Me" began
picking up commercial steam. In January 1966, little over
a year after setting up his solitary office, "Sunday and
Me" reached the national Top Twenty.

By this time, Barry and Greenwich were getting positive signals that Diamond was headed for stardom—he
had caught the performing fever once again. Neil found a

friend in Fred Weintraub, owner of the Bitter End club in Greenwich Village who later became his first real manager. Weintraub allowed him to play at the Bitter End on slow nights. Soon, Diamond became one of the house acts, filling in on weeknights, scant afternoons, and in warm-up slots. The club didn't even bother to put his name on the marquee or in display advertising until his first Bang Records release.

Diamond had learned little about performing from his "Clown Town" days and was still awkward and insecure onstage. It took time for him to develop any sort of stage banter. His early attempts were so clumsy that Weintraub forbade him to talk between songs until he became steadier at it.

He was also reluctant to use his own backlog of compositions and so was forced to fill out his shows with songs he had learned at summer camp like "If I Had a Hammer" and "La Bamba." Audience response was polite at best and never enthusiastic.

Meanwhile, Barry and Greenwich were looking for a recording deal for Diamond and arranged an audition at the offices of Atlantic Records. Gerald (Jerry) Wexler, famous for his production work with the classic rhythm & blues acts the label showcased, felt that Neil had a future after hearing him (accompanied by a brand new, jet-black Everly Brothers/Gibson guitar) run through his songs. Wexler signed him on the spot but didn't feel that Diamond was particularly suited to the soul-based label.

Looking for an appropriate place for Neil in the Atlantic business family, Wexler handed his contract over the very next day to good friend Bert Berns, whose label, Bang, was independent but distributed through Atlantic. The label's name was an acronym of Bert (Berns), Ahmet (Ertegun, Atlantic co-founder), Neshumi (Ertegun, Ahmet's brother and Atlantic co-founder), and Gerald (Wexler). The recently formed company was riding high on the success of the McCoys' "Hang On Sloopy" and was hungry for up-and-coming new talent.

Like Wexler, Berns had worked with many rhythm &
blues artists over the years, including Ray Charles and
Wilson Pickett. Prior to forming Bang, he had gone to
England to take a look at the mod/rhythm & blues
movement there, and he was instrumental in discovering
Van Morrison and Them. Morrison, in fact, would soon
be signed to Bang as a solo act, scoring a Top Ten hit in
1967 with "Brown-Eyed Girl."

Struck by Diamond's sound, Berns wanted to record
him right away.

Following months of preparation for this opportunity,
Diamond went into the studio on January 25, 1966. The
first three songs he and his co-producers Barry and
Greenwich decided to record were "Solitary Man,"
"Cherry, Cherry," and "I Got the Feeling (Oh No No)."

He later described the session: "I think I was a little
scared, but it was also very exciting. It was the first time
I had ever sung for a couple of top producers. I had great
confidence in Jeff and Ellie. They had a wonderful feel
for music at that time. Up until then, I had worked in
demo studios, making demos of my songs. It was a little
scary, but it was the big time."

It was at this turning point in Diamond's career that
his second daughter, Elyn, was born.

The first single was "Solitary Man." It presented at
least two stylistic elements that would become trademarks
of his works: the I've-got-to-make-it-by-myself lyrical
base and the sensitive-but-tough ballad style. In retro-
spect, it was an excellent choice to introduce Neil Diamond, as it was not only an encouraging first effort but it
also reflected his personality.

He was honest about the motivation behind the song:
"I'm not inspired to write. I write to express an emotion.
I was feeling very lonely when I wrote 'Solitary Man.' It
was an outgrowth of my despair."

In 1977, he said he chose "Solitary Man" as the first
song because "I knew it was something special. It struck
a very sympathetic chord inside."

But one last obstacle remained before the record could be released. For a brief period after the session, Diamond considered adopting a stage name. He believed his name may have held him down in the past, and as he told Barbara Walters in 1985: "I thought, I can't use Neil Diamond—it's too normal, it's ordinary, it's boring, and 'Diamond' sounds like somebody made it up, and I have to find a name with some character to it. Something that will be memorable."

His first choice was Noah Kaminsky. To him, the moniker had a certain Biblical sound and it was the sort of name one would expect of a symphony conductor. It sounded convincing as a real name, and to this day there is at least one reference source that reports it as his given name.

Another idea came to mind after he apparently decided on the Kaminsky tag. It was an even stranger concoction—Eice Cherry. "I thought . . . Wow! E-i-c-e . . . that sounds real cool!" he told Walters. But "the time came when 'Solitary Man' was going to the presses, and I chickened out at the last minute. I mean, the president of the company [Berns] called me and said, 'Well, is it going to be Neil Diamond or is it going to be Noah Kaminsky or is it going to be Eice Cherry?' And I thought of my grandmother, and I said, my goodness, I could never explain it to her. . . . So I said, go with Neil Diamond, and then I'll try and figure it out after that. You know . . . it worked out okay."

Sadly, the woman who influenced this decision died shortly before the release of "Solitary Man." "She was important to me; she was an inspiration. She wanted me to be successful, to have character. I hope she would be proud so I gotta go the distance—my grandmother would expect that."

The "Solitary Man" b/w "Do It" single was finally released in late March. "Do It" was recorded at the second recording date in February. He said of the song, "It was just a nice little groove thing that I wrote on guitar—real quick—couldn't have taken me more than twenty minutes to write the song. But I still like it. There's something charming about it."

An advertising campaign was assembled which described Neil as a fit contender alongside the heavyweight lyricists of the day. Early critical response in the industry trade papers was excellent, and "Solitary Man" first broke at Top Forty giant KFRC in San Francisco. Los Angeles radio stations KRLA and KHJ began playing it next, giving it an even stronger boost.

Neil later recalled the first time he heard "Solitary Man" on the radio: "I was outside of a record store in New York. I was feeling good about hearing it when I saw this little dog relieving itself on the nearby fire hydrant to my music. I'll never forget that."

"Solitary Man" did not spread far past the West Coast, as Bang's distribution reportedly had not yet become fully functional. A reorganization shuffle was reported a few weeks after the release of "Solitary Man," yet the problem didn't stop "Hang On Sloopy" from hitting number one. Neil's debut record began with a low-key response in his hometown, and finished the same way. It stopped cold at number fifty-five on the national charts.

Two months later, Bang released "Cherry Cherry," a rock & roll song in the 1950s traditional style that didn't even have an electric guitar on it. With its semi-Latin beat and call-and-response backing vocals by Barry and Greenwich, the song sounded as if it could have been a lost master dating back to the mid-1950s. On the charts at the same time as Donovan's "Sunshine Superman" and Simon and Garfunkel's "The Sounds of Silence," "Cherry, Cherry" might have sounded archaic to some. And in singing appearances on "American Bandstand" and local record-hop television shows, Neil revealed himself to be the last major pop star to wear a pompadour.

Although the rough, anti-professional "garage band" sound in hits like "Kicks" by Paul Revere and the Raiders or "Dirty Water" by the Standells—whose main influence appeared to be Kingsmen's version of Richard Berry's "Louie, Louie"—showed that a large part of the rock audience preferred the simpler, rawer forms, enough listeners decided that "Cherry, Cherry" and its old-fashioned approach was just what they needed. The record peaked on the national charts at number six.

"I'm very partial to my record of 'Cherry, Cherry' because it was done with an old, beat-up guitar that I bought many years ago, and it had a particular sound that I loved. 'Cherry, Cherry' was cut twice. The first time it was done with a large orchestra, and it was too much of a production. And so we went back into the studio, just myself and two or three other people, and we just did it. I think it was just four people."

The success of "Cherry, Cherry" made a number of industry people take notice of Diamond, particularly producer Don Kirshner. The highly touted Kirshner contacted Neil and asked if he had any other songs like "Cherry, Cherry" for a television singing group, the Monkees, he was helping to put together for Screen Gems. While Diamond had no such tunes ready at the time, he did have a song called "I'm a Believer" which he didn't feel he could properly record. He and Barry met with Kirshner and a deal was struck. Barry would produce all Diamond compositions the Monkees recorded, and Diamond would enjoy the mass exposure. But Diamond would have to sell the publishing rights to Screen Gems/Columbia Music, a mandate given all young writers contributing songs to the early Monkees bandwagon.

Diamond later regretted selling these rights as he claims to look upon all his songs as "his children." Nevertheless, three of his four songs recorded by the Monkees firmly established his songwriting talents with the masses.

Besides "I'm a Believer," Diamond agreed to sell another one of his orphan songs, "Love to Love" and two songs he would never record and release, the smash hit "A Little Bit Me, A Little Bit You" and the television show

favorite "Look Out (Here Comes Tomorrow)." Although
the Monkees were to release "Love to Love" as the single
following "A Little Bit Me, A Little Bit You" (which
reached number two and sold a million copies), the group
made a shift away from the bubble-gum set, and the song
remained unreleased in America until the 1980s Rhino
Records issue, *Monkee Business*. "Look Out (Here
Comes Tomorrow)" appeared only as a track on the 1967
More of the Monkees album.

Neil's own third single, called "I Got the Feeling" on
45s and "Oh No No" on albums, proved a solid follow-up
hit to "Cherry, Cherry," hitting number sixteen. Its
success, combined with the immediate explosion of the
Monkees' "I'm a Believer" in December 1966, made Neil
a recognized star. He would later muse: "A singing star?
. . . I wasn't a big star. I was a little star. Yeah . . . a star!"

Admirably, Diamond says he wasn't jealous of the
Monkees' success. He had good reason to be, as "I'm a
Believer" turned out to be the biggest hit of early 1967. By
comparison, it left such competing titles as the Beach
Boys' "Good Vibrations," the Beatles' "Penny Lane" b/
w "Strawberry Fields Forever" and the Rolling Stones'
"Ruby Tuesday b/w "Let's Spend the Night Together" in
the dust. "I'm a Believer" was number one for seven
weeks and is not only Diamond's first chart-topping
song, but the biggest American hit he has ever written.

"I was real excited about it," he told the BBC in 1972,
"I'd never had a number one record before. 'I'm a
Believer' was the biggest single in the world at that time,
and that was enormous to me. I didn't particularly feel
that I wanted to do the song. I didn't care for the song that
much, and I didn't particularly care for the way I sang it.
I liked the song for what it was. It was just a simple,
happy song, and I liked it for that, but . . . if you were on
an island by yourself for ten years and they said to you,
'What one song would you like to take with you?' . . . 'I'm
a Believer' would not be on that list."

Berns made sure Diamond went through the usual

publicity rounds normal for all budding rock stars in those days: assorted lip-synch appearances on television, guest shots on radio, interviews with the teen press, and package concert tours with several other acts in which he sang one or two numbers.

Neil remembers the first real concert series he ever did on his own as a scattered bunch of dates in Florida during the summer of 1966. "I got a call from a friend of mine, Sol Sapien, who was an agent, and he said, 'Hey Neil, listen! There's some guy in Florida who wants to book your band in Florida, and he'll pay you $750 to get on stage and perform.' And I said, 'Tell me about it.' And he said, 'You'll do four performances in four different cities in two days, and he'll give you $750.' I said, 'Wow! $750 . . . that's more money than I've ever . . . great! Take it!' I went down to Greenwich Village and I bought myself a beautiful suit. I didn't know black yet. It was actually a grey suit with red pinstripes and wide lapels. I bought a new guitar strap, I bought a new set of strings, and I went to Florida. Of course, between the airfare and everything involved, I ended up with only thirty dollars, but it was fantastic. That was really the first performance."

His set still consisted mostly of old standards, plus his handful of hits. He doesn't even remember if he got any applause: "I may have blocked it from my mind. I thought that the fact that I survived those shows was good. I didn't know anything. I didn't know who I was on stage. I didn't know what I was supposed to project."

Many critics have said that as in the case of Elvis Presley's Sun Records recordings, Neil's twenty-five released songs for Bang constitute the best overall period of his career. Although Diamond regards many of the Bang songs as teeny-bop fodder, they have a sharp, unpretentious quality that he would not always equal in his later work. This aside, they represented the only time Diamond actively committed himself to the rock & roll style.

Diamond's sound of this period is characterized by a basic small-combo approach augmented by a few horns and backing vocals. Credit is due to producers Barry and Greenwich, experts in teen-beat delicacies and alumni of numerous Spector and Leiber/Stoller sessions. The efforts of the session musicians played a major role as well.

By that summer, Neil had completed his first album: *The Feel of Neil Diamond*, which matched seven of his own compositions with five remakes of other hits, including the recently popular Mamas and Papas' "Monday, Monday," the Paul Simon–penned hit for the Cyrkle, "Red Rubber Ball," and a hardly serious version of Tommy James and the Shondells' "Hanky Panky," a Barry/Greenwich composition that Neil truly disliked and recorded only as a joke to fill up the album.

"It was just that the record company wanted some familiar songs as well. They didn't know that any of [my] songs would become popular or familiar. So I did [a few] of those on the two albums I did for Bang Records—whatever was a popular hit at the time."

Everything looked promising for the album. It was good and was acknowledged as such by the trade papers. Besides, it included a couple of established hits, and it bore a color full-figure picture of Diamond on the cover that practically yelled "This is one intense guy."

It reached number 159 on the national album chart.

Bang had not yet discovered how to market albums, and *The Feel of Neil Diamond* was a hard item to find even in its day. In spite of its connection with Atlantic, Bang would not have a bona fide hit album during Berns's lifetime.

Neil's next concert booking was on a fifteen-act concert package that took him to the Hollywood Bowl and the Cow Palace in San Francisco. In his 1972 interview with Murray the K, he described his first performances in California: "They said, 'Hey, come out and play the Hollywood Bowl.' I thought, 'My God! The Hollywood Bowl—I've just been on stage for the first time two weeks ago.' They said, 'Come out anyway, we don't care.' I went there, got out in the Hollywood Bowl, and found out that I was very afraid."

For the occasion, he premiered his new look: "Every-thing *black*. Black boots, black shoes, black shirt, black pants, black guitar. I got myself a black cowboy hat, black clothes, and the guitar on my back, and the whole audience just went 'Whooaa!' . . . And it blew my mind. I couldn't follow it because I didn't know how to sing or anything, but it was fantastic!"

He continued to dress in black on stage to give himself a more mysterious or at least tougher persona. This stance was not new; Johnny Cash was already becoming known as "The Man in Black" to his fans.

One of the most important developments at this time was his inspiration to write "Girl, You'll Be a Woman Soon." In late 1985, Diamond told a Detroit audience that the tune was written after he replaced the closing act after the first night. "We went out on a tour which covered thirty-two cities, and the tour lasted for twenty-eight days. Now that was a rough tour. It was a major rock & roll revue and there were fifteen other acts in it and I was the closing act. They fired the closing act after the first night because he had some very suggestive problems on stage. So I became the new closing act and I had to write a song for the audience. And at the time, the entire audience was made up of fourteen-year-old girls. I felt like a teacher. . . . This song came out of that."

The poor showing of *The Feel of Neil Diamond* was disappointing, but the follow-up singles were doing too well for spirits to be low. The public also loved the rhythm & blues–flavored "You Got to Me," the dramatic poor-boy lament, "Girl, You'll Be a Woman Soon," and the celebratory "I Thank the Lord for the Night Time."

Commenting on the recording of "You Got to Me," Diamond singled out one particular contributor to its success: "Jimmy McCracklin. He gives it ooomph! Jimmy McCracklin is the greatest studio musician that I've ever worked with in New York. Great harmonica player, great guitarist. He brought his harmonica that day and we said, 'Hey, we've never done a record with harmonica.' We asked him, 'Can you play something?

Can you add to it?' He said, 'All right. Whatever you
want.' To this date [1972], I think that's the only record
I've done with harmonica. And nobody's ever topped Jim
on that.

" 'Girl, You'll Be a Woman Soon' was the first recording I ever did with strings. Up until then, Jeff and Ellie
and I worked with a basic rhythm section. I wrote the
song and it was very melodic, and we figured what the
heck, we'll go out and do it with strings. Not too many
people were doing things with strings. We went out and
did it, and it was beautiful. I've always loved strings.
Violins can break your heart when they're used right and
they cry the right way. . . . I love it for that and many other
reasons. I won't forget about it."

Diamond then went out on the road by himself. "I'd
done some hops and lip synchs when I recorded for
Columbia so it came easily enough," he said in 1976.
"When the first records came out, I went out and played
. . . everything from bowling alleys to gigs on the top of
flatbed trucks in parking lots. The way I worked was to
use a pick-up band wherever I went. I'd meet them an
hour before the show, rehearse a little and hope they all
started playing when I did."

He still played the Bitter End regularly and made his
solo Los Angeles debut in mid-December 1966 at Dave
Hull's Hullabaloo, the Hollywood teen dance club. The
Los Angeles Times review allowed for the club's bad
acoustics in pointing out that Neil needed stage presence.
Among the complaints were "an incompetent band,"
Neil's "impossibly flat" guitar and singing that was
either off key or lyrically indecipherable.

It took much practice and more bad reviews before Neil
developed an honestly good live act. One Toronto reviewer remarked the same year: "Many musicians I talk
to say Neil should stick to his composing. His songs are
great and voice is fairly good, but good stage presence is
absent. The night I saw him, he seemed bored on stage.
He projected a let's-get-this-over-with attitude."

The problem was actually Diamond's dislike for working the cabaret circuit. He couldn't wait to get out of it. "When I played small clubs in Greenwich Village, the sound of ice cubes in a glass became as grating as chalk on a blackboard."

Another reason that many of the articles published about Diamond at this time placed equal emphasis on his writing and his performing was that many older and more pretentious columnists felt that songwriting was bound to provide a longer professional life than singing. Although Neil continued to think of himself as a writer first, the press of the period was only beginning to think of rock talents as having any lasting merit.

When "I'm a Believer" established his ability to write multi-million-selling hits for others as well as himself, many suspected that he could become one of the country's leading tunesmiths. However, the "alternative" rock audience—whose influence was highlighted by the release of the Beatles' "Sgt. Pepper's Lonely Hearts Club Band" in June 1967—was now starting to turn against the Brill Building–inspired sounds. The Brill Building was about to become synonymous with the bubble-gum genre that started with the Monkees and ended with the DeFranco Family.

The "bubble-gum" image gave Diamond some trouble when, after penning "A Little Bit Me, A Little Bit You" expressly for the Monkees ("That was written more on purpose for them and it was probably less inspired because of it," Diamond later said), he had trouble following it up with hits for anyone but himself. Cliff Richard's "I'll Come Running" and Lulu's "The Boat That I Row" were big sellers in England, but most versions of his compositions struggled commercially. Ronnie Dove's "My Babe" (which Diamond produced), the Angels' "The Boy with the Green Eyes," Graham Bonney's "Back from Baltimore" (originally given to Dove), and John Davidson's "Flame" (the song Herb Cohen remembers as the first complete song Neil ever played for him in high school) all were very minor hits.

Diamond hardly endeared himself to the feminist movement in 1972 when he commented on Lulu's version of "The Boat That I Row": "I remember my reaction when I first heard it was that it was not a girl's song. It was too strong to be sung by a girl. It's a man's song to do. So I felt that Lulu's version was wrong because she's a girl. I think she's great, but . . . it comes on too strong for the kind of women that I like. . . . It's not a feminine song."

In 1967, Diamond discovered and produced a Cowsills-type group called Penny Candy. Although the group was signed to Kama-Sutra records, they apparently never released a record.

"I can't possibly do all the songs I've written myself, so I give them to people I feel can do the best job with them. I've been told I was crazy to give the songs to the Monkees, but I think they brought in greater sales than I would have because of their TV exposure."

He maintained that he wasn't snobbish about bubble-gum music. "I think there's room in the spectrum for happy, commercial, musical cotton candy, too."

In the meantime, Diamond's own records continued to sell. His second Bang album, *Just for You*, which included his own version of "I'm a Believer," made a fair-sized dent in the charts despite the fact that one-fourth of the selections were duplicated from *The Feel of Neil Diamond*. Apparently, the commercially minded Berns decided to simply delete the first album and reissue some familiar single-released cuts on the new record so that another round of recording sessions would not have to be commissioned. This was a common occurrence at Bang: Neil's label mate Van Morrison somehow found his *second* album called *The Best of Van Morrison*.

Although established, Diamond was becoming discontented over several things. Above all, his success was only a temporary help to his marriage. Even with fewer money problems, Neil and Jaye found that the years had taken away much of what they had in common.

Diamond's initial success had enabled them to move into a rented house in Massapequa, Long Island, but its distance from New York's music center in Manhattan, coupled with Diamond's road appearances, only frustrated Jaye. For years, Jaye had complained of what she felt was the inordinate amount of time they spent apart. (In 1969, a song about it appeared, entitled "Where Do You Run To," but went unsold.) By the time "I Thank the Lord for the Night Time" was in the Top Ten, the strains were ripping the marriage apart.

He recalled this decline: "It was almost as though our destiny was preordained. We were to be married, have children; the best we could hope for was a little house on Long Island. We'd live the lives our parents wanted us to live. I didn't really begin to think about myself and my life until I began to travel and remove myself from that peer group. And I realized that wasn't what I wanted at all, and things began deteriorating from that point."

In addition, he began to feel conscious of the growing division between the teeny-bopper audience who listened to Top Forty and the maturing new FM crowd. To him, the acts more clearly destined for prolonged success were the ones that catered to the latter group. This audience preferred music like Bob Dylan's *Blonde on Blonde* or the Rolling Stones' *Aftermath*, music that challenged the status of the classic songwriting of the 1930s and 1940s. Dylan and the Stones were singing music that would be remembered long into the future as the important works of the time.

More and more, it was this sort of respect Diamond craved, and he felt that he could only get it by courting the college and post-college audience. Not only did he begin to tour campuses almost exclusively, but he started talking to the teen magazines differently—his way or not at all.

Chafing at the prospect of continuing to do interviews consisting of little more than his vital statistics, his favorite color, and the kind of women he liked, Diamond began to talk more about his songwriting inspirations and his views of the music scene. In the summer of 1967, Diamond wrote—or had ghost-written from taped interviews—first-person articles for *Hit Parader* magazine that explained some of his philosophy:

"When people ask me what artists have influenced me, I have to say no one. The things that do influence me are things and emotions. Not a song, because that is another person's interpretation of emotions. Other songs don't influence me to write songs, only people [influence me].

"For example, recently I was performing in San Francisco. When I finished, I walked to the back of the hall and I saw a girl crying. I walked up to her and said, 'What's the matter? Can I buy you a Coke? Will you marry me?' I tried to make her smile. She had had a fight with her boyfriend, who was in the band playing at that very moment. Just the sight of her standing against the wall, apart from the millions of kids out on the floor dancing . . . had an effect on me. She must have really been feeling bad to cry in front of all those people. I went back to my hotel and wrote a song. That motivated me to get something down on paper. Generally, this is the way I write.

"Usually writers get up in the morning and just start to write. It's very difficult for me to do that. I have to write when I feel like it. Once I start a song, I don't stop until it's finished. Once it starts coming, it's difficult to stop. I'll sleep for a couple of hours, or eat, but I'll get right back into the song. So, when you ask me which artists or songs or albums have influenced me, I have to say there are a lot of artists I respect.

"There are young writers who can compare with any of the great writers of the past. That's why I always laugh when people put down rock & roll. Rock & roll is a point at which creativity can start . . . it's relatively new now. Rock & roll developed a lot in six years. But six years ago you could see the potential. There are people writing in the rock idiom now who will be here twenty years from now writing good music. It's a very exciting time.

"I try not to think commercial. I try to think of things I like. If an idea doesn't kill me, I won't bother with it. When I was freelancing, I wrote to other singers' specifications—what they thought was commercial. When I did that, I was never happy with the songs and I never had hits, either. So I decided to do what I wanted and bomb or succeed on my own.

"It looks like everybody is doing what they want now. There seems to be a trend toward experimentation. It can only be good. We always need good new sounds. What's good will rise to the top and the rest will be discarded. Right now we are going through a renaissance."

He was also tapering off in his work for other artists: "I've been getting a lot of offers to write songs now. Sometimes I will sit down and write for other people, but generally my performing and writing songs for myself takes up most of the time. You can't do too many things and do them well. So I didn't want to water down my writing by writing for too many people or water down my performance by taking up my time with something else."

Diamond's own major creative step at this time was the song "Shilo," a cut from *Just for You* that was his first deliberately personal song. A story of a lonely and neglected boy who reverts to conjuring up imaginary friends when he is ignored by family and friends, it was Diamond at his best up to that time. "Shilo" proved to be a watershed for Diamond, even while "Kentucky Woman" rose on the charts.

"Kentucky Woman" was a hit, even for Deep Purple eleven months after Diamond's success with it, and was pretty good for a song written in the back seat of a car by a tired-out performer. "I wrote 'Kentucky Woman' outside of Paducah, Kentucky. I was touring and I was just dead tired and I probably needed some kind of companionship. And that's when I thought of 'Kentucky Woman' and unfortunately, there weren't any around or there weren't any available at the time. I probably wouldn't have written the song if there were!"

By this time, Diamond was tired of being hustled to the

various media like so many consumer goods. Not only did he feel "Shilo" would help him achieve the more dignified public image he wanted, but he also truly loved the song. It wasn't that he disliked "Kentucky Woman," he just felt that "Shilo" should have come first.

"Shilo" resulted in Diamond's leaving Bang. He wanted to see it released as a single, while Berns felt the song was too moody for commercial safety and refused. Even as "Kentucky Woman" soared up the charts instead, Neil persisted in his desire to give "Shilo" a chance.

The success of "Kentucky Woman" did nothing to change Berns's mind. The best deal he would offer Neil for the single release of "Shilo" was to extend his contract with Bang for another two years.

This enraged Diamond. He became so angered that he wanted to quit Bang immediately. When careful legal examination of his Bang contract indicated that he did not have to turn out any more new recordings, he stopped giving the company material.

As Diamond explained to *Rolling Stone*, "When I told him [Berns] I wouldn't record for him anymore, the heat began to get really intense. Bert started threatening me because I was his biggest artist and he wanted more of the same. At that time, Fred Weintraub was managing me. About two weeks after our real big blow-up, somebody threw a bomb into the Bitter End, and we knew it was related to this whole thing."

Though the bomb was actually a mere smoke-bomb that did little but stink up the room, shortly thereafter Weintraub was mugged on the street, and Neil became fearful for his family and friends. He borrowed a gun and sent his family out of town. "Things seemed to cool down, and so I just left it at that."

Although no evidence of Berns's alleged role ever surfaced, the business climate cooled after his death from a heart attack on December 31, 1967. Berns's widow, Ilene, who inherited ownership and management of Bang, emphatically denied that Berns would have tried violent means to influence business associates.

In any event, Neil felt safe again, and started looking seriously for a new label. In leaving Bang, Diamond also disassociated himself with the Barry-Greenwich production team. He never again worked with Jeff Barry and Ellie Greenwich, whose divorce in 1967 had effectively curbed their creative partnership as well. Barry went back to the bubble-gum factories, becoming the main force behind the Archies and Andy Kim as well as starting his own label, Steed Records. Greenwich stayed in regular pop A&R and briefly attempted to emulate Carole King's success as a singer/songwriter. Both are still active in the industry.

"Jeff and Ellie are tremendous talents," Diamond said. "Jeff is a genius and they complement themselves so beautifully. I used to sit back and watch them. They were right on; they did the thing and they did it right. I'm not sure Jeff has enough confidence in himself to really extend himself, spread his wings. He thought, as Bert Berns did, in terms of the single—the catchy thing, the hook, selling a million records.

"Don't get me wrong, that was fine. I was thrilled with that. Be realistic—I knocked around and broke my hump and lived in Woolworth's for eight years, so this [success] was a whole new thing to me. . . . But then, after a while, I began to have experience, enough confidence in my ability to want to spread out a little bit more and do other things.

"I'd go out of my mind if I had to write 'Cherry, Cherry' and 'I'm a Believer' again. I mean, they were fine then, and I enjoyed them, but to write them now, or to write them again for any length of time, to consistently come out with those kinds of records, well. . . ."

During those early meetings (when he was negotiating for a new record deal), I was quite impressed by Neil's grasp of the business. He knew about music, but he also knew how record companies worked. If his voice ever fails, he could easily become a successful record executive. But he was also supremely confident in his talent; no question in his mind that he would become a great star.

—Clive Davis
Clive: Inside the Record Business (with James Willwerth)
William Morrow & Company, 1974

4
And the Singer Sings His Song (1968-1970)

Davis made the above observation as a result of Columbia Records' attempt to sign the widely sought-after Diamond in 1968. Warner Brothers and MCA's Uni label were also expressing interest in the fledgling superstar.

Davis had a handshake agreement with Diamond's manager Fred Weintraub to bring Diamond into Columbia's fold. Davis believed the agreement was de facto and even sent Diamond a welcoming telegram. But Davis would have to wait another five years before Diamond would return to Columbia.

A last-minute concession from Uni, which offered Diamond one of the biggest money deals to that date for a rock performer, caused Neil to drop Weintraub's agreement with Davis. Davis was angry and nearly arranged to have all CBS artists boycott the Bitter End, but he and Weintraub eventually made peace.

Uni, short for Universal City, was the newest and most rock-oriented of MCA's record divisions—Decca, Kapp,

Coral, and Brunswick—all of which were suffering from declining sales; most of their commercial action was in the country and western market.

MCA faced increasing trouble keeping up with both Columbia and RCA in the rock market. Uni tried to establish a good reputation after having a number one hit with the Strawberry Alarm Clock's "Incense and Peppermints," but this song was a known fluke. The group reportedly didn't want to record it, and a friend of theirs who never joined the band sang the lead vocal. Thus, Uni could not bank on repeated success from the Strawberry Alarm Clock. Clearly, Uni was looking for someone else they could build into a superstar act.

Diamond, at the time of his signing in April 1968, was easily Uni's most famous personality. His contract called for eight albums at a $250,000 guarantee per disk. The contract also gave Diamond the artistic freedom he wanted on the heels of the "Shilo" controversy. Uni also promised better sales promotion than he had received with Bang. These details were similar to a concurrent deal that the Steve Miller Band signed with Capitol Records, but Diamond's signing was more celebrated because he had recently tied Frank Sinatra in *Cash Box* magazine's year-end poll for Male Vocalist of 1967.

Signing with Uni also gave Diamond a chance to work with new producers in different music locales outside New York City. His first Uni recording session, for example, took place in Memphis, and was produced by singer/songwriter Chip Taylor, who was famous for composing "Wild Thing" for the Troggs and "Angel of the Morning" for Merilee Rush. Taylor worked with Diamond long enough to produce the milestone "Brooklyn Roads" b/w "Holiday Inn Blues" single.

"Brooklyn Roads" was basically an extension of the biographical sentiments developing in "Shilo." "Brooklyn Roads" delved into the lonely city-born child's adolescence, sharing his hopes and dreams of one day conquering the rawness of the city.

"The fact that I'm from New York is reflected in everything I write. All my songs have the tensions, the loves and the hates, and the nostalgia created by a big city. It's inborn. The first song I wrote when I changed record companies was 'Brooklyn Roads.' "

The disc's flip side, "Holiday Inn Blues," had Diamond's touring band on the track and even mentioned most of them by name in the lyrics. This was the first time Diamond did not use session players in the studio. He wanted his band on it, as they had shared life on the road with him.

At the time he said, "That's what it's really like. The hardest thing about performing is the traveling. . . . I wanted to write about what we think, about what we go through on the road, so 'Holiday Inn Blues' came out." When a reporter said, "I bet the Holiday Inns appreciate it!" Neil added, "Yeah, we'll probably get sued next week!"

"Brooklyn Roads" was Neil's most carefully crafted single yet. He really had high hopes for its success, but the song ran into trouble in the marketplace, partly due to the competition—Neil Diamond himself.

Bang had already released "New Orleans" and "Red Red Wine" as singles riding the success of "Kentucky Woman" to reap as much as possible from the twenty-five song catalog Diamond had left them. And as if the radio and retail overexposure of Diamond they had created wasn't enough, Bang decided to finally release "Shilo" as a single, pitting it against the release of "Brooklyn Roads." The two singles nearly canceled each other out, with "Brooklyn Roads" stalling on the national charts at number fifty-eight. This release of "Shilo" bombed, but it would return again in a later reissue. Diamond's next album, *Velvet Gloves and Spit*, was released after this chart war, and it was the most notable casualty. The glut of Diamond material caused him to lose his popular momentum. When finally released, the album was a sales disaster.

The first Uni album, originally to be titled *Two-Bit Manchild*, had a close-up picture of Diamond on the cover of early pressings. It appeared in stores over six months after the release of "Brooklyn Roads," as Diamond needed more time to finish it to his complete satisfaction. After all, this was the first album over which he would have complete control. He enlisted the aid of Tom Catalano, the man who signed him to Columbia Records back in 1963, to help him finish the record in Los Angeles.

In 1968, he was still working on the album. "I've got everything in it from rock to comedy—more Copland than country, I guess. None of these are just commercial songs like I've written before. 'Cherry, Cherry' is just music to dance by, but in the album I want to say a few things. I've tried not to settle for any line that doesn't say exactly what I mean.

"When I wrote songs like 'Solitary Man' and 'Brooklyn Roads,' I wrote directly from experience; nobody had a right to that much of my privacy. Autobiography should be kept in a drawer. A composer doesn't have to do that. He can just write honestly and enough of himself comes through without pushing it.

"I like songs that give me chills. My album won't be full of soul-shattering, heart-rending, tear-jerking songs, but I hope they reach some people. I really hate so-called rock critics who dissect songs that were just meant to be heard by some fourteen-year-old kid in Wichita. These guys sound like someone trying to explain a joke after it's over. Why bother?"

He added that he wrote songs by singing into a tape recorder and then transcribing them: "I couldn't do it any other way. Composing on paper is like stopping to brush your teeth in the middle of making love."

Diamond also exhibited his first fleeting signs of keeping up with the 1960s Now Generation: "The adults who make sweeping put-downs of rock just look silly, because it's obvious what they say doesn't matter. Rock will be the folk music of the future . . . *Sgt. Pepper* . . . still will be good music fifty years from now. Take out a Patti Page recording that's only fifteen years old and see if you like it. The fact is that pop musicians are the torch-bearers of the new American culture. We picked up the torch from the nothing generation which gave us World War II, the Korean War, the Vietnam War, alcoholism, and more mental illness than ever before. Thanks to them, these days it takes nerves of steel only to be neurotic."

Neil's progress in putting together *Velvet Gloves and Spit* was also slowed by a project he had started before he signed with Uni: forming a celebrity anti-drug organization. P.A.D. (Performers Against Drugs) was announced in the teen press as an effort to show that the pop scene was not entirely in favor of experimenting with drugs, a problem that had reached epidemic levels.

Ideally, the project would have entailed enlisting other performers to do benefit concerts and promotional work for the cause. To drive the point home, Neil included a song on *Velvet Gloves and Spit* called "The Pot Smoker's Song," a sardonic novelty with monologues by real recovering addicts edited in between the verses. The teenagers in the song were patients of New York City's Phoenix House rehabilitation center.

"I feel a certain responsibility to tell addicted young-sters and the ones who are curious about psychedelics that the drug scene is the wrong way to go about things. There are other ways to solve problems," Diamond explained.

Asked for the root of his concern, he said, "I really can't answer that. It would be like telling you why I breathe . . . or eat . . . or sing. I think it's like the poet John Donne said—'No man is an island'—and like the Bible tells us—'Do unto others as you would have them do unto you.' I don't think we have an alternative. We have to care and 'do unto.' If we don't, we won't have anyone to 'do unto.' Right? People are like a religion to me. I enjoy being with them and listening to what they have to say. If you enjoy something—or someone—then automatically you don't want anything to hurt or harm them.

"You know, when the hippies first became known I thought they might have something with their love credo. I agreed with them. But too soon it became evident that though they may have loved each other, they really didn't care about the rest of the world. In a way, they were just acting the same as the narrow-minded people they were putting down. And I think they put too much emphasis on drugs. Drugs really don't turn you on. . . . They just turn your life off and shake up your head a lot. At least that's what I think."

P.A.D. turned into an alarming failure. Roughly half the performers asked to participate declined, mostly because the organization's bent seemed so contrary to the popular opinion of the record-buying generation. Artists were afraid of injuring their position with the counterculture, especially in a time when everybody was supposed to stand for something. The appearance of embracing "the squares' " values could have cost more than a few performers heavily in record and ticket sales.

When Diamond saw that all he was going to get were artists with "clean" images and no pretentious myths to protect, he knew he was beaten. His own dip in popularity at this time—caused by his overexposure—might also have lessened his chances of rallying support.

The anti-drug group established him as a conservative spirit in a liberal time. His Top Forty fans approved, but the FM audience he desired scoffed. As late as the release of *Tap Root Manuscript* in 1970, *Rolling Stone* could get away with saying, "If someone gives you this album, listen to it . . . but I wouldn't recommend blowing your dope money on it."

A few months later in 1968, he grudgingly modified his views: "I have mixed feelings about marijuana; it has no more effect on me than a good screwdriver, but I'm against legalization. If you legalize pot today, sixty million people will be smoking it tomorrow, and there'll be

two million of them who can't handle it. There are
enough things around already that people can't handle—
like guns and alcohol."

Two more singles, "Two-Bit Manchild" and "Sunday
Sun," were released prior to the release of *Velvet Gloves
and Spit*. Uni pushed "Two-Bit Manchild" heavily to
radio stations, releasing eye-catching red vinyl DJ-only
copies. Some stations played the song, while others,
especially in the South, favored the single's flip side, a
six-minute novelty called "Broad Old Woman (6 A.M.
Insanity)." The piece gives listeners a bit of Neil at work
in the studio. Recorded presumably in the wee hours of
the morning after an all-night session, the record began
life as a rough song that he just could never complete.
Despite its unfinished state, it has a good beat, and some
programmers actually preferred it. One week, jukebox
operators in Chattanooga unbelievably reported it at
number one in plays. However, Neil never put "Broad
Old Woman (6 A.M. Insanity)" on an album.

"Sunday Sun" had a genuine groundswell of support
on the West Coast and lived a chart life similar to
"Solitary Man." Despite several weeks of airplay on the
RKO radio chain, the record stalled at number sixty-eight.

It was not only the P.A.D. backlash that kept *Velvet
Gloves and Spit* out of record review magazine columns.
The music itself took an increasingly straight-pop attitude with guitars. For all its qualities, it was too serious
for the teenyboppers and too staid for with-it types.

The inside picture of the original cover reflected the
album's problems: it showed a shirtless, hairy-chested
Neil still wearing a semi-pompadour hairstyle. He is
standing by an assembly line of partially made manne-
quins in a curious, quasi-impressionistic composition. It
might have been a statement on the manufactured quality
of most pop music, but then again, it might just have
been an ugly picture.

Originally intending to provide a spoken introduction
to each song, Diamond eventually decided against it,

stating that his songs were complete within themselves and introductions were trifling. He later pronounced the album disappointing, despite his observation that it had allowed him to stretch artistically.

Almost simultaneously, he began assaulting the Bang reissue campaign by remaking "Shilo" in the hope that the new version would become the definitive one. While this strategy failed in America, the Uni-released "Shilo" later became a smash hit overseas.

The most significant aspect of *Velvet Gloves and Spit* was his association with producer Catalano, with whom he would continue to work throughout 1974, and who played a large role in shaping Diamond's middle-of-the-road sound during that period.

Neil's involvement with the production of *Velvet Gloves and Spit*, along with his shift in recording base to Los Angeles, signalled the end of his marriage to Jaye. He had been on the road so much during the year doing college tours, club dates, and recording the album, that he and Jaye had hardly seen each other for months. He admitted being the first to walk out the door: "I just decided to split and leave it all behind. In a sense it was running away."

The split was not particularly amicable, and when he grew a beard and began wearing trendy clothing he wasn't just trying to be hip. The new image was adopted to avoid the private detectives whom Jaye had hired to follow Neil, suspecting that he was seeing someone else.

He met his second wife, Marcia Murphey, sometime before 1969 when he guested on a network variety show on which Marcia was a production assistant (possibly ABC's "Showcase '67," on which Diamond sang "Two-Bit Man-child" and "Brooklyn Roads" on location at the Bitter End). Jaye's knowledge of "the other woman" was a sore point in the divorce; and to this day, Neil absolutely refuses to discuss Jaye by name, or what has become of her. She won custody of Marjorie and Elyn, and Neil received regular visitation rights.

Neil decided to move to Los Angeles permanently to start fresh and also to be closer to MCA's base in Universal City, just north of Hollywood. MCA's Universal Pictures was interested in Neil as an actor, and being closer to the record company made career decisions easier.

Settled in Los Angeles, Neil limited his television appearances to network shows, ultimately turning up on "The Johnny Cash Show," "The Glen Campbell Goodtime Hour," and the Everly Brothers' series. The divorce proceedings and his overall low morale made him even more reluctant to be a public figure.

In the meantime, he was building his relationship with Marcia, who was fairly private in her own right. Because she was closer to Neil's show-business environment, the pair seemed an appropriate match, and they were married within months of his divorce from Jaye.

"I'm not sure what it was that attracted me to Marcia. Maybe it was the sadness in her eyes more than anything else. I saw this girl and she evidently understood great pain," Diamond revealed. "Her forebears came over on the *Mayflower*. She's the much more American side of me and she offers me that much strength as well."

He made tentative steps to enter the acting field at Universal's insistence. During his later months in New York, he had said, "I've been studying with Harry Master George, a drama coach in New York, and I may be signing to act in a film with Universal Studios. It's another form of expression, and although I've never tried it, I think I'll be good at it. But even if I do get into acting, I think songs will always be my primary form of communicating."

His first acting job was in a cameo role as himself in an episode of "Mannix" in which he sang "The Boat That I Row" and a never-heard-elsewhere song called "Raisin' Cane." Diamond remembered the experience as unpleasantly bossy, as being treated "like a piece of meat." When a Universal screen test opposite David Hartman raised little interest ("They looked at it and immediately buried

it. Nothing came of it."), Diamond decided to forget
about acting for a time. So began over a decade of
rumored film projects that Neil was always
"considering."

In 1980, he reminisced with Hartman on "Good
Morning America": "I remember it very well. We came in
and rehearsed over the weekend. You were going to go
work out with the Dodgers—you had your baseball glove
and your baseball. You were wonderful. You helped me
through the thing, and I still have the screen test at home.
We watch it occasionally for a laugh. I think *you* did very
well, actually. It took me twelve years to get up enough
nerve to try it again."

He continued to play concert dates around the country,
concentrating on campuses because "collegians listen
carefully. When they enjoy the music, they give you an
honest enthusiastic response. They give a performer in-
centive. Any performer who believes the screams of a
young teenage audience is deceiving himself."

In January 1969, Diamond got up the nerve to attempt
his first concept album. He chose a subject that he had
been mulling over for several years: the world of the
revival preachers. He distrusted their rhetoric and had
originally intended to do something of an *Elmer Gan-
try*-type anti-hypocrisy statement.

"I went to an awful lot of revival meetings at one point,
and my original thoughts about these guys were that they
were phonies, and they were taking these people, really
taking them. And that was when I first had the idea to do
a *Brother Love* album. Then I left it for a while and when
I started to think about it again, I realized that the
intentions of these preachers were not really important
because they gave these people something. These people
are really the most desperate, tragic kind of people. . . .
Besides the poverty, my impression was that they had
nothing to look forward to, nothing. So they came to this
revival meeting. My impression of these people is that
they live within the Bible and the preachers and what

they say. I walked in there with a chip on my shoulder, but I started to feel that despite what the guy was really thinking, he was giving these people something, and that was good. So I became more sympathetic towards the character Brother Love. It was less what he was than what he gave. But . . . originally it did start as a putdown."

He continued: "I went up to Harlem, to 125th Street, to a church there, and sat in on a meeting one Sunday and it blew my mind. Because I realized, I think, for the first time that no, this was not a rip-off, these people were getting what they came for. They were finding answers. That there *is* truth in what these people say. That there is a way to guide your life. . . . Not for everybody, but for these people there was, and I started to think of it more positively.

" 'Brother Love' was supposed to be an entire album about this lecherous revival preacher, but I figured I could really capture a small part of the excitement of a revival meeting in one single."

Impressed by the emotional pull of the revival meetings, he became a fan of the gospel sound. The track that would be the centerpiece of the album, "Brother Love's Travelling Salvation Show," was actually written on the jet flight to the recording studio. "I was on a plane to Memphis to do my first recording session down there, and I had written a melody that I was very, very strong about and wanted to record, but I hadn't written a lyric. And . . . it all came to me—the whole revival meeting thing, the whole Harlem church meeting. I wrote the entire lyric on the way down . . . and went and recorded it the next day." He later admitted that he had tried to write lyrics for it earlier, coming up with a similar verse that was to have been called "Mo, Get 'Em Mo!" But . . . "My wife hated it."

Sessions for the *Brother Love's Travelling Salvation Show* album stumbled along for a couple of months as Neil tried to come up with other songs to complement the theme. Work had begun in Memphis under the auspices

of veteran country-and-western producers Tommy Cog-
bill and Chips Moman, but Diamond wound up producing some of the sessions himself and with Catalano.
Eventually he dumped the concept, keeping only a few
tracks.

"Brother Love's Travelling Salvation Show" reached
the singles market in early spring 1969 and provided Neil
with a definite comeback. His first genuine hit since
"Kentucky Woman," it still was not an overwhelming
smash, as it suffered from a poor response on the East
Coast. The song did earn some critical respect and a
hoped-for basis of support for the album.

The *Brother Love's Travelling Salvation Show* album
was released amidst new promotional pictures that
showed the bearded, love-beaded Diamond looking completely different. In addition, the album cover boasted a
weird pop art game board that measured the listener's
awareness. This gimmick, first used with better results by
Country Joe and the Fish, barely reflected the spirit of the
music at all.

Although *Brother Love's Travelling Salvation Show* is
very similar to *Velvet Gloves and Spit* in theme and
musical tone, Neil still lacked the major artistic break-
through he needed. Sales and reviews were fair, but
Diamond was still plagued by his reluctance to work in
the rock idiom. He identified with current music less and
less, still believing that a synthesis of rock and older pop
forms was not only viable, but potentially more enduring.

The media hadn't set the definite parameters of the rock
genre. The jazz-rock sound personified by Chicago and
Blood, Sweat, and Tears, and the folk-rock sound of the
singer-songwriter pack—James Taylor, Carole King, Joni
Mitchell—had become the predominant styles, along with
a burgeoning heavy-metal sound.

Oddly, this was the best time for Diamond's sound to
come of age. His work would become associated with
these "new rock" forms and therefore establish a tenuous
relationship with the rock crowd. Similar acts who came

after the "genre-rock" era had peaked, such as Barry
Manilow, have been more excluded from rock than has
Diamond.

Neil was not really of the Age of Aquarius, and knew
it. "I never could identify with that. I never did understand . . . this rebelliousness. First of all, I was not a
teenager anymore. I was twenty-six or twenty-seven, I had
already been married, had two children at that point. I
knew I was out of it. It didn't relate to what I was trying
to do, which was essentially to try and be Alan Jay Lerner
or George Gershwin. 'Hip' was something frivolous
people had time to be. I didn't have time to be 'hip' and
'with it' and 'groovy.' I was dealing with something that
was much more important—my life and trying to write
songs that had substance. And 'hip' is bullshit. It doesn't
cut deep. It cuts for today and tomorrow."

It was probably this awareness that inspired him to
write his next single—an archetypal "big" love song that
blended his usual sensitivity with strings, horns, and a
catchy chorus. "I finished it in the motel room just before
the session. It just felt good then, when I first wrote it; and
it's felt good doing it ever since." Recorded in Tennessee
with Catalano and Coghill co-producing, "Sweet Caroline" quickly became his biggest hit. It immediately
became a pop standard—the type of song covered by
countless artists ("It's been cut by everybody from Elvis
Presley to Frank Sinatra to Waylon Jennings; Bob Dylan
sent me a tape of him doing it."), sung by guests on "The
Tonight Show," and heard as muzak played in elevators
and supermarkets.

Brother Love's Travelling Salvation Show was reissued
with "Sweet Caroline" added, and eventually sported a
new cover with a clean-shaven Neil wearing a white suede
fringed jacket. The album's new title was *Brother Love's
Travelling Salvation Show/Sweet Caroline*, and as sales
began to pick up, Uni asked for another album before the
end of the year.

Diamond was already sketching out "The African

Trilogy," and was running low on new material, but he did have an ace up his sleeve: the even more gospel-oriented "Holly Holy." A long, bizarre epic of a love relationship mixed with the imagery of religious fervor, "Holly Holy" was, and still is, considered one of his best records. One of the year's bravest singles, it easily soared into the Top Ten.

Neil was asked to comment on "Holly Holy" during a BBC interview in 1971: "That's a weird song, and I don't really know if I can explain it. But what I tried to do was create a religious experience, or represent a religious experience between a man and a woman, as opposed to a man and a god. That's essentially what this man is singing about."

He'd given up trying to explicate it further: " 'Holly Holy' is not the kind of thing you're supposed to think about. It's the kind of a piece where one line, or one word, sets off a little zinger, gives you a twinge. And that's all it is."

The accompanying album, *Touching You, Touching Me*, contained only five original compositions, along with four recognizable pop standards. Although it was well liked at the time and was the first Neil Diamond album to sell one million copies, it may have hurt his credibility with people who no longer approved of re-makes of recent hits. Neil let it pass, inasmuch as bigger plans were already in the works.

Touching You, Touching Me contained Neil's version of Buffy Saint-Marie's "Until It's Time for You to Go," a tender love song she had been unable to hit with herself. Although Diamond's cover of the song was immediately released once "Holly Holy" had peaked, "Until It's Time for You to Go" had to suffer direct competition from Bang's second reissue of "Shilo." This time "Shilo" was a reasonably sized hit, reaching number twenty-four and destroying "Until It's Time for You to Go," which could only muster a mere number fifty-three. It was obvious that Diamond's public preferred his self-penned songs over his remakes.

Diamond's sound was now established: big, dramatic ballads with plenty of orchestration and background choruses. Diamond had also finalized his new persona: a modern singer-songwriter of standard pop music with rock overtones. He was now the sort of entertainer that Mom and Dad liked as much as the kids did. He moved up in status from playing college campuses to large amphitheaters and seemed destined for media stardom on the level of Tom Jones and Glen Campbell.

As a farewell to the small-artist days of his career, he did one last show at Doug Weston's Troubador club in West Hollywood that was taped for release as the *Gold* album. The concert took place in early January 1970, with Seals and Crofts as opening act. The concert and album were well received, although most listeners today tend to think that he was still maturing as a live performer.

Neil and Marcia soon had their first son, Jesse. As during his first marriage, Diamond was highly protective of his family and allowed very little information about them to leak out.

Later that spring, word that Diamond was indeed going to join Jones and Campbell as a television star came from sources at CBS. The idea was to give Neil a variety show that would have been the summer 1970 replacement for Campbell. As with many other Diamond television projects, it never came to pass. "The budget had been approved by CBS. . . . The only thing I can think of was there was some kind of shake-up," Neil said. "It happened the same week they were dropping Skelton and Jackie Gleason, and maybe they didn't feel like bowing down to Glen, who was exerting a lot of pressure on them. They were looking for a concept, I think, and I guess they didn't want to go with one guy." (The hour was filled by a rotating-star comedy series.)

"My show would've been a different show. It would never have been a variety show. Maybe it wouldn't have gone past the summer, but it would have been something really fine, at least to my way of thinking."

Diamond, indeed, felt uneasy about hosting a regular comedy/music show, which he knew wasn't really his forte and would not do his serious-artist aspirations much good. As a result, once this opportunity fell away, he generally avoided American television until 1977.

Meanwhile, he saw a chance to fulfill his desire to gain recognition as an important songwriter along the lines of Bob Dylan or Paul Simon. As a result of the success of the live album, Bang's successful revival of "Solitary Man," Diamond could now persuade Uni to release an album consisting of half regular songs and half a connected suite which mostly lacked his singing voice. The album, which featured an enclosed libretto, would be called *Tap Root Manuscript*.

Diamond later explained that African folk music "struck me as the most sensual music that I'd ever heard. . . . The intricacies and sophistication were built on rhythms as opposed to melodic structures and time. I got interested in the African thing and started picking up on some African records and tapes that friends had gotten from missionaries, really far out kinds of things. African music is far from primitive. It's very complicated. It's immensely gutsy. There's no prettiness in it. If you read translations of lyrics, you find a very basic kind of folk thing."

He bypassed the language problem by writing most of the lyrics in English: "Most of the folk stories I had read were in English. But I wanted to write the Mass in Swahili because I just could not conceive of a Mass being written in English. It struck me as almost sacrilegious. I spoke to a few people because I wasn't sure of the proper usage of certain terms. And I did some research work with the representatives from the Kenyan Mission to the United Nations in New York and some people with the African Studies Department at UCLA.

"I didn't feel, when I finally decided to do 'The African Trilogy,' that I could really say it in one single. I wanted to do a whole piece with a thread running through it. . . .

I thought I got away from the childhood theme but the focal point around which the 'Trilogy' is written is childhood and the simplicity of it and, I'd like to think, the honesty of it."

Diamond's recording session for "Childsong" (part of "Trilogy") used the services of fifteen eight-year-old kids: "It was the most fun and also the most difficult recording session I've ever done. You can't control eight-year-old kids. They'd go crazy, they were fighting and beating each other up, and I had to go get their mothers—their parents were all sitting in the control room while they were out there singing; and I would threaten them with 'If you don't stop fighting, I'm gonna get your mother out here.' And their mothers would be glaring at them through the window, giving them dirty looks. It was fantastic, but they ran me ragged—they made me crazy, but I finally got what I wanted.

" 'The African Trilogy' took fourteen months of work and cost over $100,000. But it was one of my most crowning delights. It was just pure personal satisfaction."

The public's first taste of Neil's folk ballet was "Soolaimon," (a French bastardization of the word "salamon"), a song which evoked imagery similar to "Holly Holy" but featured a more obvious native African influence. It was a hit—it sounded not a bit like anything else out at the time, except maybe "Holly Holy." The single that actually came out on top of the album, though, was his first number one smash, "Cracklin' Rosie." It highlighted Diamond's strength in writing unpretentious pop songs and drew the attention of thousands who never realized they were listening to a song about a mass-produced domestic wine.

" 'Cracklin' Rosie' is an interesting story," he explained. "During an interview I had with a girl who was working with a newspaper in Canada, she told me that her parents were medical missionaries . . . on the Indian reservations in northern Canada. And she began to tell me what their lives were like and what experiences they had. She told me that on one of the reservations there were more men than there were women, and come the weekends or holidays, a lot of men were out of luck—there weren't enough girls to go around. And so they would go down to their general store, and they would buy a bottle of a very inexpensive wine called Crackling Rose. . . . This wine became their woman for the weekend, and they called their woman 'Cracklin' Rosie.' And that's what the song was about."

Tap Root Manuscript was an instant hit, even spawning the release of Neil's version of "He Ain't Heavy, He's My Brother," which had been successful for the Hollies less than a year before. Although it reached number twenty nationally, it too was hurt by the Bang re-release strategy, which called for waiting until after Diamond scored with a big hit single. In this case, "Do It," the original flip side of "Solitary Man" in 1966, was revived in celebration of "Cracklin' Rosie." But "Do It" stalled at number thirty-six.

Although it was Diamond's second straight million-seller, *Tap Root Manuscript* did not get the critical response he desired. Most reviewers complained that "The African Trilogy," a seven-part opus that uses the allegory of a day in the heart of the dark continent as an expression of life, growth, and death, was heavy-handed, ill focused, and not terribly soulful. The fans liked it, although most still liked the straight songs better. Many Diamond enthusiasts still see it as the ideal synthesis of black and white cultures.

Despite the critics, Diamond was in a groove.

One refreshing aspect of Neil Diamond is his lack of concern about his image, his disdain of supercool. . . . He is free from the restrictions imposed on traditional rock artists by their management as well as their audiences. He decided to call his own shots and he seems to have succeeded. It's eerily similar in the case of Bob Dylan and Paul Simon. Portrait of the Jewish male as temperamental artist. And yet it's not a question of temperament really, but talent. And singularity. It's what a Presley or Sinatra has.

—Joan Levine
Pacific magazine, 1976

5
I Am . . . I Said
(1970–1972)

Rapidly moving up from performing in amphitheaters to large arenas, Diamond sold out the Anaheim Convention Center in the fall of 1970. He had become a confirmed superstar. His albums were selling in the millions, and his fans clamored for him to make movies and television specials.

Reporters continuously badgered Diamond about an acting debut in the wake of the proposed 1970 summer variety series. Despite confiding that he had future plans to make either a film or television special, or perhaps even become a star on Broadway, he soundly dismissed the idea of a weekly series. He pushed these plans into the deep future, claiming that they would detract from his musical goals of the moment.

Diamond formed a small production company, Kingsway Productions, to seek out possible film projects. But he was still in no hurry to make the move to acting. Rumors of his starring in a remake of *Rebel Without a*

Cause featuring Diamond in the James Dean role were rife for months, yet nothing came of them. Kingsway's major accomplishment was acquiring the movie rights to Jonathan Kozol's urban-school exposé, *Death at an Early Age*. But given the spate of such insider-look films as *To Sir With Love* and *Up the Down Staircase* in the late 1960s, it is not surprising that *Death at an Early Age* was not made during this period.

The most definite step he took toward acting was doing a screen test for the first proposed film treatment of the play *Lenny*. Diamond admired Lenny Bruce and could identify with the late comedian's outlaw view of society. But after completing his test for the role, Diamond was certain he had done poorly. Depressed, he locked himself in his dressing room and reflected for hours on the power and truth of Bruce's words. Deep in introspection, Diamond finally found the courage to write the chorus to "I Am . . . I Said"—the song that tells his story more than any other.

"Bruce's language and thoughts were so violent it was almost an intellectual form of vomiting. He was just saying all those things I had been holding in, that anybody holds in, 'fuck' and 'shit' . . . and 'death' and 'kill' and all of those things that he was getting out. I found they were coming out with me. It was all the anger that was pent up within me. Suddenly, here I was, speaking words that I had never spoken before."

Before it was finished, "I Am . . . I Said" took three months of Diamond's own self-examination, a twenty-page essay he wrote in order to get his complete feelings about his relation to the song down on paper, and his commitment not to stop asking himself who he was.

"And I went into therapy almost immediately after that because there were things coming out of me that I couldn't deal with. It was frightening because I had never been willing to admit this part of my personality."

Neil's chance to get settled into analysis really came later, during his lay-off from concert touring in the middle of the decade. In the meantime, he was hit with an inspiration he needed to follow. The months it took Diamond to write "I Am . . . I Said" helped him personally as the song became his definitive statement of self. He readily admits that it was the hardest song for him to write.

" 'I Am . . . I Said' was a very difficult song because I really had to spend a lot of time thinking about what I was before the song was written. It's a very complicated song, probably because my feelings were very complicated when I wrote it. It tells of feeling lost and full of questions and doubts and insecurities and really having a need to go back home, to go back to the roots, to go back to that original security that you feel in life, and realizing that you never can go back home. That time makes things different, and it changes things," he said.

"I suppose it's a song of conflicts and frustrations as well as the lost/scared thing that I mentioned . . . I guess I do have a lot of myself wrapped up in it. I've found that for the last couple of years the things that I can become most deeply involved with are songs that reflect my feelings about things, and so that's what I've been writing about."

Diamond further explained the genesis period of "I Am . . I Said" later that same year: " 'I Am . . . I Said' didn't really come alive until I wrote one line, and to me, it was the most important line of the song. And from that line, everything else grew, because it set a standard for me. And the line was, 'Did you ever read about a frog who dreamed of being a king . . . and then became one.' And that image of a frog dreaming of being a king just sparked me so much that I went into a frenzy for three months in writing that song to keep everything on that imagery level.

"I don't know if I could write a song like that again, because it was so personal. It required me to understand, actually, more about myself before the song could be completed. I had to go through a self-analytical thing and understand myself. And I couldn't work on anything else. It was quite a time."

When finally released in March 1971, "I Am . . . I Said" became a double A-sided disc with "Done Too Soon" from *Tap Root Manuscript.* The single is clearly the best of his career and garnered Diamond unanimous praise. Even his usual detractors gave it grudging respect.

"Done Too Soon," a triumph in its own right, is a song about legendary heroes and villains who, despite their accomplishments, died because they were mortal. The names in the song make up the verses, and are dramatically sung as if the listener gets a few seconds to meet each of them. It is an allegory of the briefness of life and succeeds on every level.

By now, the Bang reissue strategy was wearing quite thin. After "I Am . . . I Said" b/w "Done Too Soon" sold nearly a million copies in reaching number four nationally, Diamond's current material sounded nothing like the old days, this single's poor showing (number fifty-one) convinced Bang to stop competing. They were to release one last single—"The Long Way Home"—in 1973, but this was to promote the *Double Gold* two-record collection.

"I Am . . . I Said" was certainly a landmark recording, but ironically, Diamond had actually done well at the *Lenny* screen test. After reluctantly returning for a second test, Diamond was offered the role by Marvin Worth, the producer of the original *Lenny* project. But United Artists balked at the idea, Diamond said in a 1986 *USA Today* interview. "They didn't think I was bankable," Diamond told the newspaper.

(This first *Lenny* film project ultimately failed and is separate from the radically rewritten production that became Bob Fosse's 1974 Oscar nominee starring Dustin Hoffman.)

By the summer of 1971, Diamond was discussing plans for a temporary retirement. The time would be spent taking life easier for a few years and performing only in the recording studio. But before the touring sabbatical could take place, he felt he had to sell out a Broadway theater and make some sort of major artistic statement in album form.

Having used up so much creative juice on "I Am . . . I Said," his next album consisted of that song, his second straight two-sided hit single, "Stones" and "Crunchy Granola Suite"—which as a tandem reached number fourteen in November 1971—and six cover versions. Critics complained, but Diamond's following was now so solid that the album was a predetermined success.

Stones was Diamond's chance to do the mostly interpretive album the way he'd always wanted, unlike the times when pragmatism forced him to record cover versions. "The album is simply a one-shot idea. I think they are all beautiful songs that I've wanted to record for a long time. Now seemed an appropriate time to put them on an album of this kind. We went through a big selection to choose these numbers and I don't think recording other people's numbers will affect sales at all."

"Stones," a sensitive and unusually oblique ballad, is said to be one of the few songs that Diamond avoids singing in concert for sentimental reasons; its inspiration has never been discussed publicly. A disc-jockey-only interview album Uni made at the time contains his longest discussion of it: "I guess if I had to sum up 'Stones,' I'd call it a desperate love song. Stones to me had always meant things that hurt people, things that cause pain. And that's what the song is about."

It was during this period that Diamond was accorded more respect than at any time in his career. The rock press might still be looking at him askance, but his popularity was such that the establishment magazines were now treating him as a possible successor to the broken-up Beatles, declining Dylan, and Vegas-ized Elvis. *Cash Box*, which had singled him out as Most Promising New Performer in 1966, named him Top Male Performer in 1971.

Feeling the time was right to close the gap between himself and the press now that journals other than teen magazines were willing to give him space, Neil took the chance to present his current views.

One of the most perceptive profiles of the period was done by Michael Ochs for *Crawdaddy* in 1971. Ochs, while allowing that Neil was "a loner preferring to live in his own private world," was among the first to point out that, paradoxically, Neil's "un-hipness" was his strength as a unique writer and performer.

Neil was perfectly aware that most writers didn't consider him that important overall: "I don't think I'll be a phenomenon until I'm dead, because then someone will turn around and say, 'Jesus Christ, look at what that man wrote.' I figure it'll take about twenty years of writing, because I'm going to spread so much good music around this world, you're not going to believe it. Right now I have the problem of not being 'in,' not being 'new.' I'm cursed by my prior success. I think if I had started my career with 'Brother Love' and written everything from that point on, I would be much bigger today because I would have gotten immediate press attention. But, in people's minds, I still have to live down that whole early part—the teenybopper thing. You see, I've never been made by publicity because I've never had it. The only publicity I've ever had was the success that I had. Finally, after ten hit records, somebody said, 'Hey, maybe we should interview him too.' "

But Diamond was still occasionally reluctant: "I don't like being interviewed because I don't feel I satisfy people's curiosity. . . . I'm just not colorful enough, nor do I want to be. I'll never make it on that level, and I kind of like it that way. The other way is just too damn flimsy. Look at Kris Kristofferson. One day the press says he's the best songwriter in the country, and the next day they say he isn't what he used to be. I'll never have the problem of having to be a 'heavy' or having to live up to a reputation as a great poet or great songwriter of our times. Nobody ever thought I was any better except me."

Neil said that he was looking for time to improve his instrumental skills, that he no longer cared to produce other acts. "I don't want to deal with other people's egos. I have enough trouble with my own."

By now, a contradiction in Neil's attitude was beginning to show. In attempting to sound self-effacing rather than bitter in reflecting on his critical standing, he often seemed confused about whether he really wanted praise.

He told Ochs that he did not want to become actively involved in political campaigns. "I was asked to do some concerts for McGovern, but I wanted to meet the man first so I could see if the feeling was right for me, but it couldn't be arranged. I do try to get my points across to my audiences, but I would never become active in politics per se."

Ochs related a firsthand observation he made during Diamond's 1971 American tour, after the first and highly successful show in Nashville: "We ran into Mac Davis, who had just finished his own concert elsewhere in the city. We all went to eat at the hotel dining room. During the meal, Neil was besieged by autograph seekers for over an hour. 'I used to hate it when people asked for my autograph,' Neil explained, 'because I could never believe that they meant it. I used to think they were putting me on, that's how much confidence I had. But it doesn't bother me at all anymore. If I didn't feel like signing autographs, I'd eat in my room, not in a public place.' Realizing that no one was asking Mac for his autograph, Neil, sensitive soul that he is, turned to Mac and said, 'I'm just letting you see what you have to look forward to.' "

But Diamond also said, "I don't want to get too famous, though. I was approached by NBC recently. They want me to do a weekly show, but I don't want it. It would make me more famous than I want to be. One of the tremendous advantages I gain by being a recording artist is that I can have the acceptance, the respect, and the independence success brings, yet still have the freedom to go where I want to go and do what I want to do without people recognizing me."

Neil had turned philosophical about his failed P.A.D. experiment and now felt that it wasn't his place to be an advisory figure. In fact, he now thought his views on dope were rather naive: "I think grass can be good if it's used with restraint and moderation. There's an old Greek philosophy: 'Do anything you want, but do it in moderation.' I feel that with grass it's very difficult for people to use it in moderation. However, I think that the easiest way for a government to control its people would be to legalize drugs, because it would take all the fight out of them. If there were no fight left in them anymore and everyone was smoking grass all day, who would care?"

He gave his view on the cover versions of his material to fellow songwriter Tony McCauley for the BBC: "Most of the cover records of my songs have been copies of my records. And I would much prefer, as the writer of the song, to hear someone's else's interpretation—a new view, a fresher view of the song. I haven't heard that too often. When I have, I've generally liked it, if not for the quality of the work, at least for the effort." He said that he felt some artists had indeed "destroyed" his songs but did not name names.

Diamond also let slip some more of his songwriting method: "I think that any writer, first of all, writes for his own voice. You can really listen to the songs of just about any writer that you can imagine, and you'll find that the songs—the way that they're written—reflect how the writer sings. Burt Bacharach cannot sing, and so he kind of grunts the songs out. And that's why they're written like this. His songs are very difficult to sing for someone who sings. My songs do reflect the way I sing. But it seems that in the last year and a half, I'm more and more conscious of my voice, because I never considered that people liked the way I sang. Just recently, a few friends of mine have said, 'Hey, you know, I really like the way you sang that.' And I've been aware of that more since then and enjoying it more because of it.

"Writing a song can begin anywhere. It never happens

the same way. It can begin just by the sound of two words together, which is the whole beginning of 'Holly Holy': the sounds of the words and the feelings that I wanted to get across. But it can begin anywhere. It can begin with a chorus, if I feel that a chorus is called for. It can begin with a line.''

He continued: "Because my musical training has been limited, I've never really been restricted by what technical musicians might call a 'song.' I've never limited it to thirty-two bars. The main objective in any song I write has always been that it reflects the way I feel, that it touches me when I'm finished with it, that it moves me along with it and involves me in what it's saying. And that's really the only rule that I use when writing. There are no limitations other than that.

"The type of song that I've been writing requires that I become involved in it—and I suppose that 'inspiration' is the right word, although it always seems so enormous to me. I suppose that being moved to write a song is more applicable to me. I have to be *moved*, I have to have a reason to write a particular song. And if the word 'inspiration' fits, then I guess that can be used. I like to use the word *moved*.

"The songs did come easily to me when I first started writing, but then I wasn't saying what I'm saying now. I wasn't delving as deeply as I do now. They're very difficult now, and take a lot of time and a lot of care, but again, the main point is that the ultimate song—the final finished song—be reflective of what I feel and be able to touch me and move me and affect me in whatever way that the message intends.''

He also explained: "Realism may be the current thing, but I believe in sentiment. It's always tough to feel, and that's what my songs are about. I want to talk about feeling, to translate emotions into something logical.''

Diamond had also grown comfortably into the role of stage performer: "Stage performances are very important to me. I want to keep growing and improving as a performer so I try to make each concert better than the one before. It's particularly exciting to perform where I've never been.

"One of the most fantastic things about the success and the excitement that I've had is that it's given me the chance to travel all over the world to meet some of the most interesting people in the world. I look back on the last six years that I've lived two lifetimes in that period."

Diamond first traveled overseas in 1971 to play sites in England, including the Royal Albert Hall and selected cities on the Continent. Over the years, his records had been available in Europe, Japan, and Australia, but he didn't find major success in any other country until he joined Uni. His success in England was major, but his popularity in Australia is perhaps unsurpassed, even in America. He would discover this during his return to touring in 1976 when he spent an entire month Down Under.

By 1972, he clearly had developed the stage presence he previously lacked. "I see myself as another person on stage. It's the person I really want to be. You know, the fantasy world up there: I can say all the things I want; speak all the unspoken words. But a happy thing: the two [identities] are getting closer and closer together. Because of that, I'm enjoying performing much more than I ever did. I'm getting satisfaction that I never got before. It's easier now."

In the 1972 *Life* magazine profile, Diamond spoke about performing and audiences: "I don't like to feel like the court jester, the clown. I'm not there to 'entertain' people. We're there to do something together. I feel like saying to the audience, 'Paying to get in is not enough. Money has nothing to do with my reason for being here. Love—that's what I want from you. I've *got* enough money!' "

When he was asked if his self-worth had improved since becoming a bona fide star, he said that success had definitely helped, especially now that he no longer felt he needed to dress in black on stage. "Until 1970, I was in hiding. I was totally uncooperative. I was sure I was a good songwriter, but I guess I didn't think much of myself as a person. I was still tied to that kid who was not popular in school, not good-looking, not good at sports. I didn't know how to talk to people.

"There was an evolution from solid black to . . . now whatever I feel like wearing, no matter what the color. The fact that I can go on stage and feel right wearing an off-white shirt is an enormous change. It's reflected in my music, in myself. I would never have conceived of being able to do that three years ago. [Black] was like a security blanket. It reflected the way I felt at that time—dark and mysterious. I don't feel that way anymore.

"I think I've just begun. People tend to think of me as someone who has been around a long time. But I've only scratched the surface. The greatest personal pleasure is being able to grow, being able to explore. It's difficult to face the reality that all the things we've been told will make you happy—money, success, security—can't get you straight inside. That's something you have to work out for yourself. I'm a much happier person now. I feel good, positive about the fact things are coming together. It may take the rest of my lifetime, but I think I'm finally in the process of getting it together."

Most of his time was now spent on the concert trail, where his audiences soon developed some basic characteristics: mostly female, varying in age from pre-teens to gray-hairs. He was drawing women over thirty years old back into arenas.

More significantly, his performing had vastly improved in the two years after his last club dates. Neil himself felt that had it not been for songs such as "Brother Love's Travelling Salvation Show" that enabled him to build production numbers, he might never have been able to develop charisma or build momentum in his act.

Robert Hilburn of the *Los Angeles Times*, a longtime Diamond fan in spite of his often-controversial devotion to hard-edged rock, reviewed Diamond's first appearance at Los Angeles' Greek Theater in 1971: "The important thing to realize about Diamond at the moment is that he is interested in exploring his potential as both a performer and writer. He is concerned with artistic growth. Thus, he is interested in winning respect as well as applause.

"Though most of . . . the material was familiar, there was a constant feel of artistic challenge about Diamond's artistic performance. He changed the arrangements of some numbers, restructured his phrasing on others, mixed the sequence of songs (between his early, essentially bubble-gum material and his more serious, autobiographical material) so that the audience could never fall into the comfortable, but unstimulating position of being able to predict what was going to happen next.

"There were, to be sure, some growth pains. The show's pace seemed to slow too much when Diamond tried to point out the humor in some of the early, unpublished material he wrote. In his effort to bring new interpretations to his songs . . . he seemed at times to be taking away from the free-flowing spirit of the song.

"But the distractions were minor. By the time Diamond got to the closing 'Brother Love' (the third encore number), he had much of the audience clapping in time with the song's irresistable gospel-rock rhythm. He received one of the most spirited standing ovations of the Greek season at the end of the show.

"By refusing to stand still musically, Diamond won the best of both possible worlds . . . he won both the applause and respect of his audience. A major triumph."

Diamond's next single was "Song Sung Blue," the genial sing-along that provided him with his second national number one hit and fourth million-selling single. He told an Australian audience in 1976 that the song came to him during a frustrating period when his inspiration was low: "I put a recording on the phonograph, and it was a compilation of Mozart's concertos.

The very first cut on the album was very, very special—his Piano Concerto no. 21. And I sat there and listened to it, and it struck me that this was something I could write words to and even complete the melody to. It just had that sing-along kind of quality. . . . Thank you, Mozart, wherever you are."

Nevertheless, Diamond admitted that the song was almost forgotten. It was the last track completed during a recording session for his upcoming album *Moods*, and he felt at the time that it was only good enough to be a flip side. He luckily changed his mind, as "Song Sung Blue" turned out to be his biggest-selling single ever.

The release of *Moods* in July 1972 set the stage for the rest of his career. Diamond had been working with producer Tom Catalano and string arranger Lee Holdridge for a few years now, but their collaboration jelled perfectly in this album. Diamond had completed the transition to "adult performer"—that is, an almost completely non-rock singer. It was well received by the young urban professional crowd but stirred consternation among those who felt him rapidly growing older.

Moods was his most successful album to date; in addition to "Song Sung Blue," the album contained the ballad "Play Me," which became number eleven in the nation, and the gospel-tinged "Walk on Water," which reached number seventeen.

" 'Play Me,'—I've had people say, 'Jesus, there's a couple of lines I wish you'd change.' It's crazy," Diamond complained about digs at the song's heavy sentiment, not to mention the use of the non-word "brang."

"Let one line reach. Let it not add up to anything and touch you. And lets you *not* understand it. There are no rules, you see. That's the beautiful thing about it. And the best things I've done are the things that people don't really understand."

Moods was the final studio album Diamond would release with Uni Records. Neil owed MCA (which had now merged all its labels together under the now-familiar

corporate name) one more album under the terms of his
old contract, and he decided it would be a double-record
set taken from one of his last 1972 shows. The venue
picked for the recording was the Greek Theater, where he
had previously received his most enthusiastic reception.
Diamond considered this picturesque amphitheater, lo-
cated near Griffith Park in Los Angeles, his favorite
concert hall.

But first, he needed a new recording contract.

After a bidding war in which CBS almost lost him to
Warner Brothers (reports at this time said Diamond was
"unhappy" with MCA), Clive Davis finally got Neil
under contract. The contract guaranteed Diamond $4
million plus additional royalties over a ten-album period.
The deal enjoyed a very brief reign as one of rock's biggest
contracts before Elton John re-signed with MCA and
Paul McCartney re-signed with Capitol for $8 million
each later in the year.

With the contract issue settled, Diamond concentrated
on the upcoming series at the Greek. He believed his
planned album would have to be truly representative of
his career thus far, yet sound fresh enough to sustain his
fans while he took his vacation from the concert stage. He
felt he had to put everything he had into these particular
shows in his adopted hometown.

Promotion for the August 1972 shows was the heaviest
of any of his dates up to that time. Neil expanded his set
to around two hours, with no opening act (the Everly
Brothers were originally supposed to appear) and no
intermission.

Ten years later, Diamond still remembered the magic of
the Greek concerts: "Just before I went on stage, Bob
Hilburn was backstage with me and he asked me if I was
nervous and I said, 'No, I'm not nervous at all.' And I
went out and did a show and it worked beautifully.
There's a certain sense of anticipation before you go on
stage, your adrenaline is flowing, and if it doesn't happen
naturally when you hear the audience out there, then you
force it to happen. You do things in your mind that make

it happen, and usually once you get in front of the audience, you're thinking about too many other things to worry about nerves. Once you make a commitment and once you step onstage, there's almost nothing that can stop you from doing a performance the way you want to do it. You feel almost no pain, you feel almost no tiredness when you're onstage."

The first concert was on August 18, and Hilburn found it anything but wanting: "More of a triumph, in every measurable way, than his stunning show last summer. Diamond's performance was a virtual model for an entertainer who wants to make a personal, distinctive musical statement. Most of all, Diamond gave of himself. From the care in production (including quadraphonic sound and elaborate lighting/staging effects) to the intensity of his own performance, Diamond takes advantage of the live encounter to prove he is even better than you thought he was.

"[Because of his impending sabbatical] . . . the Greek shows represent the farewell to a period in Diamond's artistic life. But, significantly, he didn't let the importance of the evening lock him into a rigid format. Instead, he remained in control of the evening, sticking close enough to business to give the evening a sharp sense of pace and dramatics, but remaining loose enough—he interrupted his planned sequence to meet audience requests—to give a human, spontaneous quality to it.

"Significantly, Diamond seemed to approach each song with a sense of purpose, a determination to prove its value."

Hot August Night reached the stores in time for Christmas and was an immediate hit. Just as "I Am . . . I Said" had previously quieted the cynics, so did the live album; it showed Neil's performing strength at its peak. It had the longest chart run of any Diamond album, still a best-seller as late as 1974. In Australia, the album was still in the Top Ten when Diamond came there on tour in 1976.

Later in 1972, Diamond got to fulfill his wish to play

Broadway. And even he never thought the stand would be so monumental. For one solid week, covering seven nights and fifteen shows, he was the toast of Broadway. His one-man show, at the Winter Garden Theater, was contracted at $250,000 per night and sold out every performance within a day. His was the first solo concert series Broadway had seen since Al Jolson. "For any performer who walks onstage, the ultimate is Broadway. Right here, home, in New York. Broadway. And there's no better way to close out my concert career than to do it on Broadway.

"I figure after I finish at the Winter Garden, I'll have satisfied an old ambition. I'll have played every historic theater I ever wanted to," he told the *Lost Angeles Times*.

Neil was even excited enough to exhibit some ego to Joyce Haber: "I have had over the last six years more hits than any other artist in the world, including the Beatles and Simon and Garfunkel. And more records sold than any other artist in the world. It's been consistent. I consider myself one of the best songwriters in the world today. People don't know it yet, but they will, maybe five years from now. . . . You'll look back later and say the Beatles did this and Neil Diamond did that, and I don't know who's going to come out ahead."

The New York run was capped with the feature pictorial in *Life* later in the month, and a subsequent private benefit performance for the Robert F. Kennedy Memorial Foundation—his first discernibly "political" activity.

The benefit led to a brief association with the Kennedy family. The press got a lot of mileage out of this friendship, with one gossip magazine ridiculously implying that Neil was having an affair with Ethel Kennedy.

"I liked the Kennedys because of their family-mindedness, because they're close-knit, because they had a sense of responsibility and obligation toward other people," Diamond said later, while admitting, "I'm not sure whether you ever know that you're friends with the Kennedy family."

The highlight of Neil's Hyannis Port experience came during his benefit performance, when Ethel and Eunice Shriver both wanted him to sing their favorite songs, apparently joking that they would be angry if he played the other's favorite. (Eunice liked "Sweet Caroline," while Ethel favored "New York Boy.") As it happened, Diamond could choose only one and sang "Sweet Caroline." At that point Ethel, in an instant of light-hearted indignation, walked on stage and dumped a glass of beer on his head! "I think it was a joke," Diamond later commented.

He went home to dry off and stayed there for four years.

Neil Diamond:

It all began three years ago when I heard you commu-
nicate ... feelings. You shared the living of your life—the
pain, the joy, the dreams, the challenge, the questions,
the memories. You are a true poet of our times, Neil. You
have reached out to people everywhere. I am proud and
grateful that you are sharing Jonathan Livingston Seagull *with us in creating, composing, and singing a*
unique musical narrative for the film. It is fulfilling for
each one of us to work with you.

—Hall Bartlett
Hollywood Reporter trade ad, February 28, 1973

He's too slick now, and it's not as much from his heart as
it used to be. [However,] Neil is extraordinarily talented.
Often his arrogance is just a cover for the lonely and
insecure person underneath.

—Hall Bartlett
People, April 5, 1982

6
Flight of the Gull
(1972-1974)

Neil Diamond would ultimately take forty months away
from the stage. The performing sabbatical afforded him
the time to reacquaint himself with family and friends
and to reexamine his life. But Neil couldn't relax until
after he had completed his next studio project, which
would turn out to be one of his most trying career
experiences.

The album was the soundtrack to the motion picture
adaptation of *Jonathan Livingston Seagull*. In the early
1970s, the Richard Bach book was the country's reigning

pop philosophical sensation. It sold millions of copies and had a middle-American impact that other works such as Kahlil Gibran's *The Prophet* never had, despite critical reaction which generally termed it interesting but light.

Jonathan, a bird whose aspiration is to transcend the meager existence of a seagull by expanding his flying power, is banished from his flock for being a troublesome rebel. He spends the rest of his life an outcast and eventually is escorted to the afterlife where a mystical authority figure, Chang, teaches Jonathan that his strivings are worthwhile. Chang teaches Jonathan a highly developed sense of awareness before sending him back to Earth.

Upon returning to his old flock, Jonathan finds a similarly expelled young gull named Fletcher Lynd Seagull living on the edge of his dreams. Jonathan helps Fletcher and a group of young disciples by imparting his spiritual guidance. But they are attacked and once again banished by a fearful flock establishment. Their hopes for the future, however, are undimmed, and Jonathan leaves Fletcher in charge of the new brood as he moves on to help other flocks.

Neil liked the allegorical fable and was receptive when producer/director Hall Bartlett, who had acquired the film rights, asked him to score the film.

As Diamond said at the time, "I identify very closely with Jonathan: his defeats, his triumphs, and his philosophy. I suppose a lot of other people do because I can't imagine any other reason for the enormous success of the book."

Bartlett told the *Los Angeles Times*: "Neil is one of the true musical poets of our time. He was my first and only choice for this unique and demanding assignment."

Bartlett first contacted Diamond about writing the film's music during the Winter Garden shows in October 1972. Neil was looking for a special theme for his first album under the much-publicized CBS deal. And he was planning to use the long touring absence to broaden his creativity: tentative projects included a symphony and a stage musical.

Neil was wary about participating in the *Jonathan* project at first. Knowing the book would look highly unusual on film, he told *Seventeen,* "Oh, my God, what are they going to do? Are they going to make it in animation, making the birds move, their mouths move? Are there going to be humans in it?"

Bartlett's asking for Neil's decision directly following the grueling Winter Garden shows proved to be a mistake. Diamond was exhausted and sorely needed time to recuperate. He told Bartlett of his reluctance to begin a new project so soon but, always the workaholic, called back after a few weeks of rest to ask if the offer was still good.

Principal photography on the film had already begun, so Bartlett was able to show Diamond some preliminary live-action film footage of the seagulls. "The photography is some of the most spectacular I've ever seen. Hall Bartlett . . . did a fantastic job. Now it's a matter of the story and songs. I'm aiming to write the most beautiful music I can, music that will expand the story.

"I'm starting from zero, studying film scoring, rereading *The Prophet* and books on philosophy to build up my vocabulary. I'm trying to formulate my approach, decide on the type of lyrical language to use, the attitude, where the best places for songs would be. The producer wants me to be the voice of Jonathan, but my feeling is that it may be better if the ballads and instrumental score are separate, like a stream of consciousness that runs along with the film.

"Jonathan has become a part of me and I've become a part of him, too. Jonathan represents Everyman—every man's aspiration and dream of going beyond what he is— and I identify with that more closely than the reality of it. I haven't been excited about a project for a long time. It's what I need, something to make me stretch, to go one step further than I've gone so far and develop a fresh approach. . . . Jonathan says the ultimate is to fly straight up and know the meaning of truth, beauty, love, and kindness. It's the most beautiful premise in the world to devote myself to."

Many Hollywood producers dismissed the notion that a *Jonathan* film could work. First, there was the question of how to do it; then, how to market it. It was widely believed that the novel was overexposed, and that the story needed a rest from the public eye for at least several years. Popular speculation was that *Jonathan* would not age well. Thus, buying the film rights appeared to be a bad investment.

Diamond later said that he was aware of the risk but believed in the concept. "I was warned by several people about the dangers caused by the overexposure of the book. Because of the book's success, there will be some people who won't like the film regardless, and there will be some people who will like it regardless. . . . Because of this, I think the film has to overcome a lot of preconceived notions. But I think it will. The film is really an entity unto itself."

On February 26, 1973, *Daily Variety* reported that Diamond had signed with the film project, which would be a Paramount Pictures release. The first hurdle was to determine which record label would release the album. A clause in Diamond's CBS contract allowed him to negotiate soundtrack album deals independently from his normal album commitment. A meeting the following week between Diamond, Bartlett, and Clive Davis, which included discussion of Diamond's score concepts and viewing of rough film footage, ended with an agreement with Columbia to handle the album.

Producers normally pay scorers a set price regardless of how much of their material is actually used. In return, producers offer no guarantees how much, if any, will make the final cut. But to assure his participation, Bartlett allowed Diamond's contractual condition that at least forty-eight minutes of music would be used in the film. This was an almost unprecedented move.

"Hall and I had a very special relationship. He believed in me. We discussed the songs—placement and so forth—but I never felt I was limited. I understand the guarantee about using all the music is unusual. I was a little surprised when he accepted that. What if the songs weren't any good? But he was a fan. He wanted me because of my music, not just that I was a name that might help the picture."

Diamond's work on the score was first complicated by a household accident in which Neil broke his right hand; it was in a cast for nearly six weeks. In the meantime, early reports in the press speculated that Diamond would be Jonathan's voice or would at least write the film's narrative. Talk of Neil writing the script may have arisen from some early hints that his songs might tell Jonathan's story in "rock-opera" fashion. Although both possibilities were brought up when Diamond signed, they were soon dismissed. He had said that one of his challenges was that "I have to figure out who's singing. Is it Jonathan, or is it the voice of his subconscious?"

Diamond's work was also delayed due to the fact that he had never before attempted to write a soundtrack and was confused about how to proceed. He told Hilburn of the *Los Angeles Times* that he learned the ground rules of scoring by asking those with experience.

"I spoke to a couple of top film scorers, Henry Mancini and Lalo Schifrin, just to try to understand what they do, what they deal with, what they had to learn. They were both very nice, very open. We discussed all kinds of things and they put me at ease. I kept asking questions and they kept saying, 'Don't worry about it,' 'No, don't worry about that, either,' and 'Just write your music and everything will take care of itself.' They made me feel very much at ease. They took away the doubts. I'm indebted to them both."

At first, in order to get his concepts for the soundtrack on paper, Diamond returned to the essay method that had helped him compose "I Am . . . I Said." He also concentrated on Eastern and Indian philosophy. Thus, the score became a college course, with the completed work serving as the term paper and final exam.

Due to Diamond's craftsmanship and the technique involved, he was far from finished when the filming neared its end. Bartlett was already talking about a semi-documentary he had pasted together for publicity while Neil still pondered the score ideas.

Despite his own commitment to the film, Bartlett found the going rough. He wanted to make the film his own way, but he found disbelievers everywhere. He told *Seventeen* magazine, "Experienced Hollywood people said 'impossible.' You can get a hawk or an eagle, even a raven to fly up to your shoulder and peck your cheek. With a seagull, forget it! They're too wild. Producers wanted to make an animated cartoon or integrate people into it."

Even original author Richard Bach, who collaborated on the screenplay, considered adding a scene in which a couple of people peer at Jonathan from a passing plane. But Bartlett was steadfast: "If you create an on-screen illusion that birds are people, then suddenly have real people in the middle of the movie, you blow everything."

Bartlett kept reiterating to the press that the film would be made his way. He told the *Hollywood Reporter*, "I was born to make this movie. I acquired the property five days after reading it, long before it was such a phenomenal best-seller. It shocked me when I discovered I didn't know how I was going to realize my ideas. I found the answers step by step."

He spent five months shooting the film, half of that time from inside a helicopter. Four weeks were spent just learning how to film the birds and determining if it was possible to herd the gulls for the aerial shots. During the first month he didn't get one usable shot.

"There's no way to train a seagull to do something dissimilar from its basic pattern working with three hundred gulls at a time. You have to find a way to actually herd the birds. That takes great coordination between the pilot and cameraman," Bartlett said.

Only ten of the six thousand birds captured for the film could be trained, and they became the stars. The one particularly exceptional bird was used for the close-ups of the Jonathan character. Five of the trained birds became exhausted before the principal photography even began in October 1972, so each bird could only be used every other day.

Bartlett was lucky to have picked a crew that believed the film was important. Only their dedication made it possible to complete the shooting. The official production schedule was scrapped because of the seagulls' behavior and Bartlett finally had to call in the United States Navy.

The Navy had been studying behavioral tendencies of seagulls since 1967 and made its findings public so that *Jonathan* could be made. They told Bartlett that gulls always fly into the wind and could not be coaxed to do otherwise. Bartlett then brought wind-making machines up to the Big Sur location to induce the birds to face each other in dramatic sequences. (Other locations used for shooting included Yosemite, Death Valley, Carlsbad, Pinnacle National Park, the High Sierras, the Mono Lake region, and the Monterey-Carmel coast.)

Bartlett also learned that the gulls could not be tempted to slow their naturally jerky head movements. While these actions might be necessary for the birds, they do not pass for good acting. A week of experiments with a high-speed, slow-motion camera finally made the gulls appear calm and saved the crew endless retakes. Even at that, more than seven hundred thousand feet of film were used by the picture's finish in April 1973. Sound dubbing wasn't completed until mid-September, a full month after the announced premiere date.

The major change Bartlett made in the story was the addition of a romantic interest for Jonathan. He did so to increase emotional accessibility: "But it's not seagull

meets seagull. It's a love story that becomes part of the
book's theme, which is the importance of the individual,
self-value, striving to realize all that's within you. Learn
to fly straight up and show kindness and love."

Outwardly, work on the score seemed to be running on
schedule. On July 25, 1973, Bartlett ran another full-page
advertisement, this time in *Weekly Variety*, to praise
Diamond's work:

"Neil Diamond: I believe that the musical narrative
that you have created for *Jonathan Livingston Seagull*
will be of enduring importance. You have achieved
everything we dreamed of together. Gratefully, Hall."

Diamond was apparently displeased with only one of
the songs he composed for *Jonathan*. It was an instrumental piece called "Harbor of Light." Although Bartlett
really liked the tune and wanted it in the film, Diamond
deleted it from the score. Neil wasn't convinced the song
was good enough to release and certainly had no intention of letting the public hear anything that didn't
personally satisfy him.

When Neil was interviewed by the *New York Times* in
September, he had finished the music to his satisfaction.
He sounded genuinely pleased with his personal growth
and the music he had been able to generate out of it.

"It took ten months of my life to write it, and the whole
project has been a learning process for me. . . . In my
surge to understand what the *Jonathan Livingston* story
was about, I got myself involved in philosophy and
religion. As a result, I began working with a yogi—as
friend, student, teacher, that kind of relationship—for
about six weeks, meeting every day. It was fascinating—
really my first exposure to serious religion. I guess
working on the music for the film really changed my life
somewhat."

Ben Fong-Torres told a less ostentatious version of this
anecdote in *Rolling Stone* three years later: "There is a
story that is told—usually by Diamond, in fact—that
during his sabbatical, a Hare Krishna showed up at his

door with incense and literature. Diamond invited him
in, talked with him, then showed him his work in
progress. The young man ended up meeting with Diamond every day for six weeks. Diamond put him up in an
apartment, rented him a car. And when the youth asked
him to join him in India so they could sit in a cave,
Diamond said he'd love to—except he had to finish this
Seagull thing. But he gave the man airfare to India."

Also in September 1973, Neil went to the Columbia
Records annual sales convention and, at Davis's request,
gave the keynote address. Diamond brought along a
thirteen-minute segment of *Jonathan* scored to the song
"Be." When the clip was finished, he received a standing
ovation.

Spirits were high at both Paramount Pictures and
Columbia Records. The companies thought they were
guaranteed success, as the $1.5 million film already had
$5 million in advance bookings. To insure the continued
success of the film, Paramount launched a huge promotional campaign. Meanwhile, Columbia lined up radio
and television commercials and print ads and outlined
plans to display *Jonathan* paraphernalia at retail outlets.
They hardly needed to push the album, as it was presold
before the score was even put on record.

Coincidentally, Neil and Marcia purchased their
$500,000 Malibu beachfront home that same month.

Variety had announced that the West Coast premiere of
Jonathan would be held on October 30 at the Village
Theater in Westwood, California. The proceeds would
help International Orphans, Inc. build a children's village in Beaumont, California. The date for the world
premiere was then announced for the Sutton Theater in
New York on October 23. An accompanying charity ball
would be held that same night on the Starlight Roof of the
Waldorf-Astoria Hotel.

The *Jonathan Livingston Seagull* album was in stores
in early October. Dressed in the most formidably expen-
sive-looking cover Diamond had ever released—a heavy-

stock booklet with full-color seascapes, portrait shots and Hallmark-type lettering—it looked marvelous. So high were the expectations for both the music and the treatment of the story that the album debuted higher on the charts than any of his earlier works. Reviews only trickled in at first, with most writers hedging their bets until the movie was released. Most found the album apart from the movie to be inherently incomplete.

"Be" was issued as the first single but was not a major hit. A deliberately oblique and heavily orchestrated ballad, it was earmarked by most radio programmers as having little air appeal and got little airplay in most markets, including Los Angeles. But the disappointment of "Be," which stalled at number thirty-four nationally, did not hurt the momentum of the album. It soon reached number two and within months became the biggest-selling soundtrack of all time. It held that distinction until 1978 when it was surpassed by the *Saturday Night Fever* soundtrack. *Jonathan Livingston Seagull* remains Diamond's best-selling album in America.

The album's success turned out to be the last good news associated with the movie. The troubles began on October 10, when both the *Hollywood Reporter* and *Variety* gave only mediocre reviews to the 114-minute film and suggested that its commercial prospects would be hard to predict. Both agreed that the movie was too long.

The next day, Richard Bach asked the Los Angeles Superior Court for a preliminary injunction prohibiting the exhibition of the movie, claiming the screenplay was dramatically altered without his consent. Bach charged that the film as it now stood was unfaithful to the book and totally unacceptable. The author sent telegrams to critics who had seen the first screenings, informing them that the film lacked much of what was in his original screenplay and that he was never told or consulted about the changes as his contract had stipulated. He urged the reviewers not to file stories until they saw a version of *Jonathan* that he approved.

Bartlett refused to comment, saying only that the issue "will be decided in court, not in a series of emotional, preposterous telegrams." Bartlett's laywer contended that Bach did have a limited right of approval, but that it did not extend as far as Bach insisted.

After seeing the film with an audience, Bartlett said that he would not rule out shortening the film—now even he considered it too long. Although at least one invitational screening audience did like the film, a wave of negative criticism from the entertaiment trade papers was already expected.

On October 16, Diamond filed suit against Bartlett, seeking to enjoin the film's release. Neil alleged breach of contract, claiming that his rights to artistic control had been violated. He contended that the completed version of the film he saw September 28 had five minutes of his music removed without his approval and twelve minutes of music he did not write added without his approval. As such, the score was "no longer fairly representative" of his music.

Diamond was also dissatisfied with the fim's credits. He claimed that he was to have been listed as "Music by Neil Diamond," with his name printed 75 percent as large as Bartlett's. But the film also gave songwriting credit to arranger Lee Holdridge, who had orchestrated Diamond's material and had written the twelve minutes of new material at Bartlett's request. The suit asked for deletion of Holdridge's music, the reinstatement of Diamond's five minutes, and the contractually entitled credit.

Paramount Pictures, named in both suits as a legal matter of course, offered no comment on the matter as their involvement only constituted release and distribution of *Jonathan*. In picking up the film for distribution from Bartlett's independent production company, Paramount agreed to a hands-off policy regarding the content of the movie.

In asking that Diamond's suit be dismissed, Bartlett blamed Diamond for the bulk of the problems. He claimed that Neil did not comply with mutual decisions the two had made regarding song selection and placement, and that he felt Neil did not make sufficient effort to promote the film in conjunction with the soundtrack album. Bartlett also stated that many of Diamond's complaints had either been ironed out during production or had never previously come up. In particular, Bartlett alleged that Diamond contributed so little in actual original music that he was forced to ask Holdridge to compose music to fill out the score.

The biggest factor in Bartlett's favor was that Holdridge sided with him. Holdridge had worked with Diamond since "Holly Holy" and was a firmly established part of the production team. He stated that Diamond had failed because of his inexperience and misunderstanding of the scoring process. Holdridge also said that Neil's level of technical expertise was so low that he had to give him substantial help in extending the orchestral score. He also accused Diamond of disregarding the timing requirements and cues for dialogue provided by the film crew.

Holdridge's claim was backed up by *Jonathan*'s music editor, John Hammell, who claimed that both Diamond and producer Catalano approached the project with an arrogant attitude. He pointed out that much of what Neil complained about was simply normal film scoring procedure. And Hammell objected to Diamond's "profane and curt language" in stating that he did not care about the dialogue and that it would have to be adjusted to his lyrics.

In his rebuttal, Diamond backed down on some charges but strengthened others. He said he disregarded the timing instructions because he was working under his and Bartlett's original agreement that his music would provide much of the film's narrative. However, he denied that he or his production team had been lax in paying attention to Bartlett's demands. He claimed that many of Bartlett's individual points, such as the complaint over the deletion of "Harbor of Light," were motivated by prior discussion between the two of them.

It was apparent that communication between Diamond and Bartlett had never been quite as smooth as it had appeared.

On October 17, *Weekly Variety* reported that a shorter version of Bartlett's original *Jonathan* film would replace the first prints seen by critics. Bach still did not approve of this revision and told the publication that he wanted an additional forty minutes added. This would have made the already long picture a staggering 157 minutes.

Diamond's suit was supposed to be heard before Bach's in Los Angeles Superior Court the following day—October 18. However, Superior Court Judge Campbell M. Lucas decided to hear both claims the same day and said he would deliver separate decisions within the next two days. He didn't get the chance—a last-minute compromise by all parties resulted in his granting a continuance while matters were changed.

This meant that the premieres could be held as scheduled, as well as the opening New York and Los Angeles engagements. The only change was an addition to the opening credits of a statement that it was still a work in progress.

The benefits were successes. The demand for tickets to the Los Angeles affair was 20 percent greater than the original projections. Numerous celebrities attended, but Neil was conspicuously absent on both coasts.

While the parties were in Judge Lucas's chambers trying to work out a satisfactory settlement, the nation's film critics were attacking the film viciously. Disapproval of *Jonathan* was almost unanimous, with at least seventeen pans from the New York critics alone.

Before seeing the film, most critics admitted they believed that the book was either unfilmable or vastly overrated. After seeing the movie, few changed their opinions. Most of them described the script as either pretentious or silly. The fact that none of the voice-over actors—including James Franciscus, Hal Holbrook, Juliet Mills, and others—were given screen credit became the source of uncomplimentary jokes. Few had any qualms about the cinematography, but most also picked on Diamond's score as bombastic and overbearing, both in the poetic aspects of the lyrics and the emotional tones of the music.

Judge Lucas handed down his decision on November 5. He ordered that the film be changed after November 20 to reinstate Diamond's missing music, including parts of "Dear Father" and "Anthem." The credits would now read, "Music and Songs by Neil Diamond . . . Background Score Composed and Adapted by Neil Diamond and Lee Holdridge . . . Music Supervision by Tom Catalano."

Bach was not an unconditional victor. The judge felt the author had not acted soon enough in reading a production script and was partially to blame. He ordered Bach's name off the screenplay credit and that Bach be mentioned only as the book's author. But Bach won in getting Jonathan changed from Bartlett's "social reformer" back into his own "individual in search of perfection." The twenty-five pages of changes ordered in the script was the most substantial alteration of a film already in release up to that time.

Bartlett asked for and received eight more days to make the changes and was forced by the court to cancel any press conferences during that period regarding the film's reworking. On the day the new *Jonathan* was sent out in distribution, Bartlett spoke his mind at a California town meeting at the Greater Los Angeles Press Club.

"Neither [Diamond nor Bach] had made a film before, and they didn't realize every motion picture is a collaborative effort. But those differences have been resolved, and I know Diamond is satisfied with the results. I hope Bach is, too, but I can't speak for him because he's out of town."

Unfortunately, there was no denying at this time that

the film had already earned the status of box office failure. Given the $2.1 million Paramount paid for distribution rights and the initial $700,000 publicity budget on top of the negative cost, *Jonathan* looked like a break-even proposition at best. By year's end, it had grossed less than $3 million.

Word of mouth was as negative as the press had been. Some educational groups gave the film a recommendation as a suitable family film, which probably resulted in numerous kids being taken to a movie whose slow pace and thick philosophizing were contrary to their interests.

Many wondered why such a popular literary item failed to provide a presold audience of any size. Though no one wanted to admit it at the time, it may have been that the *Jonathan* phenomenon was already just a fad on its downswing.

The particularly amazing aspect of the seagull saga, though, had to have been the immense success of the soundtrack album. Despite being mostly instrumental, receiving terrible reviews, and being attached to a flop film, it sold in the millions. The *Jonathan Livingston Seagull* album placed Diamond in the select group of artists whose relative unpopularity among critics was counterbalanced by fans who not only appreciated him as an entertainer but revered him as a bona fide artist.

While it is true that the second single, "Skybird," was his worst non-reissue showing (at number seventy-five) since the early Uni releases, this was the Diamond album that never should have had singles pulled from it. The LP was still on the charts long after the film was playing eighth runs. By 1975, the *New York Times* reported that the album had grossed $15 million in American sales and $5 million overseas.

Jonathan the film did find a few pockets of popularity around the globe—particularly in Australia, where it was re-released during Diamond's 1976 tour. The new acceptance led Bartlett to try to re-edit the film and replace the dialogue with straight narration; as he told the *Los*

Angeles Times: "All the publicity probably left people thinking that Hollywood had ruined another well-liked book and so nobody went to see the movie."

Bach was reportedly helping with the new version and trying to get it re-released in America. But *Jonathan* never flew again, except at revival film houses.

Holdridge and Diamond never worked together again. Holdridge has since gone on to become a successful film scorer, with *Mr. Mom* and *Transylvania 6-5000* among his credits.

"I guess I was pretty naive when I became involved with *Jonathan*," Diamond said later. "I come from a very independent medium—records. If you have established any kind of track record, you can do what you want, and because of this attitude, the record business has grown tremendously. The people in the business have a healthy respect for the creative artist. There's no such animal in the movie business. After *Jonathan*, I vowed never to get involved in another movie again unless I had complete control.

"It was quite an experience. It took one year of concentrated work and I honestly don't know what it took out of me. It probably gave me more than it took. But it was the hardest year of my life."

*It's difficult to imagine that singer-composer Neil Dia-
mond still experiences periods of frustration, discontent,
and fear in his illustrious career. But those times do
indeed exist for him—and he has a unique way of
dealing with them. He drops out.*

—Barbara Zuanich
Motion Picture

7
Stargazer (1974-1976)

Since his day at Uni, the fear of becoming too popular
and overexposed plagued Diamond. He feared he would
burn out: too many records; too many appearances; just
too much of Neil Diamond.

Despite a shyness in front of cameras, and despite the
mistreatment he felt he received on the set of the "Mannix" show, the real reason he avoided television and
movies was this fear of overexposure. He had tasted its
bitterness when Bang and Uni singles battled on the
charts and he vowed he would never again fall prey to
such problems.

He had seen so many of the artists from his Tin Pan
Alley days fall quickly from the public's grace. With hit
after hit and sellout after sellout during the early 1970s,
Diamond still feared joining popular music's casualties
whose careers were done too soon.

This fear was among the three primary reasons for his
sabbatical; the other two were his need to lead a normal
family life and honest fatigue. With the *Jonathan* experi-

111

ence behind him, Diamond was ready to relax. He used the opportunity to catch up on the life he had rushed through during the eight years in the public spotlight.

"I feel you have to stop performing every once in a while. It's kind of a forced sabbatical to give you time to rest, reconsider, reflect, and look at what you do from a different perspective," he had said back in 1972.

"Every time you go out on the road, it tears up your life. It tears your roots, even if only for three or four days. It breaks a flow. It did to me anyway. It broke the flow of my life, so I stopped performing . . . just because I wasn't excited about the road anymore. I didn't feel I could give it everything I wanted to. I love performing, but only under my conditions, which are that I want to do it, that I'm excited about it, and that I can give everything to it."

In the 1970s, it was rare for performers to sustain successful careers without the benefit of the live audience. During the 1960s, Elvis Presley was the first artist to stop performing live. His concerts were replaced by a multitude of sub-par movies, and his career suffered. The Beatles stopped touring in 1966, but pioneered the use of videos like "Penny Lane" and "Strawberry Fields Forever" for television. The Rolling Stones followed up with their own videos, but they soon found the need for concerts.

Yet Diamond, who refused to be on television, had yet to be in a film, and whose first video would appear in 1985, was going to become totally inconspicuous to the public until his next album. And then he only planned on granting a few interviews. Fans would have to be satisfied with his records.

Diamond was warned about the cost of a prolonged absence from the public. But even workaholics get tired. Some have families. He took the time to get closer to his son Jesse, who had reportedly been traumatized by Neil's long absences while on tour.

As he would explain in 1976: "After the Winter Garden engagement, I felt burnt out. I had been on a merry-go-round since I was 17; in my early years I played as many as 130 cities a year. I was warned by my manager, my agents, my friends, and my fans not to quit, that it would be dangerous to my career, but it was important for me to get away. I had to find myself as a person, to remove myself from the celebrity out there in front of the audience. I wanted to enjoy all the things I had missed—Christmas, birthdays, socializing with my family and friends. Also, I had a son, two-and-a-half, who was going through a difficult period. That was the final clincher."

He elaborated further that same year: "One of the reasons I quit in 1972 was that I felt it was important for me to get a concept of who I was again. You can get so lost in what the public thinks you are, what the reviewers and record companies think you are. I just wanted to withdraw and find out who Neil Diamond was.

"The way for me to live, I've found, is . . . to be a complete person. That's my goal now; not just a complete songwriter or complete performer, but a complete person, which includes being a complete father. . . . I was haunted by the memory of [Jesse] when I would leave. He and Marcia would be standing in the window, both of them crying. I just felt I couldn't have the joy of performing unless I took care of business first. The relationship is fantastic now. I've had three years to spend with him; fishing, reading books, drawing together, playing music together, teaching him, learning with him. He's five now and much stronger."

Diamond, who had begun to study himself during his work on *Jonathan*, wanted the time to delve deeper. He needed to relieve the pressure of his vicious cycle: write songs, record albums, plan tours, go on road trips, and start again. He did not want to stop writing songs; he just didn't want to write them on deadline. The touring sabbatical allowed him more time to think about what he was writing and how he was doing it. He brushed up on his musicianship, and he devoted more time to writing.

"I've got lots of ideas, but I don't really want to talk

about them now. Whenever I do talk about things ahead
of time, they never seem to work out. I want to move
ahead without any limitations. I want to find new ways of
expressing my music: new forms, new attitudes, new
modes of performing. It's important to set new goals, new
plateaus for yourself. Otherwise, you begin to lose your
enthusiasm and your work eventually suffers. You can't
stay in the same place and keep your interest up. It's time
for me to make that move now. That's why I want some
time off. I want to study piano. I want to learn the
technical language of music so that I can better commu-
nicate with the musicians."

Diamond spent most of the next four years writing
songs, enjoying family life, and finding himself. In
addition, he continued psychoanalysis. In 1976, Diamond
told Australian interviewer Michael Schildberger that at
one point he saw his analyst three to five times a week.
Much of the treatment centered around explorations of
his lyrics and what they meant to him.

He also read some two hundred books—sort of the
college education of which he never really took advantage.
During his 1976 Australian tour, he named *The Lives of
a Cell* as the book he enjoyed most during this period—
his scientific leanings were still latent.

He brushed up on his chess, which he has enjoyed
since high school. And he found time to ride his motorcy-
cle through the hills of Malibu, a pastime he took up
while living in Long Island. Diamond explained his
affection for riding by calling it his one fling with
physical danger.

He went on real vacations with his family to Europe
and South America. He made certain that his parents
were able to retire. He went fishing.

He collected his thoughts.

By summer 1974, Diamond celebrated the release of his
MCA hits package (*His Twelve Greatest Hits*) and had
written enough songs to begin a new album. The new LP,
to be called *Serenade,* was another effort to beef up the

literary quality of his writing. His inspirations from romantic poets were obvious, and the lyrics of several of the numbers were the least linear in meaning of any up to that time. Nothing on the album could really be considered rock music, although two cuts were reggae-inspired.

While *Serenade* was still in progress, Diamond decided to give more interviews than he had originally planned. He later admitted that he understood Columbia's disappointment in the lack of a hit single from *Jonathan*, noting that the company probably expected another Diamond album that had at least two hits on it. Despite the soundtrack's success, he felt guilty and wanted to make it up to the label with a good effort to support *Serenade*.

He made the interview rounds and even allowed a *Los Angeles Herald Examiner* reporter into the studio for a while. ("Wander around if you want. Ask questions. Nothing bothers us, not even earthquakes.")

Diamond reconfirmed that he still thought of himself as a writer first: "When I'm not writing songs, it's like I'm dying. When I am writing well, it's like I'm reborn. Performing . . . is not as close to the core of me. Writing is like my shield or my banner or my emblem. It's a reflection of me. I don't let anything get in the way of writing."

He also talked about the fickle nature of success: "Sometimes when you are the most successful, it is the hardest on you. There was always a certain criticism of Janis Joplin, about how she could honestly sing the blues when she was making a million dollars a year. Well, I felt for her because she obviously couldn't handle the million dollars and adoration and acceptance. She was really singing the blues when all that was going on. Paying dues can be one of the most exciting and least pressured times of your life. You don't have anything to protect or defend, either your image or your reputation. You're just doing it for the love of doing it. The pressures come later.

"I've learned to deal with most of the pressures. One of

the biggest problems is deadlines. That's one of the greatest pressures on me. But, generally, I've been lucky. It is a difficult business. I've seen so many artists and writers become acclaimed, famous, and then be discarded. They're built up and then deflated. You have to keep struggling against that. You can't really relax. It's like a man's territorial imperative. A guy works, establishes his area of control, then protects it. Because of the fickleness of public taste, however, you have to keep expanding in some way to survive in the entertainment business. They call it broadening your career."

He also admitted he had developed a stronger ego: "Well, of course you have to have some amount of ego just to be able to stand up on a stage in front of ten or fifteen thousand people. Because you have to assume that you're capable of entertaining them or motivating them or moving them. I don't really understand it beyond that. Every performer that I've ever met has a certain ego. [Otherwise,] they wouldn't ever step in front of an audience or in front of a microphone. Beyond that, it depends on the individual how far it goes and how far they get swallowed up by the potential of their ego."

Diamond continued to avoid any hint of controversy in his song topics, as he had done ever since the anti-drug debacle. "I still believe that you have to be very careful about the public position you're in, because you do have a soapbox, and you have to be very careful about what you say. Being a writer, you can construct things and say things that maybe convince people of certain things. But they're not necessarily right. So I generally stay away from that. Most of my music involves personal relationships and certain introspective observations."

To help awaken Europe to the upcoming release of *Serenade*, he agreed to be a guest on Shirley Bassey's British Christmas Special of 1974. It was his first television appearance anywhere since his last tour of Europe in 1971. He not only got a chance to work with one of his favorite female singers in a duet of "Play Me" with Bassey,

Diamond's earliest publicity photo for Columbia Records during his first contract with the label in 1963.

*In the studio during the recording of "Clown Town"
in 1963.*

The Bang production team. Left to right: Diamond, Ellie Greenwich, Bert Berns, and Jeff Barry in 1966.

Jasper Dailey

Neil appeared in 1966 on KHJ-TV's "Boss City," Los Angeles' answer to "American Bandstand." At Neil's right is host Sam Riddle (also a KHJ-AM boss jock at the time). Surrounding them are members of Jr. Walker and the All-Stars and various studio dancers.

Michael Ochs Archives

Lacking the flashy stage persona that would later become his trademark, Neil appeared in small clubs during 1968.

Appearing on "The Everly Brothers Show" in 1970, Neil got his chance to play with his longtime musical idols, Don (right) and Phil.

Backstage at the Greek, August 23, 1971, Neil greets Los Angeles County Supervisor Warren Dorne.

Cultivating a superstar sneer in Los Angeles, 1971.

While visiting with his former New York University fencing coach Hugo Castello, Neil took time to pose with the 1972 varsity fencing team.

The Palomino Club in North Hollywood provided the meeting place for two musical legends, Neil and country superstar Waylon Jennings, in 1972. Neil's hand is in a cast after he broke it in a household accident.

Woburn Abbey, 1976.

Michael Jacobs Photojournalism

The frog who would be king in all his glory at Woburn Abbey, 1976.

At the 1980 Grammys, the crowd went wild as Barbra Streisand joined Neil for an unannounced performance of "You Don't Bring Me Flowers."

Rehearsing at the Aquarius for the 1986 television special, "Hello Again."

In Los Angeles during a 1986 party.

Neil and Marcia at a film premiere in 1986.

but he also plugged the new album. And the next day he premiered the first single from the album—"Longfellow Serenade"—at the end of a BBC radio interview.

During the show he also spoke of his next-door neighbor in Malibu—Elvis Presley. "As a matter of fact, we live next door to each other, so we wave to each other over the fence every once in a while. [Living next to him] does have its problems. You know, Elvis has a group of people in front of his house, and I have a group of people in front of my house, so occasionally he will send his people over to my house; they'll call me up and say 'Is Elvis here?' and I'll say 'No, he's next door.' And then I'll send my group of people over to his house. It's kind of fun. He travels quite a bit, but we do see each other every once in a while. [I've never written specifically for him,] although he's recorded a number of things . . . there's 'Sweet Caroline' and 'And the Grass Won't Pay No Mind.' "

When Diamond returned to Los Angeles, he found Columbia's promotional campaign for *Serenade* in full gear. Columbia was seeking to make it clear that Diamond was an established artist. The record company practically convinced people to think of *Serenade* as one of the best of the year even before it was in stores. Reaching number five nationally, "Longfellow Serenade" was his first Top Twenty single since "Walk on Water" and his biggest hit since "Song Sung Blue" two and a half years earlier. It harkens back to the days of Neil's high school rhymes and devotion to Cyrano de Bergerac. Neil explained it as basically the theme song of a fellow who wooed and won someone with the help of Longfellow's poetry.

It hardly seemed to matter that most critics were disappointed by the album. His fans had learned to consider Diamond's critics as the enemy—those who misunderstood. As Neil's devoted following bought *Serenade* in overwhelming numbers, the general consensus in the music press was that Diamond achieved more when he reached for less.

Many younger journalists stopped taking Diamond seriously, due to his refusal to rock, and because their frame of reference was the new cutting edge of rock personified by David Bowie. Although Bowie was slowly abandoning his Ziggy Stardust antics, he had helped force a new identity on Elton John and others.

Whether or not Neil chose to recognize it, Elton was now his competition. It would have been utterly ridiculous for Diamond to adopt Elton's wild style and flair for outrageous suits, shoes, and glasses. But Elton's immense popularity with teens did cut into Diamond's youth base. Diamond would continue to have young fans but could never again hope to approach the numbers he once enjoyed.

His next release did nothing for his popularity among teens. "I've Been This Way Before" was about reincarnation, and it reflected the marked change in Diamond's music more than any other single song. It was his latest gospel number; but it didn't have the fervor of "Brother Love's Travelling Salvation Show" or the soul-searching of "Holly Holy." "I've Been This Way Before" is a ballad with no power or depth, and it only picks up steam near the end. It barely cracked the Top Forty, struggling to number thirty-four.

It is an interesting song, however, because it appears to have greatly influenced subsequent balladeers, particularly Barry Manilow.

The third single from the *Serenade* album, "The Last Picasso," didn't even break onto the national charts. It failed not only because Diamond was losing his foothold in the teen market but also because of its reggae style. Few reggae-flavored songs received support in the United States. In the first half of the 1970s, only Johnny Nash's "Stir It Up" managed to approach the Top Ten.

After the *Serenade* sessions, Neil retreated to the resting portion of his concert layoff. He did not talk to the press at all during 1975, choosing instead to spend more time immersing himself in family life and clearing up some business matters.

During that time, Neil established a permanent office suite on Melrose Place in West Hollywood. He also signed with the Management III agency and Jerry Weintraub in particular. The company, which has also handled Frank Sinatra, Bob Dylan, the Beach Boys, John Denver, and the Moody Blues, was involved with his career until October 1985.

Weintraub became Diamond's fourth manager, following Fred Weintraub (no relation), Bob Thiele, and Ken Fritz. Fred Weintraub and Diamond parted when Neil moved to Los Angeles and Weintraub left New York and became involved in independent filmmaking in Miami. Thiele was in charge during the early and bleak Uni era and quit managing Diamond to go back to record production. Fritz had been successfully handling Diamond's glory period, but he could not equal the industry connections or the concert-booking ability of Jerry Weintraub.

Besides arranging touring itineraries and promotion for his clients, Weintraub's co-owned Concerts West subsidiary had staged concerts for most of music's superstars, including Elvis Presley and Led Zeppelin. Weintraub has been a personal manager since the late 1950s, and his business ties include all facets of the entertainment industry. Weintraub, another workaholic and a fellow Jew from the Bronx who had relocated to Malibu, promised continued success and unparalleled tours and provided a bridge between records and other entertainment fields.

While continuing his touring sabbatical and press blackout, Diamond was working. His next project was a collaboration with his new neighbor in Malibu, Jaime "Robbie" Robertson, leader of the Band. They met and became friends in the spring of 1975; and although Neil was not really fond of the Band's rustic folk/country rock sound, he did find enough in common with Robertson to listen to some of his musical ideas.

One night when the conversation turned to the early 1960s, Robertson mentioned that he had also spent a brief time on Tin Pan Alley before deciding to go to New Orleans. After they shared anecdotes about some of the

people they knew, Robertson suggested that Diamond do
a concept album about the Tin Pan Alley days. Diamond
had to think about the idea a while—those days may have
had some excitement for him, but there were also plenty of
hardships. He was reluctant to dredge up bad memories,
but the idea intrigued him. Neil came up with an idea to
do a group of songs not connected by plot nor directly
autobiographical.

"Over a period of months, we met out on the beach and
talked almost every Sunday. He had passed through that
[Tin Pan Alley] scene on his way [from] Canada . . . and
it turned out he knew some of the characters that I knew.
. . . We worked very closely on the thing for a year, having
long discussions about the thrust and the content, so it
was a real collaboration in the best sense of the word. . . .
This was more a personal relationship between the two of
us and a mutual respect for what we'd each been through,
. . . commonly-shared disasters along the way. That period, the songwriting period, was a very rough period for
me."

Diamond explained: "[The album] is a series of recollections, and I think of it as a conceptual album. Hopefully, one day I'll be able to do it on stage as a theater
piece. It was written as a visual piece."

Robertson (whose favorite Diamond music was from
the Bang era) produced the sessions, which featured
Diamond's most extensive involvement with "name" session men—other members of the Band plus drummers
Jim Keltner (who has worked with three of the solo
Beatles), Jim Gordon (Eric Clapton's band) and Russ
Kunkel (Jackson Browne, Carly Simon, among others),
Toto pianist David Paich, saxophonist Tom Scott, as well
as Dr. John and James Newton-Howard. Robertson co-
wrote "Dry Your Eyes" with Neil; it would ultimately be
covered by Frank Sinatra who called it "a hell of a song."

"We thought [we were] an odd combination, too. . . .
But we thought the combination of the two would create
a third thing that neither of us had experienced before."

The recording went smoothly and might even have inspired Diamond to turn it into a double album. But Columbia insisted on having it delivered in time for the start of his comeback tour the following spring. The album was named for the sounds of New York City: *Beautiful Noise.*

Response from the CBS organization was favorable, if not downright fanatic. "I played it for Columbia Records and I said, 'No, no, I'm not finished with this yet, because there's still some things I want to do.' I turned around, and the president of the company lifted it right out of my hands, and he was out the door. It was just hysterical. The president just ran out with it."

Columbia was excited for a very good reason. *Beautiful Noise* was the best of the three albums Diamond had delivered thus far, succeeding both artistically and commercially to the extent that it suggested that Diamond had finally recorded the album of his career. It surpassed the studio quality of *Moods*, yet contained the freshness, magic, and vitality of the live *Hot August Night.*

Diamond succeeded here because he seemed to have kept his artistic goals firmly in mind before the recording of the album, and came closer to meeting these aspirations than on any of his other records. The main thrust of the work is always in place, and the lesser moments are few and not extreme. Most importantly, *Beautiful Noise* is one of the few times he truly appeared to step out of his introspective self to interact with the outside world—a task he has always been much better at doing than he has claimed.

The title track, as fresh as sea breezes caught full in the face, brought Neil's Broadway influences to the forefront in one of the best songs of his career.

The album's momentum coupled with a growing fervent longing for the stage drew Diamond back to performing. "I got itchy about wanting to be in front of an audience again. I wanted to test myself again. Besides, being on stage is a real upper. It makes you write better.

When I write a song, I imagine how it's going to work in front of an audience. It's the only real test. A concert is also a treat for the performer. It's like the lollipop after I finish the hard work, which is writing the songs for an album. But this will probably be my last major tour ever. I'd like to perform again, but physically and emotionally you just can't do it and be a songwriter and be a father and be a husband and have time to develop your own concept of yourself."

He elaborated in the *Los Angeles Herald-Examiner*: "You know, in fencing there's an expression called 'blade hunger,' and it refers to the fencer who's on the sidelines, watching the bout in progress. It's the desire to get into the fray: put on your outfit, take out your weapon, and get out there and do battle. I think to a certain degree I had that blade hunger over the last three or four years. I would see people onstage and I would feel little twinges of wanting to get back into the battle, to do it again myself. It wasn't any all-encompassing thing, because I felt what came out of that period was very positive."

Diamond assembled a touring band, many of whom continue performing with him today in the Neil Diamond Road Racing Team—NDRRT. For this comeback tour, the band consisted of Dennis St. John (drums), Tom Hensley and Alan Lindgren (keyboards), Richard Bennett, Emery Gordy, and Doug Rhone (guitars), King Errisson (percussion), Reinie Press (bass guitar), and Linda Press (backing vocals). All were experienced session players from the Los Angeles area; most had worked with him on earlier records.

He was understandably nervous about performing again. It had been four years, and all those warnings about how his fans would discard him were running through his head. The one place he felt sure about was Australia, where *Hot August Night*, the country's all-time best seller, remained in the Top Ten after three years. It was once estimated that one out of every four Australian households owned *Hot August Night*.

The other advantage Australia provided was that if he proved to be rusty, at least the hometown fans wouldn't know about it. He joked that Australia was so far away from America, no one would hear about it if he did fail. Besides, he owed Australia. He was the continent's most popular recording artist, and 98 percent of an opinion poll audience named him as the artist they would most like to see in concert.

He had no reason to worry. Following wildly enthusiastic tune-up concerts in Sacramento and Salt Lake City, he arrived in the land of the koala in early February 1976 and found the press core properly geared up to receive him. For days afterward, he answered questions over and over again: why he semi-retired; what he did in the interim; what he thought of the *Jonathan* film; if he was afraid to come back; and so on.

Normally wary of interviews but hoping to "show the man behind the myth," Diamond agreed to a one-hour nationally televised interview conducted by Schildberger. Diamond looked pleased, for the most part, with the questions on friendship, the sabbatical, and his childhood. But he looked put off when cornered into talking about topics he usually refused to discuss: his finances, his cigarette smoking, politics, and religion.

He explained that for him, money meant privacy and freedom. The material aspect of it did not concern him. "First . . . you must buy your privacy when you are a public person. You must live in areas that are exclusive simply because you want to go about your everyday life like everyone else; and if you're too much in front of the public, then you can't do that. Everybody wants their two minutes or their ten seconds, which seems very small . . . but when you realize there are thousands and maybe even hundreds of thousands that want that time. . . .

"Money also in a sense means freedom: the freedom to stop performing for three years, the freedom to study and read and to get to know myself. Also, being in the public favor is extraordinary and exhilarating, but it's not something you can count on for the rest of your life. And so you hope you can put enough in the bank so that when the public finally says, 'We no longer like you. We like that person,' you don't have to go around and work at jobs you don't want to work at."

Diamond declined to reveal his personal worth. "I don't really know. After a while, it gets very complicated. It's a business, really, and I'm one of the employees of the business. I receive a salary."

When Neil was asked to tell the audience the kinds of things he spent his money on, Schildberger, perhaps expecting details of extravagance, learned that Diamond had average tastes. "Anything . . . a new pair of shoes, as many record albums as I want, the best hi-fi system, the best guitars."

Diamond talked about his smoking, saying that his doctors had already warned him that he was unnecessarily shortening his career. He admitted that he had tried changing brands, self-control, even hypnotism—all to no avail.

He also bemoaned the fact that in his opinion, America was mostly devoid of any real political thinkers. He said he would only actively support those individuals he felt honestly considered the future of mankind.

Concerning religion, Diamond said he believes in God but not organized religion. "[Religion] means a great deal to me, but I'm not religious. I tend to be very spiritual. Organized religion is created by people who are fallible."

Having finally completed the last interview, Diamond, rather uncomfortable in the role of being "the biggest thing around," was only too glad to take the stage.

The concerts were not just well received; they seemed indicative of some sort of "Diamondmania." From the announcement of his first show at Auburn, New Zealand on February 14, ticket requests from all over that part of the globe poured in. Promoters David Frost (the noted interviewer) and Robert Patterson called the tour "the biggest ever, in box office terms, outside the United

States" and doubted that Bob Dylan could have filled some of the halls Diamond did. With great reviews, great box office, and an incredible rejuvenation of his record catalog in both Australia and New Zealand, Diamond was the star of the season.

"I could have crammed the Australian dates together, done the tour in two weeks, then split. But from now on, I've promised myself that it's going to be fun. We spread the tour over a month. . . ."

He told a radio audience later that year: "The Australian audience had been waiting. I had never been down there to perform and they'd been so great that I just felt it was the natural place to start it off, and as it worked out, it was one of the most extraordinary experiences that I've ever had. I couldn't even begin to describe what it was like. It was beyond pandemonium, it was beyond anything. It was insanity after a while, and it was just beautiful. It's an exotic place. We swam in the Indian Ocean, we went to the Sydney Opera House, and we met great people and hung out in the pubs with all the drivers. It was an extraordinary experience."

The pinnacle was a free concert at the enormous Sydney Sports Arena broadcast by the national television network at the end of his tour. The 255,274 people in the crowd is the largest audience Diamond has ever played before, and four million more saw the live feed in their homes. He gave a fine performance. The concert, never seen in America, is a much more satisfying experience than either of Diamond's two NBC-TV specials shown in 1977. Neil shows far more candor, spontaneity, and enthusiasm.

By April, he was back touring in America and Canada. *Beautiful Noise* had been warmly received by the public, although it was now obvious that the rock writers, poised to jump on the up-and-coming New Wave bandwagon in the United Kingdom, were no longer interested in "middle-aged" Diamond. For every Robert Hilburn who pointed out that *Beautiful Noise* was his hardest-edged and best studio work, there were many who brushed it off as lacking the vitality of the younger acts.

Columbia waited until June to release the first single, "If You Know What I Mean." The archetypal drinking-after-hours ballad about remembering old times and the paying of one's dues hit number eleven. Oddly, his follow-up single, the bouncy "Don't Think . . . Feel" could not crack the Top Forty (number forty-three) and the ultra-late release of the album's title track sparked no interest at all.

The relatively poor showing of the singles could not put a damper on the achievement factor of the album. Most of the songs are indispensable in understanding Diamond: where he came from, how he did it, and what it meant. Although Diamond, even in this work, found it somewhat difficult to clearly express himself (note the vagueness of "If You Know What I Mean") at all times, *Beautiful Noise* is an honest triumph which fairly begs for film treatment. Diamond would move to free more time for such endeavors at the expense of his concert schedule.

What he did was to devise a less-stressful method of touring. A start-stop schedule allowed him to tour for six to ten weeks, then spend at least that much time at home. This was accomplished by bunching the shows together within a particular geographical area. It proved to be a key element in keeping his family together while driving fans living in the wrong area crazy.

Following the first scattered Southwestern America and British Columbia dates, Neil took two months to prepare for the concert that would "officially" open his North American tours. After refusing to play Las Vegas show-rooms for years, Diamond agreed to be the first performer at the new $10-million Aladdin Center for the Performing Arts, the gambling center's first legitimate concert hall. He was paid $650,000 for five shows in early July 1976. The 7,500-seat facility sold out in two weeks at then-staggering ticket prices of $20 and $30.

The drama that preceded the Aladdin engagement overshadowed the concerts themselves. After an anonymous caller told police that Diamond had a cache of cocaine in his home, fifty Los Angeles police officers surrounded Neil's Holmby Hills home near Westwood. (The family preferred to stay here most of the year because it was less susceptible to snoopers than the Malibu house.) An officer called the house on the pretense that there was a prowler in the area. When Diamond opened the door, the investigators handed him a search warrant.

The police searched the house from top to bottom, uncovering no cocaine but discovering a small amount— less than an ounce—of marijuana (possession of such a quantity for personal use is a misdemeanor in California). Neil reportedly handed each officer an autographed copy of *Beautiful Noise* as they left the house. He was issued a summons but not arrested, and he was eventually sentenced to a six-month drug rehabilitation course, which he completed in 1977.

Later, Neil tended to agree with *Rolling Stone* that the bust might have been an attempt by organized crime to take some of the steam out of the Aladdin opening. Attempts to find the informer or establish a conspiracy failed. Ultimately, the emotional impact of the raid was too much for Marcia, and the Diamonds moved to Malibu on a permanent basis.

The bust surprised many, especially in light of Neil's earlier vehement anti-drug stance, but did little to diminish his popularity. The shows at the Aladdin came off without a hitch; Las Vegas reviewers loved him as much as the audience did. But Diamond has refused to play Las Vegas ever since.

The show introduced America to the new Neil Diamond performing techniques. More than just a singer performing his hits, Diamond became a personality. He not only continued to ask his audiences to sing along with him on "Song Sung Blue" but now also traded banter with patrons in the first few rows. The fifteen-minute *Jonathan* segment was introduced, as well as music from *Serenade* and *Beautiful Noise*. The new material scored as high with audiences as did the old songs. But most importantly, Diamond was more confident of his ability and had become a much more relaxed performer. He hadn't lost any of the intensity of the *Hot August Night* era, yet he conveyed a certain ease that made audiences feel at home.

This personal touch, combined with Diamond's trademark sincerity in live settings, created a demand for return engagements throughout America. His fans, eager to see their idol after four years, bought virtually every ticket printed for each arena. Diamond had become the first pop attraction at New York's Forest Hills tennis stadium in years. Stadium officials lifted the ban on performances that was instituted after drug-related murders at the site during a concert five years before. Due to Diamond's more mature audience, they were sure that serious problems would not occur.

Entering the shows each night were fans and disbelievers alike. Leaving their seats after seeing the new and improved and rested Diamond were fanatics and fans. In every city they asked the same question: When would Neil Diamond come back? He was now consistently receiving much higher praise for his concert performances than for his recordings—and would do so to date.

Diamond had one challenge remaining: Could *Hot August Night* be duplicated? It was now time for him to find out with a return to the Greek Theater.

With the possible exceptions of Frank Sinatra and the late Elvis Presley, Diamond is probably the pop master of audience manipulation. He knows just how to get everyone instantly in the palm of his hand and make them do whatever he wants.

—Larry Kelp
Oakland Tribune/Eastbay Today

8
Let Me Take You in My Arms Again (1977–1979)

Los Angeles, the entertainment capital of the world, had become the adopted hometown of Neil Diamond. Beginning with the 1966 success of "Solitary Man," through the recording of the *Gold* album at Doug Weston's Troubadour, to the accolades for his Greek Theater concerts spawning the *Hot August Night* album, Neil had found his most ardent supporters in Los Angeles. The laid-back atmosphere of the city was conducive to his high pressure style of creativity.

Still, the thought of a comeback performance in Los Angeles was nearly too much for Diamond to bear. Playing New York was easy—it was home. Headlining in Los Angeles became a trial of acceptance much like pledging a fraternity—one slip could result in utter failure. He wanted the city to embrace him, and he risked rejection in achieving his goal.

Neil disliked admitting it, but scheduling Los Angeles concert dates at the Greek Theater put a terrible strain on him as a performer and as a human being. After being so successful in a city where success can fade quickly, he had walked away for four years. Now he dared to return with hopes of regaining his preeminent place in the pop performing world. If his performing comeback was to be complete, Diamond would once again have to win over Los Angeles. The Greek Theater shows would either reestablish him in the performing field or signal the end of an era.

On the day of the opening concert, Neil admitted his trepidation: "The legend has grown up and built around the last engagement we had here at the Greek," he said. "There's been enormous worldwide [attention] and so I was just a little nervous about it. What could I present in this show that could ever top what people have in their imaginations? And so I was a little nervous about [performing at the Greek again], but I knew that if and when I ever came back and played Los Angeles, this would be the place to play. It's very special from a performer's point of view. It's a small place compared to the kinds of places we've been playing—the setting [is] nestled in the trees in the hills and it's a very extraordinary place to play."

The eight Greek shows, running from September 13 through 20, broke all previous sales records: 37,000 tickets were snapped up by 11,000 fans in three and a half hours. Though Neil might have lost some potential audience among youth over the years, his ranks of devoted fans continued to increase.

The engagement revealed changes in Diamond's appearance and demeanor. Gone were the long hair, beaded denim, and the bluesy growl of a Muddy Waters or Janis Joplin. In place of these, Neil sported a clean-cut image accompanied by vocals as clear and straightforward as they sounded on vinyl. No longer "forever in blue jeans," he wore casual browns perhaps more reminiscent of a business mogul than a pop superstar.

Despite the toning down of his image, Neil was still an effective showman. He delivered his new material from *Beautiful Noise* and *Serenade* with a definitive bravado.

The highlight of each Greek show was the performance of "Song Sung Blue." Instead of merely asking the audience to sing along, Diamond pulled celebrities out of the audience to sing on stage with him; included in these impromptu choruses were Helen Reddy, Henry Winkler (singing in the style of "the Fonz"), Diana Ross, Roger Miller, Red Buttons (who didn't know the words), basketball great Jerry West, and local critic David Sheehan.

The Greek shows were a rousing success and proved beyond any doubt that Diamond was back. Diamond was once again asked when he would return. He gave the same answer everywhere: "We'll be doing more shows. We're back, we're going to be doing lots of exciting things. I'm sorry that there were so many people who couldn't get seats, but we will be doing more shows in the Los Angeles area and, hopefully, next time we'll play venues where more people can get in and we don't have the problems of people unable to get tickets and going through those kinds of hassles."

The final Greek appearance was taped by television crews for Diamond's first network special, shown the following February on NBC. The accompanying live album bore the name which has become associated with the event: *Love at the Greek*.

"The Neil Diamond Special" showcased the singer in his own familiar surroundings—the stage. For years CBS and NBC had been asking Neil to do a variety special. But his distaste for traditional variety shows was well known; he repeatedly vowed never to do one. However, televised highlights of a concert were a satisfying compromise for Diamond and the network. NBC had Diamond singing and even had Reddy and Winkler as guests during the final "Song Sung Blue" segment. Diamond only had to be himself. NBC had asked time and again and had agreed to do the special under his supervision; Diamond felt he could lose nothing but his anonymity.

After working on the special with film editors for three months, Diamond gave a number of interviews to promote the special; and the subject of each article was the loss of his anonymity. As he told *Billboard*: "I've been an anonymous superstar for a long time and I've liked it that way. People don't know what I look like. People go around imitating me and there are two guys in jail because of it. The show will make me recognizable and I'm not totally happy about that. I've been away four years, hiding and trying to be an anonymous person. As a writer you have to be an observer and the key of observing is being anonymous."

In all the stories, he kidded that he would now "have to buy banana noses and fake mustaches and long fright wigs" to do his observing.

During this period Diamond participated in a piece of rock & roll history. Fresh off the Robertson-produced *Beautiful Noise* and *Love at the Greek*, Diamond was invited to perform in the Band's farewell concert at Bill Graham's Winterland in San Francisco on Thanksgiving Day 1976.

The group—Rick Danko, Garth Hudson, Levon Helm, Richard Manuel, and Robertson—invited their friends and a capacity crowd of five thousand to a $42,000 traditional Thanksgiving dinner, complete with 220 turkeys and all the trimmings.

Robertson got many of the group's closest performing friends to join the concert. Besides Neil, the Band's guests included Bob Dylan, Ronnie Hawkins (who had discovered them), Ringo Starr, Eric Clapton, Neil Young, Joni Mitchell, Dr. John, Muddy Waters, Van Morrison, Ron Wood of the Rolling Stones, and Paul Butterfield. Studio footage of Emmylou Harris and the Staple Singers was added to director Martin Scorsese's film of the concert, *The Last Waltz*.

Each artist performed songs with the Band, joined in the closing number—Dylan's "I Shall Be Released"—and also agreed to be in Scorsese's film and on the accompanying soundtrack album.

Diamond sang "Dry Your Eyes"; it was the stiffest

performance of the night. He seemed out of place in all of this, even though he had brought along his own drummer, Dennis St. John. The leisure-suited Frog King looked about as compatible with the rest of the guests as Frank Zappa would on a Jerry Lewis telethon.

After all, his own music was quite unlike the Band's. In fact, his music was different from everyone else's at the concert, and Diamond's uneasiness was never more apparent than in his reluctance to be included in "I Shall Be Released."

Perhaps it was only stage fright or awe at being on the same stage with superstars like Ringo Starr and Bob Dylan. He did perform in the closing, although he spent much of the time looking offstage while trying to sing along. He even tried to walk away before it was over. Those he had called onstage to sing "Song Sung Blue" with him at the Greek Theater may have experienced the same feelings.

But his lackluster participation in *The Last Waltz* did not hurt him. The Band and Dylan proved to be the stars of the evening, and it didn't really matter how the rest of the ensemble looked or sang. If anything, Diamond's appearance mildly lengthened the lifespan of his appeal to album rock listeners.

With his American audiences completely conquered following the Greek dates, Diamond set off on a European tour May 31, 1977. Beginning in Rotterdam and playing throughout the Continent, he wound his way to England by July. There, at Woburn Abbey in Bedfordshire, he played the second largest open-air concert of his career before an estimated 70,000 fans. The show was filmed for another NBC television special scheduled for the fall. However, Diamond was dissatisfied with the sound recording and felt the repertoire too similar to the Greek special. Instead, he and director William Friedkin began working on an idea for a different kind of semidocumentary inspired by Diamond's visit to France.

Stories began circulating in July that work would

begin in August on a film featuring Diamond in his first starring role. The picture, to be called *Free Man in Paris* (after the Joni Mitchell song Diamond planned to cover on his next album), was said to be loosely based on Diamond's life during the 1960s and would be principally shot in France. Jeanne Moreau was set to co-star in the film along with Jacques Tati, Catherine Deneuve, and Jean-Paul Belmondo; Diamond was to sing and portray himself. Brigitte Bardot was rumored to be coming out of a three-year retirement to play a cameo role. Producer/director Friedkin (director of *The Exorcist* and whose most recent film was *To Live and Die in L.A.*), had been following Diamond with a camera crew throughout the European tour, shooting background footage for the fictional feature scripted by Moreau.

NBC bankrolled the project, intending to include the film in a series of four year-end entertainment specials it planned. The network invested $1.5 million in the project and planned to recover its investment by showing the picture in theaters outside the United States. Diamond said he and the others would work for little or no money.

The film's theme song was a radically rearranged version of the Joni Mitchell hit of the same name, which had originally been written about record business mogul David Geffen. Much of the subsequent *I'm Glad You're Here With Me Tonight* album had its origins in the film project.

But *Free Man in Paris* was scrapped after scheduling problems forced Friedkin to begin work on another project. Diamond, meanwhile, was awaiting the outcome of a rights' complication concerning another possible film project.

Diamond had first been contacted about starring in the second remake of *The Jazz Singer*, (originally a 1927 Al Jolson film which is regarded to be the first movie with sound) by producer Jerry Leider in February 1977. Leider was impressed with the "Love at the Greek" special and felt Diamond would be great in a film. At this time, *The Jazz Singer* was still only talk, as Leider would spend months securing the film's sequel rights, and years in getting Diamond to finally agree to star in it.

Free Man in Paris was never completed but Neil nevertheless took what remained and, with director Art Fisher, created the "I'm Glad You're Here with Me Tonight" television special. The program, which aired only ten months after his first special, combined a behind-the-scenes look at a mostly staged recording session, which Neil narrated, with footage from the Woburn Abbey concert. There was a scene of Neil working with Alan and Marilyn Bergman on the recording of "You Don't Bring Me Flowers" (which was intended for use on the short-lived Norman Lear soap opera satire "All That Glitters"), and a look back at *Jonathan* was included.

In addition, scenes of Diamond biking and strolling in France accompanied the song "Free Man in Paris," a radically rearranged version of Mitchell's hit; and shots of him playing chess with old men in the city accompanied "Morningside." He sang most of the songs from his forthcoming album and a couple of medleys of old hits.

The special aired on November 17 to moderate ratings and reviews. To most observers, the material was staid and self-serious, and offered little to non-devotees. To make matters worse, the namesake album, produced by Four Seasons member Bob Gaudio, was viewed as a disappointment by most commentators. While the album still sold a million copies, it marked the beginning of a decline in the quality of Diamond's work that continued until *The Jazz Singer*. It was particularly disappointing as it was the first studio album after *Beautiful Noise*.

Only one single—the Top Twenty hit "Desiree" (number sixteen), an unusual song that combined distorted electric guitars with a full orchestra—was released from the album in America. The song, about a young man losing his virginity to an older woman, was the kind of song the public expected from Diamond. The title

track, "I'm Glad You're Here with Me Tonight," was
another of his now-patented laid-back ballads, and was to
be put out on a single backed with the excellent instrumental "Dance of the Sabres." However, plans were
scrapped as the critical beatings continued. This second
45 and a third track, the country-flavored "Let Me Take
You In My Arms Again" (backed with "As If"), were
released with some success in Europe.

As the specials aired and his concert tours continued,
several interviewers managed to coax Diamond near
microphones. In one particular interview, he talked of his
thoughts on the importance of pop culture: "Entertainers
and performers and artists make a contribution in the
work that they do, and they go through a lot of changes
and pay a lot of dues in order to be able to do that. I think
they all make a contribution in one way or another, and
in varying degrees of quality and quantity. But it is a
contribution, and I value it. . . . I think it would be
terrible to live without it, so I have to be grateful to the
people who move me and who entertain me and can
affect me. It is a gift they give because they have a gift and
I'm appreciative. I'm really appreciative. That's where it's
at."

When asked if money was still a motivation, he replied:
"The money happens to be an outgrowth of it, and you'd
have to be a fool to turn down the best deal that someone
can offer you. I mean, we're not stupid just because we're
artists. At least somebody will tap us on the shoulder and
say, 'That guy's gonna pay you more to make the same
music you're gonna make anyway. Do it with them.' You
dig what I'm saying? No artist that cares about anything
he does is gonna let the money take precedence. The point
is, does he or the other artists have any self-respect? Do
they care about what they do? Do they give it their best
shots? Do they offer something to people?

"People who listen to my music know me; there's no
question about it. It's one of the greatest things that I
come into concerts with; when I come in front of an

audience, I know that they know me already. I don't have
to teach them anything about me. I don't have to prove
anything to them. They know me, and they're there
because they accept me for what I am. And it's a tremendous burden off my shoulders, because then I can just be
what I am.

"I'm beginning to understand what my responsibility
is. I'm beginning to believe that maybe I have a small
contribution to make. And I want to do it—just work and
be happy with whatever happens, with whatever I have,
with what little or with [how much]I have. I want to be
happy inside as a person. Then whatever happens, it'll be
fine."

The drug bust prior to the Aladdin Theater engagement and *The Last Waltz* appearance were the last
incidents in his professional life that would link him to
the rock scene. He had become a completely middle-of-
the-road pop artist. This was reflected in his next recording project, an album that was to have been titled *The
American Popular Song*. Although press coverage im-
plied that the album was the same collection that was
released under the name *You Don't Bring Me Flowers*, it
was actually intended to be another concept album.

A lack of songwriting inspiration led Neil to decide to
record an oldies theme album that would partially reflect
his roots and influences. Columbia was not in agreement
with this, since the run of all-oldies, change-of-pace
albums by established artists, like John Lennon's *Rock N'
Roll*, had peaked some time ago. Besides, the disco age
was beginning, and this led the company to fear Diamond's proposed album would be flatly rejected by the
buying public.

In the meantime, a freak phenomenon was taking place
that would result in the biggest-selling single of Neil's
career. A Cleveland disc jockey named Gary Guthrie
came up with the idea (inspired by his concurrent
divorce) of splicing Neil's recording of "You Don't Bring
Me Flowers" together with the cover version by Barbra

Streisand from her current album, *Songbird.* Quite by
chance, both versions were recorded in the same key and
at approximately the same tempo. The finished product
sounded like a legitimate duet. Although local programmers had been producing novelty records this way
for years, Guthrie's tape hit a nerve in the local listener-
ship. It soon became his station's hottest request. The
record's popularity spread to other stations and eventually
to other cities around the country. Aside from inspiring
other such splice-duets (the subject of which was usually
the recently deceased Presley), Guthrie's "You Don't Bring
Me Flowers" caught the fancy of Columbia Records
executives.

It is not known who approached Diamond and Streisand—both recording for Columbia—with the idea of
properly cutting the song as a duet. But both ultimately
agreed to record what would become the love song of the
year and a standard on middle-of-the-road (MOR) airplay
lists.

The duet shot up the charts and was number one for
two weeks. It remained on the charts for over four
months and went platinum. This was an amazing feat in
a year when almost all of the hits were either disco or
hard rock.

Some critics complained that the duet took the satiric
edge out of the composition, but that had no effect on the
millions who took it at face value. Diamond and Streisand
appeared unannounced on the 1980 Grammy Awards
broadcast and sang it live, elevating "You Don't Bring Me
Flowers" to a modern romantic legend.

In a 1982 Los Angeles radio interview, Diamond discussed his and Streisand's feelings that night at the
Grammys. "Well, I do know that Barbra and I were very
nervous. She was shaking. I tried to put on a good front
but I was also shaking. It was very exciting and it was
over so quickly that I think we were both a little relieved
that we had done it and sung the right notes and she sang
her lines when she was supposed to and I sang my lines

when I was supposed to. It was just a very special moment for both of us."

(Streisand appeared with Barry Gibb at the 1981 Grammy Awards and said, "I feel like I'm cheating on Neil Diamond!")

The single's success threw a wrench into plans for *The American Popular Song*, which Columbia wanted to be at least 50 percent new material. Neil had put together a lineup that featured versions of the Fortunes' "You've Got Your Troubles," the Walker Brothers' "The Sun Ain't Gonna Shine Anymore," Martha Reeves and the Vandellas' "Dancing in the Street," Lloyd Price's "Stagger Lee," Bob Dylan's "Lay Lady Lay," the DeCastro Sisters' "Teach Me Tonight," Elton John's "Rocket Man," a rework of his own "I'm a Believer," and a song based on B. Bumble and the Stingers' "Bumble Boogie" entitled "The Dancing Bumble Bee." The album was also to include the "You Don't Bring Me Flowers" duet, one composition by Diamond and Richard Bennett—"Money Talks" (the original title of "Forever in Blue Jeans")— and a Tom Hensley song composed especially for Diamond, "The American Popular Song."

The artwork was even completed for the record. The album cover for *The American Popular Song* became the cover of the 1982 *Heartlight* album. The unreleased inner sleeve shows a cartoon drawing of Diamond in various stages of his career—easily the best piece of art Diamond ever commissioned for one of his records. Unfortunately, Columbia blocked the record's release and this jacket was scrapped.

Neil could have tried to change the CBS view but apparently had second thoughts himself about some of the material. He decided to put together a new album under the auspices of Bob Gaudio. Most of the originally scheduled songs were only temporarily shelved, although three—"Lay Lady Lay," "Teach Me Tonight," and "Rocket Man"—have never been released.

Diamond's string-laden versions of "Lay Lady Lay"

and "Rocket Man" truly deserve to remain where they are. Dylan's country tune becomes something else entirely in the hands of Diamond, who turns the risqué love song into a labored plea for affection and a most horrendous abuse of strings. The seemingly endless "Rocket Man" just doesn't sound right in Diamond's voice; and the backup instrumentation can't seem to decide what to sound like. "Teach Me Tonight" was a pleasant surprise, at least as good as Al Jarreau's 1982 version. It would not be surprising to see it on an album some day.

The American Popular Song was retitled *You Don't Bring Me Flowers* and filled out with some Diamond originals, most notably "Say Maybe," another Diamond ballad that in the disco age only reached number fifty-five. The only remake on this album was "You've Got Your Troubles," which had its own troubles.

Despite the enormous popularity of "You Don't Bring Me Flowers," a better song on the album was the newly titled "Forever in Blue Jeans," a simple and bouncy song about the power of love over money. As Diamond would explain in concert when introducing the song, "Forever in Blue Jeans" was an idea that NDRRT guitarist Bennett had in his head for weeks but couldn't fully grasp, so he asked Neil to help him out; the resulting song became Diamond's next big hit, reaching number twenty.

Diamond was almost immediately besieged by jeans manufacturers to either lend the song or sing it himself in a commercial. He has turned down multi-million dollar figures almost yearly and as recently as 1985 turned down $10 million just to let the song play in the background of a commercial. Considering how protective Diamond is of his songs, this is a perfectly understandable response.

He was softening this hard-line stance a bit, however. After having stopped doing collaborations back at Tin Pan Alley, he had begun to reconsider as early as 1973. When he signed with CBS back then, he boasted of their artist roster and said it would be wonderful if he could work with some of the label's other talents. He did not get around to doing this until his work with Robertson on *Beautiful Noise* in 1975, and tried again with "You Don't Bring Me Flowers." The success of "Forever in Blue Jeans" on top of the duet—both collaborations—finally convinced him to work with other writers. His personal mellowing also probably made it easier to break down his creative walls.

Diamond thus began a temporary songwriting relationship with sophisticated French singer-songwriter Gilbert Becaud. The first hit for the pair was "September Morn'," an old-fashioned cabaret ballad that would reach number seventeen in early 1980. "We met after a concert that I did in Paris and decided to meet the next day . . . I met him in his apartment in Paris and there was a piano there and we both started talking about music and said, 'Well, let's see if we can come up with an idea together— just now, right at this moment, because the feeling is very good.' . . . And we came up with the general idea and the melody for 'Septemeber Morn'. It was the beginning of a new relationship for me and, really, the making of a new friend." He remarked to *Billboard* in 1979: "Now I see that it's more fun to write with someone, sharing the agony and the ecstasy."

Becaud soon starred in his own French television special, which was beamed over to Canada's French-speaking Quebec Province. Diamond was a guest, via satellite, and talked with Becaud about their writting all the songs for *The Jazz Singer*. When Becaud suggested that "Septemember Morn' " could be in the film, Diamond readily agreed.

Since talk of Diamond's starring in *The Jazz Singer* had begun circulating, with reports having him agree, then not agree to be involved with the project, gossip began to surface concerning his involvement in alternative projects. This had partly been fueled by Diamond's contribution of a song, "I Seek the Night," to Clint Eastwood's film *Every Which Way But Loose*. Neil had allowed Eastwood's costar Sondra Locke to sing the song in the film rather than record it himself. Pre-release talk about the Eastwood film had Diamond appearing in it, even in a cameo role.

Why? Even though no hard proof ever existed, now that the tabloid press had Diamond committed to starring in a film (or so they believed), if he was unsure about doing *The Jazz Singer*, he would certainly replace it with another project.

In January 1979, a story had Diamond reportedly planning to buy the American rights to Tim Rice and Andrew Lloyd Webber's musical *Evita*. He was to stage it himself, portraying the lead role of Che Guevara as well. *Los Angeles* magazine claimed that Raquel Welch, Faye Dunaway, and Ann-Margret all expressed interest in the role of Eva Peron, but Rice himself said no stars had yet been signed.

Almost simultaneously, *People* reported that producer Jon Peters had plans for a film version of *You Don't Bring Me Flowers* with Diamond and Streisand in the lead roles, with Barbra possibly directing. Although it could not have materialized at this time because of Diamond's almost-final commitment to *The Jazz Singer*, Neil said at the time: "Barbra has an extraordinary feel for filmmaking, and I'd love her to direct our movie. She never tries to get by just on her name."

The *You Don't Bring Me Flowers* film had faded from current memory by the birth of Neil and Marcia's second son, Micah, on St. Valentine's Day in 1979. He once said to KIIS-FM listeners in Los Angeles: "I'd have to say that my proudest achievement has been my kids. They give me more satisfaction, real satisfaction, than anything I do. Everything else pales and takes second place to that—my best music, my best performances, all that takes second place to just waking up in the morning and seeing my son Jesse come in in his pajamas and having breakfast with him. I've yet to find anything as satisfying or as beautiful as that."

Diamond had already allowed Jesse to help King

Errisson and Vince Charles on percussion during a few concerts. The first time was before an enthusiastic sold-out crowd in Indianapolis. Zack Dunkin of the *Indianapolis News* quoted Diamond's introduction of Jesse, who played on "Beautiful Noise": "It's such a tremendous thrill for me to turn around and see my son on stage. I'm going to break him in early, because when I'm eighty and can't go on and do it anymore, he can."

For months now, Diamond had been experiencing increasing numbness of his right leg. He had been able to hide this from his audiences by restricting his stage movements. Neil later said he'd been losing feeling in the leg for some time; a look at his appearance on the 1979 Grammys—when he presented the Best Album award to *Saturday Night Fever*—showed that he walked like the leg was in a splint.

In late February, Diamond was doing his now custom-ary encores of "Forever in Blue Jeans" and dancing on stage at San Francisco's Cow Palace when he collapsed and could not get up again under his own power. Stage hands carried him off the floor, and the show was halted. Unable to walk, he was rushed back to Los Angeles' Cedars-Sinai Medical Center. Exploratory surgery revealed that he had a cancerous tumor on his spine. Neil wanted to finish his remaining tour dates, but doctors told him that he faced paralysis and possibly death if the tumor was not immediately removed.

"I had felt that something was wrong for a number of years. I was losing some of the feeling in my right leg, but it happened so gradually that I was able to convince myself that it wasn't anything serious," he told Robert Hilburn in 1983. "It was really a life-or-death situation. They didn't know how much damage had been done."

Neil had never been more frightened. Even if he lived through the dangerous operation, there was a chance he might still be permanently paralyzed. He gave his consent, checked his will, and wrote his farewells to all his friends and family.

On March 16, the tumor was removed and two of Neil's vertebrae were replaced in a delicate nine-hour operation.

In a 1986 "Entertainment This Week" interview, Diamond recalled that when he was being wheeled into the recovery room, "I saw my wife and said, 'Honey, I don't know if I'm going to be able to [perform] anymore. But I'll tell you what, as long as I can sing, you'll put some sequins on my wheelchair and wheel me out there, and we'll try it anyway.' "

Diamond's admirers' concern for his health ranged from the ridiculous to the revealing. During his Cedars-Sinai convalescence at least two fans disguised as nurses tried to sneak into his carefully guarded room. But Diamond realized he had friends out there beyond the footlights. "I was moved by the amount of mail I got, from kids to nuns. [It made me realize that] I wasn't locked up in a hole I call the recording studio for a year without touching somebody's life."

By June he was walking again. He returned to the Cow Palace and resumed the concert tour that had been interrupted. He also cut a couple of tracks to fill out an album tentatively titled *Songs from the Ark,* a portion of which became part of the *September Morn'* album, the other portion being the genesis of *The Jazz Singer.* (*Songs from the Ark* was an obvious reference to the religiosity of the upcoming *Jazz Singer*).

Ironically, *September Morn'* contained half remakes and half originals, including material dumped for *The American Popular Song,* as well as some passed-over items written for *The Jazz Singer.* The album's second single, "The Good Lord Loves You"—not written by Diamond—was an inexplicable commercial bomb (number sixty-seven). Besides the title track, an excellent Carole Bayer Sager song called "That Kind," a Diamond-Hensley tune called "Jazz Time," and a Diamond-Becaud masterpiece, "Mama Don't Know"—clearly his best song since "Walk on Water"—there was nothing else truly substantial on the record. It might have been wise to delay the release of this otherwise dreary album.

Musically, Diamond would more than make up for *September Morn'* with *The Jazz Singer* soundtrack. Determined to create the best music he had ever written, Diamond would make no other commitments for the duration of *The Jazz Singer* project. The results would be debatable but the album was Diamond's best in quite some time.

*Neil is a very, very dedicated, serious artist. He is
contemplative. He has managed his career brilliantly by
not making a lot of precipitous moves, and the pace at
which he wants to accomplish things is perhaps a pace
that's unique to him. He can afford that luxury . . . but
deserves it, also. He's a very talented and gifted artist. I
have extraordinary respect for Neil Diamond. I have
often thought about the trials and tribulations of making this film. I've also thought about the highs that we
had . . . and the lows . . . and if I had to do the thing all
over again, from beginning to end, I'd do it again. I don't
know whether Neil or EMI would, but I know I would.*

—Jerry Leider,
The Jazz Singer producer
Interview with the authors, 1984

9
Amazed and Confused
(February 1977–
February 1980)

It was not Diamond's idea to do a remake of *The Jazz
Singer*, the 1927 Al Jolson cinematic milestone which is
considered to be the first "talking" picture. The notion of
remaking the sentimental story of a Jewish cantor and his
rebellious son originated with producer Jerry Leider, who
spent better than two years courting Diamond for the role
that would finally put the singer in films.

The saga of the third remake of *The Jazz Singer* (the
second version, made in 1953, starred Danny Thomas)
actually began in February 1977, when Leider returned
to America after several years of working in Europe as
head of international filming for Warner Brothers. Leider
had begun developing his own independent production

147

company when he tuned in to the "Love at the Greek" special. He immediately became intrigued with Diamond as a performer who might easily direct his talents to movies. He was unaware of the countless others that had approached Diamond through the years.

By coincidence, Leider had made a lunch appointment with Tony Fantozzi, an old friend whom he hadn't seen in two years who, unbeknownst to Leider, was part of Diamond's management group. Leider began asking Fantozzi about Diamond's possible cinematic future and discussed his feeling about the singer's crossover potential. Leider was impressed by Diamond's magnetism and forcefulness and felt that Neil's talents were equal to those of Al Jolson, Frank Sinatra, and Elvis Presley, who had all made the successful transfer to celluloid.

At the mention of Jolson's name, Leider suddenly said, "Why don't we do *The Jazz Singer* again?" Fantozzi suggested that the rights to the story must be owned by Warner Brothers, who had produced the previous two versions. Leider's first independent production was contracted with Warner Brothers, so he agreed to check into obtaining the rights.

Fantozzi arranged a conference between Diamond and Leider in March 1977, which led to a meeting after a Diamond concert in Houston. Leider recalls that despite reports of Diamond's apprehension, Neil appeared eager to be involved. But inner anxieties over the project would cause Diamond to take the better part of two years to definitely agree to involvement. He feared that a poor film could force him into premature retirement. "Maybe I'm afraid to tackle something new, like making a movie, . . . if it's a flop, it could be all over for Neil Diamond."

During this time he began to ask his concert audiences if they wanted him to star in a film. Diamond said he had used this method in the past with songs he wasn't sure about including on upcoming albums. "I've found that I can ask them things from the stage. I've done it with songs . . . if they like it, it goes in the album—*Bam*! If not, it makes you rethink it a bit. They're very truthful. They're for you. That's why they're there. But you can feel it if they don't really like something. They still applaud, but not as strongly."

But as Leider attempted to secure the film rights, Diamond began his short-term involvement with the *Free Man in Paris* project. Leider believed so strongly in the remake possibilities that he still pursued the property. While *Free Man in Paris* was being scrapped and turned into the second NBC special, Leider was still busily obtaining the remake rights. And Diamond still hadn't given him a definite "yes" on a film contract.

Securing the remake rights was not an easy task. The original 1927 Jolson film, though produced by Warner, had been sold in a package deal with other Warner features to United Artists in a massive pre-1948 film buyout. When Warner decided to do the 1953 Danny Thomas remake, it obtained the sequel rights, which were not even discussed when the original film was produced. Thus, United Artists owned the 1927 film and Warner owned the 1953 version and apparently all subsequent versions.

Each studio felt it had some rights to the project. Leider wanted and needed complete clearance so he struck a deal with both companies. Each would receive an up-front option payment, additional rights fees as the picture developed, and a percentage of the profits.

Because of this odd arrangement, Leider was unable to successfully negotiate the complete option on the rights until October—six months after the project's conception. The Warner pact was completed first; the United Artists deal was closed on Yom Kippur. Leider telephoned Diamond to inform him of the Jewish New Year's present.

At first, it appeared MGM would make the movie as the company had expressed early interest and actually financed the first development. Leider hired Jerome Kass in January 1978 to write a screenplay. It was completed by summer, but MGM rejected the script and Kass was fired.

MGM wanted to continue development. Leider met with the agents of writer Stephen H. Foreman; he had been impressed with a script Foreman had written for director George Roy Hill at Universal. After a month of discussions, Foreman was signed to write the script.

At this point, MGM refused to continue financing the film's development unless a deal with Diamond was consummated. Neil, his representatives, and Leider met with MGM officials and agreed on a contract that would call for the singer's participation only if he approved the screenplay. Nothing was written in the contract concerning the music; however, Leider explained that it was "a given" that Diamond would have control of the songs and soundtrack album.

Meanwhile, MGM did a series of research tests conducted by a Westwood, California, marketing firm. Shortly after Foreman's script was completed, MGM abruptly dropped the film. Leider has surmised that a combination of the research report and Kass's heavily ethnic script led to MGM's decision: "There was some concern about the title—*The Jazz Singer*. Were we making an updated version of the old movie? And if so, what validity did it have today? Was it a twenties' movie? Did the kids want to see it?"

There were many negatives about the concept of the film on the research report. Some in the studio's upper echelon wanted to further modernize the remake by changing the cantor's role into a school teacher or a college professor. Leider said he considered this an honest effort by Dick Shepard, Ray Wagner, and Frank Rosenfelt at MGM to circumvent their apprehension about the film's premise. "They weren't being obstructionists, and they weren't being destructive. They were being constructive. And like many situations, we just couldn't solve the problems," Leider said.

MGM felt their differences with Leider were irreconcilable; at the end of of August 1978, the film was put into turnaround. This released Diamond from his contract, as he was signed only as long as the studio agreed to the script.

The film was far from dead, although Diamond, who had begun to talk of a movie version of *Beautiful Noise,* might have thought so. The idea surfaced at Paramount Pictures, the acknowledged king of movie musicals at the time. Paramount had just scored big with *Saturday Night Fever* and planned to follow it up with *Grease.* But nothing more than talk was generated about *Beautiful Noise,* although Paramount did list it as one of its upcoming films for 1979.

Fantozzi arranged for Leider to meet with Gary Dartnell, head of EMI Pictures in America, only a day after MGM rejected the *Jazz Singer* script. An impressed Dartnell called Lord Bernard Delfont, the new president of EMI. Delfont agreed that the film would be a great project for EMI as long as Leider could guarantee Diamond's commitment. When Leider replied that Diamond was still interested, Delfont made the deal over the telephone, agreeing to finance and distribute the film as long as the soundtrack album was included. This meant the album would be released through Capitol Records, EMI's American record division, rather than Columbia.

The Jazz Singer was the first deal for Delfont since becoming EMI's chief executive in May 1978. He had been named to the post after heavy losses to EMI's record division and a proposed merger with Paramount Pictures that had failed. *The Jazz Singer* became his top priority, as it was projected to bolster EMI's sagging fortunes. Delfont visited Neil at Malibu on three occasions in an attempt to get a signed contract. In a September 1978 conversation, they agreed to meet backstage at one of Diamond's upcoming Toronto concerts to discuss a contract. The project hinged on Diamond's signing. Delfont told Diamond that he believed in him and the film, and personally asked him to do the picture. Impressed with Delfont's gesture of confidence and faith, Neil replied that he looked forward to it.

Of the project, Delfont said, "This is part of my campaign to get EMI moving again. We saw *The Jazz Singer* as a clean family story which would appeal to audiences as much today as it did in the original version. And we see Neil as very big box office indeed."

Speculation emerged about the possibility of Paramount coproducing the film, but this proved to be born out of Delfont's previous association with the major studio, and Diamond's tertiary commitment with Paramount concerning *Beautiful Noise*.

From fall 1978 to the beginning of production in January 1980, the film went through an extended preproduction period during which Foreman again rewrote the script and Diamond began to write the score. Although Diamond had said on Becaud's television special that the two of them would write the score, Becaud ended up only co-writing five of the film's twelve original tracks; one of these, however, was "Love on the Rocks."

The rumors of Diamond's casting in an *Evita* film and as a costar with Streisand in the *You Don't Bring Me Flowers* movie peaked at this time but Leider maintains that he was unaware of any serious thought Diamond might have given these ideas. Besides, Leider said, Diamond was too busy working on the score.

Leider had begun the search for a director and talked to a number of people, including Michael Apted, who went on to direct *Coal Miner's Daughter*. But he hired his original choice, Sidney J. Furie, in February 1979. Leider liked the work Furie had done on Diana Ross's screen debut, *Lady Sings the Blues*. And he felt assured that Furie was passionate about doing *The Jazz Singer*.

All work on the film had to be postponed for six weeks because of Neil's bout with spinal cancer and his painful rehabilitation. Although Diamond reassured Delfont that once he was physically able he would star in the film, neither EMI nor Leider had a signed commitment from him. Nevertheless, Delfont told the EMI officers in Los Angeles, Barry Spikings and John Cohn, to put the film

back into development. Then, Harriet Helberg was
signed on as casting director. While the script was
developed by Foreman, Furie, and associate producer Joel
Morwood, Diamond's commitment became more and
more questionable.

By May 1979 Leider had lost all hope of signing
Diamond to the film. He met with Spikings and Cohn at
the Cannes Film Festival and told them of his frustration
over not having Diamond's name on a contract. With
option days fleeting, they decided that alternative actors
should be considered. (Leider had flown to Omaha in
April to see Billy Joel in concert but never met with him.
Leider said the only other person ever considered was
Barry Manilow.) At Cannes, Leider showed Spikings and
Cohn videotapes of Barry Manilow, and after consulting
Delfont, Leider was authorized to negotiate with
Manilow.

Attempts to coax Diamond into signing an agreement
continued during negotiations with Manilow's representatives. Word leaked to the press about EMI's latest
contract offer to Diamond—$1 million for acting and a
guarantee of $3 million for the soundtrack.

An offer was made to Manilow and a counter-offer was
made, which meant negotiations were nearing a close.
Gossip columnist Rona Barrett, at that time the Hollywood correspondent for ABC's "Good Morning America," unwittingly helped EMI's cause by reporting on
Leider's negotiations with Manilow twice in two weeks
on national television.

Diamond finally became aware that Manilow might
get the role if he did not make a decision. Realizing he
had to act fast, he flew to London with his attorney David
Braun and Fantozzi. Delfont, Bhaskar Menon (head of
Capitol Records), and Braun concluded the deal, and
Diamond signed the contract at a London press conference. The latest press reports about the highlights of the
contract had been accurate.

Manilow's agents were understandably upset at Diamond's sudden change of heart. But Manilow later commented that it was Diamond's film from the outset, and he felt it was handled fairly.

It should be noted, however, that the whole affair emphasized the professional rivalry between Barry and Neil, which remains stronger than ever. In fact, Manilow cut the semi-novelty "The Last Duet" with Lily Tomlin around this time—no doubt about what record inspired it—and both parties have ribbed each other from the concert stage on occasion. When Ray Stevens released "I Need Your Help, Barry Manilow" the following year, Manilow sent him a telegram thanking him for not doing a satire on Neil instead.

Diamond's insecurities had struck again and had this time prodded him to make a film. He told syndicated columnist Marilyn Beck, "It was a matter of nerves. A matter of being scared to death about making my first movie. [But] I was afraid that if I didn't take advantage of the chance to enlarge my audience, I could lose what I've built. Fear is a strong motivating force in everything I do."

Diamond was to portray assistant cantor Yussel Rabinowitz, the latest in a long family line of cantors at a synagogue on the Lower East Side of Manhattan. But Yussel, always intrigued by popular music, discovers, with the support of his musician friends, that he has real talent in that area. His friends urge him to join them in Los Angeles and pursue a singing career. He does, against his father's and his wife's wishes. Becoming entertainer Jess Robin, he is transformed into a sensation within weeks and falls in love with his gentile publicist and agent, Molly Bell.

The character—on the surface—does not seem to differ too much from Diamond himself. As Neil commented during one post-production interview, "I didn't need to become an actor, you know. I've had other offers in the past and turned them all down. But this part is very special. I identified with it very stongly. There are many,

many aspects of it that related to my life. The film is
about Jewish immigrants, the struggle to start a new life,
the American dream. My grandparents were immigrants;
they came from Russia and Poland to this country. I've
grown up hearing the legends of that Atlantic crossing,
their first sight of the Statue of Liberty. Their stories were
told and retold at family gatherings."

Having secured Diamond, Leider's next monumental
task was to sign Sir Laurence Olivier, whom Diamond
had often called the world's greatest actor. In fact, it was
Diamond who first suggested that Olivier play his tradi-
tion-bound father. As Diamond remarked to Army Ar-
cherd in *Variety*, "I wanted someone who'll act me off the
screen!"

Diamond placed a call to Olivier in London. The
beginning of the conversation was reported as follows:

Diamond: Hello. This is Neil Diamond. I hope I'm not
disturbing you.
Olivier: You certainly are not.
Diamond: I'd like to talk with you about a part in a
movie.
Olivier: I'm delighted to talk with you. I would love to do
your *Sunshine Boys* on the stage here in London.

After a brief pause, Diamond was able to convince
Olivier he was not Neil Simon and actually succeed in
obtaining Olivier's agreement to do the film. The previous year, Olivier supposedly claimed to have never
heard of Bob Dylan.

Diamond was understandably nervous about co-starring with the great Olivier. In the 1986 "Entertainment
This Week" interview he said he discussed this with
Dustin Hoffman who co-starred with Olivier in *The
Marathon Man*. "I was traveling somewhere and I
bumped into Dustin Hoffman in an airport, and I
cornered the guy and said, 'You may not know me, I'm
Neil Diamond and I'm making a movie in a few months
with Laurence Olivier and I'm scared to death. What do

I do?' And he gave me some great advice: 'Try and relate
the character you're playing in the film to your fear of
Olivier in real life and it'll all come very naturally.' And
I did. I was scared to death of him, but I wasn't afraid of
that fear anymore.''

Production was set to begin in December in Los
Angeles, with some concert footage to be shot early in the
twelve-week schedule rather than after completion of
principal photography as was previously planned. As the
starting date grew nearer, the script problems stemming
from a disagreement between Foreman and Furie on an
ending for the film were becoming volatile. Furie labelled
Foreman's script, which closely resembled the plot of the
original, old-fashioned and asked for a rewrite. But Foreman was committed to developing another film and left
The Jazz Singer.

Leider decided that Herbert Baker, a friend of over
twenty years, was a logical successor and introduced him
to Furie. They agreed on the script, and Baker was put to
work combining Foreman's adaptation of Samson Ra-
phaelson's original play with some new ideas. Baker's
script was satisfactory but too long at two hours and
twenty minutes. At Baker's suggestion, Arthur Laurents
was hired to further synthesize the script. (Laurents
requested no billing for his work, although he later
changed his mind, only to be denied.) But it turned out,
only bits of Laurents's dialogue survived in the finished
film.

While the script problems continued, Leider worked on
securing the female lead. Delfont directed Leider to talk
with Jacqueline Bisset but a satisfactory agreement was
never reached. Leider flatly denies reports that Bisset
asked for $1 million and 8 percent of the gross to co-star.
He said she simply didn't want the part and opted for
other roles she was offered. Diamond phoned her and
attempted to persuade her to change her mind, but she
refused.

Furie's first choice for the part had always been Lucie

Arnaz, whom he had seen on Broadway. He even discussed her with Leider and other production members. But he changed his mind when he saw Deborah Raffin in the television movie *Willa* (which Leider had produced). The female lead character written by both Foreman and Baker more closely resembled Arnaz's personality than Raffin's, however. So Furie ordered the character rewritten, and the role underwent many personality and name changes within a few weeks' time. After a lengthy debate, Furie and Leider decided the female lead role of Jess Robin's manager-lover would go to Raffin. After meeting Diamond backstage in Denver to discuss the role, Raffin signed on January 4, 1980, reportedly for $250,000, only a fraction of what Bisset was said to have wanted. Shooting was to start the following week in Maricopa, California, which was doubling for rural Texas.

With only a week's notice, Raffin was signed on the basis of new concepts in a proposed script. When she reported to the set for rehearsal and wardrobe fitting on the first day of filming, she found the set in disarray as Furie and Diamond were discussing the still-unfinished script. She had learned a southern accent to play the poor farm girl that Furie originally requested, but the part had changed to that of a woman from a rich Pasadena family—a complete turnaround. Coupled with changes in dialogue and story content, it was no longer the part she had signed to portray.

Furthermore, Furie had not resolved his indecision on a lead female actress. He said he wasn't sure which way to go and, if given the chance, might consider filming with two different actresses in the role and then decide which footage to use. Raffin quickly became disillusioned with what appeared to be a demeaning situation. Finally, Michael Viner, Raffin's manager and husband, asked Leider if she could be released from her contract.

EMI announced its "general unhappiness in accepting the inevitable—that her (Raffin's) assignment was no longer the role she had signed to do and it no longer suited her." Raffin withdrew from the film in exchange for an unspecified payment. Simultaneously, though coincidentally, EMI Films signed her to a two-picture non-exclusive pact for *Deadly Encounter* and *Dry Hustle*, projects in which she would have a hand in producing. She never faced the cameras, never rehearsed, and later told the *Los Ageles Times* that if the experience had happened at the beginning of her career, she would have quit the business.

I really am sorry to see that Neil hasn't done anything else. You know, he was making a big transition from a singer to actor. I think that he's a very much more charismatic singer . . . he didn't quite capture that in the movie but I think that would come with other movies.
—Franklin Ajaye
Interview with the authors

10
Love on the Rocks (March 1980– January 1981)

Raffin was not the only one surprised and confused by the constant changes. Furie was apparently never satisfied with any completed version of the script. So he purposely cast the minor roles with actors he found to be comfortable with improvisation. In fact, several people hired for these bit parts agreed that improvisational experience was practically a prerequisite before Furie would cast them. He reportedly would show the actors the few written lines he had prepared for them and say, "Don't worry, we'll fill it out later."

Thus, memorizing lines was either unnecessary or foolish. How a film could be completed within a reasonable time frame without a proper script was a question Furie could never answer. It would be his undoing.

Burly Kansas-born character actor Hugh Gillin played the bartender in the saloon where Jess Robin finds himself singing "You Are My Sunshine" after giving up on Hollywood. Gillin said that when he auditioned for the part, Furie made sure of his improvisational ability.

"He said, 'Actually , what I'm interested in is people that
have had some improvisational background. . . . the
reason I'm [asking] is because of Neil. This will be his
first film. He's never done a film before and we don't want
to burden him with a big script and learning all those
lines.' "

Furie again asked Gillin about his improvisational
skills, and according to Gillin, explained that he was
going to hire character actors who could ad-lib to support
Neil to make him look better. "I didn't get a sense of Neil
Diamond being a problem," Gillin said. "I don't think
he's a wimp. He came into the scene and he did the best
he knew how. I knew what I was doing with my character
and we worked."

Even though Gillin was hired for his improvisational
skills, he said, "People think they like improv better
because it's easier, because you don't have to learn all
those lines. But that's bullshit. You really need the
structure of a good script."

Janet Brandt, who played Jess Robin's Aunt Tilly, had
previously worked with Furie on the films *Sheila Levine
Is Dead and Living in New York* and *Hit!*, and she was
comfortable with his style. She told of Furie's reassurances
that her part would grow after she asked him how she
could play the part without any written lines. " 'Don't
worry, don't worry,' he said. 'We're going to improvise
scenes and we'll work it out that way.' It was a one day job
as far as I knew, and I ended up working three months."

When Brandt was hired, Olivier sent his own speech
coach over to her dressing room to teach her the same
Yiddish accent as Olivier was using—he had the good
sense to see that the actors who played Robin's family
members spoke with the same pronunciations. But
Brandt had to tell the surprised coach about the planned
improvisation. Needless to say, Brandt was given lines.

Although Brandt worked three months, nearly all of
her scenes were edited out. She only appears in the party
scene at the synagogue celebration for Cantor Rabinowitz
(Olivier).

When production began in Maricopa, Neil was playing the disillusioned and frustrated Robin, who had just
quit show business but would not admit defeat by returning to New York. The only written part of the script
called for Robin to ask the bartender (Gillin) for a job as
a singing cowboy. The scene called for the bartender to
offer the singer a drink, even though it was before 8 A.M.,
and the singer would accept. The punch line was that the
bartender refused to employ the singer because he
wouldn't hire anyone who drank before eight in the
morning.

Furie stayed in the background while Diamond looked
as though he wished he wasn't the focus of attention.
Gillin started to familiarize himself with the bar. "Pretty
soon I looked up, and there's some guy with a god-
damned old straw hat on, a straggly beard . . . . I'd always
seen pictures of Neil Diamond with his spangled suits on,
one of those Hollywood rock & roll guys and all that shit,
so I say, 'Who's that scrubby-looking bastard?' And they
bring him over and they introduce him. And he's real shy,
kind of quiet."

The cameras began to roll. Gillin was following the
script, and Diamond suddenly deviated by saying "Why
don't you give me a chance?" Gillin said a "little light"
clicked on in his head—he thought he was expected to
improvise; the dialogue quickly deteriorated into a battle
of wits.

Gillin: I don't hire anybody that drinks before eight
o'clock in the morning.
Diamond: Why don't you give me a chance?
Gillin: Well, what do you do?
Diamond: I play the guitar.
Gillin: Oh. Why don't you play me a tune?

Figuring he had brought the scene to its logical conclusion, Gillin explained, "I leaned back and said, 'Why
don't you play me a tune?' Now it's in his lap—I don't
have to do nothing. I figured all you have to do with Neil
Diamond is say 'play me a tune' and the damned fool is

going to start playing a tune. He looked at me with those big cow eyes and said 'Weeell, what do you want to hear?' And I felt like saying 'Dooon't ask me what I want to hear. I don't know your damned songs. Don't ask me that.'

"Well, shit, now it's in my lap. I can't think of any of his songs. The only thing I could think of was 'You Are My Sunshine.' You sing that as a kid at camp. Well, his eyes just glazed over. And then he said, 'Ahhh, alllll right. That's something my old daddy taught me.' And he got his guitar and he just started playing it. We just had two or three takes on the scene.

"It felt so good, I started singing along with him, and the next thing I said was 'Hell, you got yourself a job.' "

What Gillin didn't realize at the moment was that he had created the need for a whole new scene, in which Diamond would perform in the saloon. When the scene was finally shot four weeks later in a country-western bar in the San Fernando Valley, Gillin noticed that Diamond was not nearly as relaxed and placid as he had been during the first days of filming. "That night I had a sense that with all the activity and all the people, . . . he seemed a little more harried and frustrated."

The night after Gillin and Diamond filmed that first scene, Liza Minnelli, Cher, and Donna Summer were all being considered as replacements for Deborah Raffin. All were quickly dismissed in favor of reverting back to Furie's original choice. Within days, Lucie Arnaz was offered the role and accepted it. But she was co-starring with Laurence Luckinbill in the Broadway production of *They're Playing Our Song* and could not leave it for another few weeks. The solution was to move up the scheduled New York location scenes to accommodate her.

Out of the sequences that Furie wanted to complete before moving the filming to New York was the scene of Jess Robin as a cantor before being offered stardom. The scene was to include an original Hebrew melody written by cantor Uri Frenkel, who portrayed a cantor and acted as technical advisor, and sung by a young bar mitzvah student, portrayed by David Coburn. But Diamond wanted something more traditional. Cantor Frenkel wryly suggested the all-purpose, all-occasion "Hineh Mah Tov." Neil approved.

But neither Frenkel nor Diamond could play it on the piano. And as Neil struggled to find the tune, Coburn, who had played the piano since he was five, started to help Diamond—much to everyone's delight. "I'm standing next to him at the piano and he's trying to figure out the chords to the song. I'm saying, 'No, Neil, it's A-minor here, D-minor here,' and the crew was getting a big kick out if it—that this kid was teaching Neil Diamond how to play the piano. He got a big kick out of it too."

This rapport between Neil and Coburn led to an expansion of Coburn's part. Furie wanted more interaction between the two, and so Coburn and his mother were brought along to New York.

The problems on the set of *The Jazz Singer* continued to mount. Furie had been using six or more cameras to catch even basic action where three are normal. Many scenes took twice the time usually required. In addition, Diamond was said to be keeping to himself—talking only when spoken to and constantly accompanied by at least one of his entourage.

More than one member of the crew and cast described Furie as arrogant, acting like he and Diamond were on a higher plane than everyone else on the set. They repeatedly saw a marked difference in the way they were treated and the way Diamond got Furie's constant attention. Furie had control of everything on the set except Diamond. Following a take, he often asked Diamond's opinion. After giving Diamond an instruction he would then ask Diamond how he felt about it. Diamond would sometimes politely agree to what Furie told him and then would do what he felt was best. Eventually, Furie lost the respect of most of the crew members.

As in the case of virtually all of his movies, Furie refuses to comment on *The Jazz Singer*. (During the shooting he did liken his relationship with Diamond to that of "a doctor with his patient.") Leider said he felt Furie never acted less than professionally in his duties. He added that Furie's interaction with Diamond was nothing more than an attempt to make the singer feel more comfortable in the unfamiliar surroundings of a film set.

Franklin Ajaye, the actor/comedian who played Bubba, Jess's best friend in the film, said that he understood Furie and enjoyed his style of direction. "I think an actor likes someone like Furie because he's going to give you a little freedom and yet direct you also. As far as the story changes, I just think he explored the scenes from a performer's standpoint. Anytime you're trying to make a movie, and you're trying to figure out what's going to work, there's a little confusion. I thought that he was a little confused, but I kind of accepted that because I know it's artistic temperament. There are a lot of good cats like that. Francis Ford Coppola [is] obviously a confused cat on his movies, but he turns out a good movie. You know, *The Jazz Singer* is still good after all. Sidney's an artist, there's no doubt about that. Artists always have problems with business people."

Ajaye also said he thought the morning meetings between Furie and Diamond were understandable. "Nothing out of the ordinary—just the star and the director [having] their meeting in the dressing room before the day's shooting and deciding where they want to go."

Before the production could leave for New York, further problems arose when the press publicized complaints by Catlin Adams, who played Jess Robin's wife Rifka, that the dialogue in at least one scene was demeaning to women. Adams claimed that a bedroom scene called for her character to disregard everything she believed in just to please her husband. She was to accept changes in her own life for no other reason than that it pleased her husband. Denying reports that she was disenchanted with the whole production, Adams admitted she would have

quit if some lines in the script hadn't been removed. She
said that actors are role models and should be aware of
what they do on the screen.

Diamond caught walking pneumonia while shooting
on location in New York and spent a couple of days in bed
during the two weeks of filming. Gossip columnists
erroneously blamed the delays on Diamond's moods,
accusing him of leaving the set early to jam with other
musicians in local clubs (something completely out of
character for him). They were correct, however, in implying that the picture was going over budget.

David Coburn's scene required that he wear the same
clothes he had worn at the Goldwyn Studios in Los
Angeles to match what had already been shot. But it was
winter in New York City and the windchill factor neared
zero. He was to run across the street to the synagogue,
practicing his bar mitzvah as he ran. Despite a hand
warmer and a parka at either end of the run, the cold
almost froze the microphone to his chest. Coburn also
had to dodge traffic which wasn't stopped, and Furie had
him run it close to fifteen times. The footage was never
used.

Leider and EMI both now began to question whether
Furie had a finished script. He promised great things for
the ending, but when the producers saw what Furie and
Baker had agreed upon, they were disappointed. Furie
was reportedly determined to have Olivier's character die
at the end of the film, although he knew he was about the
only person who felt this way.

In addition, one report which Leider denies stated that
EMI determined Furie's finished script would have
doubled the shooting schedule and sent the budget sky-
rocketing over what was then considered the $12 million
negative cost, already up from $10 million. Leider knew
about Furie's use of the multiple cameras and, while not
defending the unusual technique, would not directly link
the unorthodox and seemingly costly film procedure with
Furie's eventual dismissal from the project. "I think

Sidney felt that this was the best way for him to get the kind of performance from the combination of actors he was using. It was a technique that he thought was the best for him to use in this situation. You know, it's a strange thing, but if it works, you can shoot a lot of footage all day but at the end of the day you still have three pages finished. So, it is not necessarily a more costly approach to filming. It's unorthodox, but if you're looking to do three pages a day and you rehearse all day long, and you do a three-page setup with five cameras, and you get a more spontaneous response that way—it could work."

The crew returned to Hollywood at the end of February, but Furie was no longer their director. On February 29, the producers and Furie decided that their "creative differences" had driven an irreconcilable wedge between them and that Furie would be terminated from his contract. On March 3, the day Los Angeles shooting was supposed to resume, the film industry trade papers carried the story.

Leider did not deny Furie's dedication to the film but did cite the "creative differences." Furie and the producers differed in their concepts of the second half of the film. Others close to the film have cited Furie's inability to get the most out of his actors or crew.

Shooting at the Goldwyn Studios and various Los Angeles locations stopped for two weeks while Leider searched for a new director and familiarized himself with the script and Furie's master shots. His decision to hire Richard Fleischer was no doubt influenced by the fact that Fleischer and Olivier were friends and had previously worked together. Leider stressed that neither Olivier nor Diamond ever had the right of directorial approval—as had been rumored.

Leider said the pick-ups—scenes reshot after Furie's departure—were done after the final script had been settled upon and Richard Fleischer had assumed directorial command. He said they reflect a "pulling together" of the script in an effort to condense what was already done and to allow Fleischer to approach certain aspects of the film in his own style.

Coburn remembers his own amazement at being called back to do his pick-up with Diamond after having spent hours rehearsing and seeing six cameras shoot his page and a half of dialogue. "I only had this short little scene . . . and there was supposed to be this one close-up of me. In the six cameras, [Furie] didn't get one clean close-up. Neil's shoulder kept blocking my face. He'd breathe and my face would disappear for a second. Fleischer needed to call me back six months later at the end of the summer to reshoot the scene, and my voice had changed." Coburn was concerned about his voice because he didn't know whether Fleischer planned to use the old soundtrack. He could not sing in the same key anymore, and as he tried to match his earlier performance, his voice kept cracking. I said, 'I can't stand this, my voice is cracking!' And Neil said, 'Don't worry. I'm making money because my voice cracks.' "

Leider said that pickups were necessary but were in no way an attempt to remove any directorial credit Furie might have held. When Furie later brought a case against Leider and the film to the Director's Guild, an arbitrator was assigned. But before a decision could be reached, Furie withdrew his complaint, prompting Leider to call Furie "gracious."

In the few days separating Furie and Fleischer, press coverage of the production intensified. A variety of biting charges were reported: Furie had expected to be fired as a scapegoat for making changes ordered by Diamond; the film was in danger of either being scrapped or totally reshot; the producers weren't going to pay the cast and crew during the hiatus; Diamond still hadn't finished the score; and that no one as yet knew how the movie was going to end.

Barry Spikings publicly refuted all the charges and pledged EMI's full support of the project and Diamond.

"The entire production crew of more than fifty people, as well as the cast, remain on full salary during our brief hiatus. My enthusiasm for the movie, and that of my company, continues unabated. Neil Diamond will emerge as a major motion picture star. During the hiatus, Neil is rehearsing and prerecording new numbers for the second half of the picture. *The Jazz Singer* is our major Christmas release for 1980."

Spiking's statement was also intended to reassure theater exhibitors who harbored doubts about the existence of a movie. To further bolster theater owners' confidence in the film's completion and delivery date, Neil agreed to make a rare personal appearance at the "Show-a-Rama" industry exhibition on April 9 in Kansas City. He and Leider presented a nine-minute clip to prove there was a movie which would be released on time.

Fleischer began filming again on March 17—the day Herbert Baker turned in his final script and left the production. It was a shortened version similar to the one he had done before Laurents was brought in to help. Under the guidance of the veteran Fleischer (whose previous musical film had been *Doctor Doolittle*), shooting returned to the schedule with a definite finale in mind.

Ajaye said that the project's change of direction was obvious. "When Richard came in . . . I learned not to question a lot of things. You know, it's not my movie; it's their movie. Richard came in and he didn't have the time, and I think he's someone who stays close to what was planned. Craft is good, and I think Richard's a craftsman. And Sidney's an artist; so, you know, the producers have to know coming in what they want."

Fleischer had a firm grip on both the crew and the stars. Diamond, without Furie's constant adulation inflating his ego, calmed down and acted more professionally. Douglas Nigh, who played a technician in a recording studio sequence, and Mike Pasternak, who played comedian Zany Grey, had both worked under Fleischer and spoke highly of Diamond's professionalism on the set.

"Contrary to what I'd heard, I never saw him lose his temper or do anything that I would consider obnoxious. I was amazed that he always seemed to know his parts so well—everyone else seemed to be blowing their lines and things. Diamond acted like someone who was happy to be working and happy to be making the kind of money that he probably made . . . so happy that he could slap everybody on the back and say 'How the heck are you!' "

Nigh, whose scene was shot close to the end of the production, saw a more low-key mood on the set as the crew was anxious to get done. Although he tended to think Diamond was keeping to himself somewhat, he did like Diamond's attitude. "When he came out onto the set, he was always professional—you know, very meticulous in what he did, very precise—quite an adept craftsman, much better than I'd anticipated he'd be."

In December 1980 Lucie Arnaz told an Associated Press reporter that Diamond appeared more at ease under Fleischer's direction and had gotten used to working on the set. "Can you imagine anything more intimidating than playing opposite Laurence Olivier in your first picture? Yet Neil learned to relax. He realized he didn't have to run the whole show, and he relaxed and sat back and learned."

Ajaye felt Diamond not only did a creditable job but is not given credit for some of the work he put into the film. "He was inventive at times; surprisingly inventive, because he's a quiet guy. He's kind of an inward guy. He might do a scene and slap you on your back, try to add a physical element in the relationship between the two characters. It'd be kind of a surprise to me because like I said, he's kind of inward—he was really trying to come out of himself.

"Now when he would sing during those sequences, I would always notice there would be a sparkle in his eye that would really add to his performance. You could see that he knew what he was doing as a singer and he could really come across with much more energy. I think he did a good job. He's believable, and I think that's all you really want."

Fleischer shifted the focus of the film away from the improvisation and test shots to the chemistry between Diamond and Arnaz. Ajaye talked about the way Fleischer was able to take control. "We had to do things quicker . . . he was more of a quick worker. Richard came in . . . and he's got things planned: 'quick, let's hit it.' He was very professional, which is probably why they brought him in there. They knew he could bring them a good product within a certain time."

Fleischer also contributed some humor to the rehearsals. In one scene shot near Venice Beach, Olivier was to walk up to a house and ring the doorbell and Diamond was to greet him. After several takes, an unsuspecting Neil opened the door and found a beautiful blonde rollerskater instead of Olivier.

The film's concert finale was shot at the Pantages Theater in Hollywood. It took about eight days to set up the lighting and eleven cameras to prepare for the Diamond miniconcert. There were 350 extras as well as an audience of 2,000 who had all been given free tickets. There were door prizes and gifts like official Diamond tour jackets, albums, and tickets to the premiere or a *Jazz Singer* screening. A live Dixieland band and free hot dogs, popcorn, and drinks were in the lobby. Leider himself served as emcee for the day, helping to warm up the audience.

When Fleischer needed additional set-up time, Diamond helped out by performing some of his older hits in addition to "Hey Louise," "Summerlove," and "America."

The final piece of bad press during production was a report that Olivier had grown so tired of the setbacks that he called the whole operation "trash." He was supposedly angry to be filming scenes he termed "embarrassing"; he reportedly called the pick-up scenes "doubly embarrassing" although he earned a bonus of $100,000 for a week's extended shooting.

Olivier "categorically denied" the story the next day, saying he had "nothing but respect" for the entire production, including Leider, Diamond, and Fleischer. He wrote each of them apologetic letters assuring them of the report's inaccuracy. He explained he was having dinner with friends and the word "trash" came up during some small talk but had nothing whatsoever to do with *The Jazz Singer*. Olivier said it was obvious that a reporter happened to be listening to his conversation and assumed the worst.

"I don't believe he ever said that about the film, nor did he know who did. He's much too professional of a man to do it," Leider said.

Principal photography on the film concluded April 28, only three days behind schedule, and reports of the May 6 wrap party at Goldwyn Studios revealed no hard feelings among the surviving cast and crew.

Having made a favorable impression at "Show-a-Rama," the producers set out to preview the film at the Cannes Film Festival in mid-May. At stake was a chance to remove the stigma of all the bad press coverage and to assure international distributors that a salable product existed. Leider assembled a twenty-six-minute promotional trailer; Neil and Lucie agreed to make guest appearances.

The Cannes audience went wild with approval. Diamond was finally vindicated. "Despite all the problems, all the adverse publicity, I never lost faith. I always knew this project was a good one. I had many movies offered to me before I did *The Jazz Singer* but nothing excited me as this one did. I simply could not refuse it."

Making the film had been a trial for everyone, but ultimately no one bore the brunt of it heavier than Diamond himself. He had known what he could be getting into (his experiences with *Jonathan* left deeply imbedded scars) and was concerned about how he would deal with the pressure. When the chance came to exercise control, he took it—sometimes unwisely, but always sincerely. Even Leider, who had the most to lose from any mistakes, defends Diamond's actions: myriad requests for script improvements, conceptual changes, the familiar Diamond moodiness, and the intensely protective attitude toward the music and the lead role.

The tabloid press, eager to exploit the "expanding-stardom" angle, took advantage of Diamond's vulnerability in his unfamiliar surroundings. A demand for lurid *Jazz Singer* stories was created, just as it had been for Barbra Streisand's *A Star is Born* remake four years earlier. It may not have affected the quality of the film, but it most certainly influenced the film's reception.

Diamond kept a low profile for the rest of the year. He had intended to tour during the film's opening but instead waited until the following spring. As post-production progressed on schedule, Diamond stayed at home, resting his back and writing the songs for his next album, *On the Way to the Sky*.

The film was not only ready on time, but it became the first major holiday-season release exhibited to distributors. Prior to the full-length screenings in October, the Cannes promotional film was shown to assorted advance press conferences and theater conventions. In addition, an uncontroversial short feature on the making of *The Jazz Singer* was shown on pay television networks.

The New York premiere, benefitting the Will Rogers Institute in Westchester County, was held at the Ziegfeld Theater on December 14.

Diamond told ABC-TV's "Good Morning America" that he was on his way to the New York premiere at the Ziegfeld Theatre when word of John Lennon's death reached the airplane. He said he became "visibly shaken" when the pilot relayed the news to the passengers. He added that a moment of silence was immediately observed.

At the premiere, Diamond talked about Lennon. "He

made all of this possible for every writer, every performer who has doors open to them today—he made possible. He made this picture and this opening possible for me, for a million reasons."

The Los Angeles premiere took place three days later at the Plitt Century Plaza in Century City. The Women's Guild of Cedars-Sinai Medical Center, who sponsored the event, declared it the most successful benefit of its kind in their history. Several other benefit showings were held, including one in Madrid the following year attended by the royal family.

Although the nationwide opening was not scheduled until the week after the Cedars-Sinai event, there was already talk of at least two possible film projects for Diamond. The *You Don't Bring Me Flowers* project was tossed around again, but eventually forgotten; Ray Stark expressed some interest in producing *Death at an Early Age,* which had now rested in Diamond's hands for almost a decade. The project is still talked about on occasion as a possibility.

(Ironically, Stark had turned down Diamond's request to do the soundtrack for his John Huston-directed project, *Fat City,* years before because he had never heard of Diamond at the time!)

The Jazz Singer soundtrack album was released in November to immediately favorable response. It quickly became Neil's biggest-selling album since *Jonathan Livingston Seagull,* and it was his best since *Beautiful Noise.* The first single release, "Love on the Rocks," just missed the national number one spot; the second single, "Hello Again," the film's central love theme, hit number six, and "America," which has since become one of his most enduring songs, reached number eight.

Reader's Digest sponsored the British release of a five-record, fifty-seven-song boxed set of Neil's Uni/MCA–period recordings. A Bantam paperback novelization of *The Jazz Singer* had an initial printing of 200,000 copies, beating the movie to the marketplace by several weeks. Diamond himself submitted to a round of promotional interviews and television appearances.

The outlook was hopeful. The film was set for a ninety-city, 250-theater national opening on December 19, followed by broader release in mid-February. Everyone was preparing for a large-scale success, especially after the enthusiastic reactions at the benefits. And then the troubles began all over again.

The critics emerged from the theaters, and they weren't smiling.

A wave of almost unanimously negative reviews washed over *The Jazz Singer*. The major objections centered around the outdated and overly sentimental plot that seemed ludicrous when set in the present day.

Diamond's acting performance was almost as severely lambasted. Most writers described him as awkward, wooden, cold, or amateurish. Olivier was also singled out for scorn; more than one reviewer called it the worst performance of his career. Arnaz was generally praised; so were the film's songs. But the script, editing, photography, and the film's rather curious treatment of the modern Jewish-American psyche were all fair game for poison pens.

The bad reviews frightened audiences away, and the early grosses were disappointing. The MGM study which warned that the concept lacked youth appeal may have been accurate: the film never really reached the teenage audience—a main-stay of repeat business—that could have made the film a massive hit.

By mid-1981, the film had taken in $14.25 million in American grosses—not very impressive, considering that the film's negative costs tallied $15.6 million and that returns of $30 million-plus would have made the film a worthwhile investment.

The situation was not hopeless, however. A handful of critics did take the film to heart, and Diamond's own devoted fans supported *The Jazz Singer* strongly. Together with the early media blitz, enough enthusiasm was generated to keep the film from going out of release prematurely.

The advertising was changed to emphasize the successful soundtrack, and a few weeks after release, one critic's encouraging open letter was used in the display ads to convince the public that his peers had been unfair. More significantly, several exit polls taken around the country indicated that the vast majority of people who actually saw the film genuinely approved. One survey based in Los Angeles, Cinemascore, ranked it in a tie with *Ordinary People* as the highest-rated film of the year!

Ultimately, its release abroad put *The Jazz Singer* in the black. The film enjoyed particularly large followings in Australia and Great Britain, but the largest international market for the picture was South Africa, where it outsold major American hits such as the Richard Pryor–Gene Wilder film *Stir Crazy* and Clint Eastwood's *Any Which Way You Can*.

Cable and commercial television showings in the following years settled *The Jazz Singer* into a comfortable place in history. And Diamond's devoted fans have made it one of the most popular videocassettes ever.

It is hard to say exactly what Diamond gained by making the film. He was richer, of course, but the film was so closely identified with him that he was fated to carry most of the burden for the project's shortcomings. During production he was exposed to some of the most humiliating press he had ever received, and the relative non-success of the picture (not to mention the scathing critical reviews) endangered his chances for an acting career.

To Diamond, getting through the film was as important to him as the message he tried to convey. He told Larry Kart of the *Chicago Tribune*, "While we were making *The Jazz Singer*, they kept telling me, 'Don't worry, it's just a movie.' For most of the past three years, my life was draining out everyday with fear and anxiety and uncertainty. But now that it's all over, I agree with them. . . . It's just a movie, one that will entertain or not based on its own merits.

"We worked very hard to retell this classic, which I think is worthy of retelling, and to retell a little bit of the Jewish experience, as much as we could understand the confines of reality. The world is not Jewish and does not understand Yiddish or mezuzahs or yarmulkes or saying Kadish or any of that stuff, but I loved the idea of getting some good, positive propaganda into the film.

"So much of it reminds me of my grandparents and their kind of life. They were immigrants and taught Yiddish to me as a child. I wanted Yiddish in this movie, I really wanted it. In fact, I tried to convince them at one point to have the whole opening in Yiddish with subtitles like they did in *The Godfather*. Yiddish is a beautiful language, and I wanted to do my bit to keep it alive."

Neil could honestly feel grateful for the experience of making *The Jazz Singer*. Although hurt by the film's reception, he could now finally claim that he had committed himself to an acting role and followed through to completion. He had abandoned much of his fear of losing anonymity and in the process had done a job that had, on most levels, satisfied himself, satisfied the people closest to him, and satisfied his fans. As he has explained since the release of *The Jazz Singer*, "We made the movie for fans, not critics."

It was quite a night. The (Inglewood) Forum was filled to a capacity seldom seen in these rock-recession years, with even the behind-the-stage seats sold out. Some ticket holders had been scalped to the tune of $70, some reportedly much more. Cars were lined up outside for more than 40 minutes in some cases, with the Forum's parking lot filled to bursting and the folks at Hollywood Park next door taking advantage of the situation by raising their usual rate by 200 percent. And that was just Monday; by the time his local run ends this coming Sunday night, some 130,000 people will have run the same gauntlet to see singer-songwriter Neil Diamond.

The seven-night stand marks Diamond's first local performances since he last played the considerably smaller Greek Theater seven years ago. His following has grown to amazing proportions—why, Diamond may be more popular than the Rolling Stones or Kenny Rogers!

—Todd Everett
Los Angeles Herald-Examiner
June 1983

11
I'm Alive (. . . ?)
(1981–1983)

After finishing his promotional commitments for the release of *The Jazz Singer* film and soundtrack, Diamond fell into a more leisurely pace of creative output. He recorded at the rate of only one album every eighteen months and spent more time with his family when he wasn't out on abbreviated concert tours.

The growth of Neil Diamond through the years is best illustrated by his concert appearances. Diamond began his career with absolutely no stage presence, totally unable to talk between songs, and with a repertoire that always featured the two songs he'd learned during his monumental summer at camp: "La Bamba" and "If I Had a Hammer." But the Greek Theater appearances which produced both *Hot August Night* and *Love at the Greek* proved that Diamond had not merely discovered the difference between performing and entertaining; he had learned how to truly captivate audiences wherever he took his show.

Diamond's concerts had solidified into a tightly knit event with just a touch of unpredictability to keep things from stagnating. He wore glittery loose-fitting shirts, which helped camouflage his mild, middle-aged spread. He kept his hair longer than current fashion dictated, diverting attention away from his receding hairline.

Following *The Jazz Singer*, and until December 1985, he opened his shows with "America"—always a crowd pleaser—complete with fireworks and laser effects. He sang his newer material near the beginning of the shows and always included a large mixture of earlier hits, skipping only the lesser Bang items. Depending on the time and location, he would perform some oldies ("Teach Me Tonight" or the Shirelles' "Dedicated to the One I Love"), something indigenous to the area ("Back Home in Indiana"), secular Christmas carols like "Winter Wonderland" or "Rudolph, the Red-Nosed Reindeer," and sometimes even "The Star-Spangled Banner." He saved most of his best-loved songs like "Song Sung Blue" and "Cracklin' Rosie," for the end, and closed with "I Am . . . I Said" or "I've Been This Way Before."

After Diamond left the stage, the band would play a fifteen-minute sampling of *Jonathan Livingston Seagull*; Neil would return in an all-white outfit to sing a medley from the film's score. After performing a small piece of "Soolaimon," the band would segue into a long climactic workout of "Brother Love's Travelling Salvation Show." Neil would then thank the audience a final time and swing into a reprise of "America."

But he altered his concerts late in 1985, and closed with

either "Heartlight," his most recognizable hit of the decade, or "He Ain't Heavy . . . He's My Brother," which, although a cover version, had some significance for Diamond and gave him the opportunity to leave the audience one last special message.

The shows are not necessarily the "incredible emotional experience" hardcore fans and some reviewers describe, but each performance is fun. There's no need for Diamond to prove anything on the concert stage. He's been around long enough. He need only be Neil Diamond to thrill his following when he steps on the stage. NDRRT is always sharp, and his charisma makes many of his post-*Love at the Greek* numbers more fulfilling than they are on vinyl. The only time he falters is when he gets too theatrical, like at his 1984 Royal Command Performance in England, when he said, "Here we go, kids!!"

The demographics of a Diamond concert audience are still quite a sight. A large portion are Yuppies: clean-cut and well-mannered thirtyish men and women, stereotypically computer programmers and assistant account executives. There are also a healthy number of middle-aged folks who normally wouldn't be caught dead at a pop concert unless it were held in Nevada or Atlantic City. Their exposure to Diamond comes from the middle-of-the-road radio stations that now give him the bulk of his airplay. Then there are the young ones: some adoring females, some Top Forty mavens, some rich conservative types who don't identify with rock, some whose interests were piqued by his oldies, and some who merely find him an acceptable substitute for Barry Manilow.

Another phenomenon along the Diamond concert trail is the wide diversity of reviews that follow him. Roughly half of the critics call him a brilliant artist and the grand successor to the Sinatra tradition; the other half call him a flat-voiced schmaltzy, stylistic reactionary. Once in a while, someone who usually likes Diamond will say that Neil was too easy on himself.

Unfavorable Diamond reviews inevitably give an editor

days of work following a concert. There are always some descriptive letters suggesting new and unusual uses for the reviewer. Most of this correspondence comes from Diamond's version of the Grateful Dead's "Deadheads." These are fans who have formed unauthorized fan clubs to meet and discuss their idol; fans who have followed him around the country on concert tours to see him perform in his favorite cities like Indianapolis and Detroit; fans who buy at least three copies of every single and album in hopes that they will go gold and platinum; fans who like Diamond regardless of the quality of his most recent material. The unsung throng that every performer secretly prays for but never admits he needs, these people alone are so numerous and so devoted to Diamond that he could press records just for them and still be commercially successful.

Columbia's faith in Diamond's mass commercial appeal was strong enough for them to re-sign him to a new eight-album, $30-million guarantee. The lucrative long-term deal came on the heels of Diamond's success with *The Jazz Singer*, but it was also due in part to Capitol Records' reported attempts to sign Neil. A rivalry between the two companies had erupted after CBS signed Paul McCartney away from Capitol; Capitol had hoped to return the favor by inducing Diamond to leave Columbia.

Work on the first record under his new deal took much of Diamond's time during 1981 after the conclusion of *Jazz Singer* publicity commitments. Neil and NDRRT also were able to hit the road for the first time in two years. One British newspaper reported that Diamond was being wooed by English impressario Alan Schaverien to tour the United Kingdom and play at least one concert on Wimbledon's Centre Court. But his upcoming release took precedence, and this British tour never materialized.

The album, *On the Way to the Sky*, was characterized by its singles—all hits—including "Yesterday's Songs" (although it reached number eleven, Manilow's "The Old Songs" was unfortunately released too close to it), "On the Way to the Sky" (number twenty-seven), and "Be Mine Tonight" (number thirty-five). The overall sound was typically mellow, with lots of strings, and only a couple of songs even remotely sounding like rock & roll. One exception, the Bang-like "Be Mine Tonight" was a pleasant surprise, with Diamond actually playing the acoustic guitar just like the old days.

The most telling song on the record is "Fear of the Marketplace," another of Neil's self-analytic autobiographical attempts. It is one of the most revealing Diamond songs of the 1980s, if not of his entire career. The tune accurately describes Diamond's outlook on life, his fears, and his self-doubt, and offers hope for a better future.

The *On the Way to the Sky* album is not only noteworthy for its cover shot—which until 1986 graced practically every concert advertisement and publicity still— but also because it marked the beginning of a periodic songwriting partnership with Carole Bayer Sager and her husband, classic pop songwriter Burt Bacharach (Diamond and Bayer Sager had previously teamed on "That Kind," from *September Morn'*. It also marked the last time Diamond worked with drummer Dennis St. John, who was replaced by ex-Elvis Presley sideman Ronnie Tutt.

Diamond and St. John reportedly had a bitter split over the production of the *On the Way to the Sky* album. The album was to be the first record that NDRRT and Neil worked on together without an outside producer; St. John was to be the producer. The two had worked together since the Uni days, and the drummer reportedly felt he had earned Neil's trust at the mixing board. But Diamond, ever the perfectionist, and fresh from the problems of *The Jazz Singer*, decided to take complete control of the album; St. John was relegated to co-producer. Hurt by what he saw as a lack of faith by Neil, he quit the band. Originally, *On the Way to the Sky* had Diamond and St. John both listed as the producers. Additionally, the album was to have contained as many as fifteen tracks. Four songs, "The Revolutionary," "It's Alright," "Another Sad Moment," and "It's Gonna Be a Good Night" were dropped from the album by its release and were not even copyrighted.

After *On the Way to the Sky*, Neil increased the number of his charity benefit appearances. He was influenced in this decision by Marcia, Bacharach and Bayer Sager, and Jerry Weintraub and his wife Jane Morgan (the same woman who sang the 1957 hit, "Fascination.") These were formal and exclusive invitational affairs that benefitted various children's and cancer-related charities. Diamond occasionally would sing a few songs like "Heartlight" and "America" at each. By 1985, he was appearing at several per year.

The success of *On the Way to the Sky*—it reportedly sold 1.5 million copies within six months—encouraged MCA to release its third Diamond collection album in America. Entitled *Love Songs*, it was a shameless attempt to capitalize on Neil's current appeal and offered nothing new. It failed to crack the Top Two Hundred.

Diamond's next album, *Heartlight*, came out in time for the 1982 Christmas season. It was essentially built around the mood created by the title cut, a ballad to the Steven Spielberg movie character E.T. Universal Pictures/MCA didn't appreciate the song and claimed copyright infringement; they eventually collected a licensing fee. Diamond told *People* magazine that he felt bitter about the charges, but that he cooled off after Kathleen Kennedy, Spielberg associate and co-producer of *E.T.*, wrote him a thank-you note for the song.

"Heartlight" was not really an inspired song, even though it was written on the Fourth of July (1982). It did, however, warm the hearts of those already enchanted by *E.T.* and was his biggest hit single since "America," reaching number five. It even helped to broaden his youth appeal a bit for the first time in years.

(Bacharach and Bayer Sager subsequently named their racehorse after the song, and it won its first race after Neil supposedly sang to it. They persuaded Neil to continue his performances while the horse continued its winning streak.)

The album itself may well have been his poorest. It lacked originality or instrumental thrust and was just too sentimental for its own good. The brightest spot, a "hang-in-there" anthem called "I'm Alive" (number thirty-five) was co-written with David Foster and has become a Diamond concert staple. The album also featured another Diamond/Bacharach/Bayer Sager composition, "Front Page Story" (number sixty-five), as its third single.

At the end of 1982, Neil finally released *His Twelve Greatest Hits, Vol. II.* Like its MCA predecessor, the LP showcased the important songs of the period it represented rather than merely concentrating on the hit singles. Thus, "Beautiful Noise" and "Be" were included over "Don't Think . . . Feel" or "I've Been This Way Before."

Diamond faced legal problems in 1983 in a copyright infringement suit over "Yesterday's Songs." A Staten Island man filed a still-pending suit (at press time) in U.S. District Court against Diamond, Neil's Stonebridge Music publishing company, and Columbia Records, alleging that Diamond "largely" based "Yesterday's Songs" on a song he had written and copyrighted in 1979.

The man did not explain how Diamond might have heard his composition, but he asked the court for an injunction against "Yesterday's Songs" as well as an accounting and payment of all of Diamond's, Stonebridge Music's, and CBS's profits from the song, along with other relief the court would deem proper.

This suit ironically occurred at the same time Diamond was about to be inducted into the Songwriter's Hall of Fame in New York City. The honor is only bestowed on songwriters with a success record coupled with longevity. Neil was inducted on March 7 along with Sammy Cahn, Fred Ebb, and John Kander.

Two years had passed since *The Jazz Singer* and

Diamond had yet to commit himself to a follow-up film
project. Although there was more talk of the *You Don't
Bring Me Flowers* movie, this time starring Diamond
and Mary Steenburgen, nothing became of it. But Diamond's manager Jerry Weintraub, a successful movie
producer fresh from the triumph of *Diner*, convinced
Diamond that it was time for another movie. Weintraub
said he wanted to produce a CBS-TV movie musical
based on "Brother Love's Travelling Salvation Show," in
which Neil would star as the preacher. Neil was to write
some new songs for the score and, in doing so, complete
the concept album he had in mind way back in 1968.

"I'm excited about it because it's going to give me a
chance to work with black gospel groups," Neil told
Shirley Eder. "Pete Hamill is writing the script. I just
want him to leave enough places in it for music. He can
put whatever lines he wants to in between, so long as
there's enough space for lots of music and singing."

Hamill reportedly went to a retreat in New England to
write the script, and he apparently returned to civilization
to show Neil the script too late. Diamond had instead
opted to do more concerts and begin work on his next
album. The movie *Brother Love* never came to pass;
ironically, plans for Barry Manilow's "Copacabana" television film were announced almost simultaneously.

Diamond also told Eder that a Broadway musical was
out for him, at least in the foreseeable future: "It would
take two years to do, and I don't know if I want to stop
performing and making records and writing records to do
a Broadway show."

More interest was generated over word concerning a
Paramount Pictures feature film based on *Beautiful
Noise* in which Matthew Broderick was considered for the
lead. Diamond was to have played one of Tin Pan Alley's
old hands showing the young kid the ropes. Neil reportedly even hoped to get Stevie Wonder and Linda Ronstadt
in the film. Apparently, a script that satisfies both
Diamond and the producers has yet to be agreed upon,
and the project is currently dormant.

At the same time, however, Hollywood trade papers quietly reported the genesis of an over-the-line crew for *Death at an Early Age* (which by this time Diamond had owned for over a decade) and mentioned Ray Stark as producer. But all this indicated was that Diamond hasn't given up on the project yet. He even said that he was planning to do *Death at an Early Age* and a third film— *The Unknown Man*—before he would begin *Beautiful Noise*. He described *The Unknown Man* as a thriller and pledged he would not do the entire score for either, though he would agree to do the title song for each if "forced."

But instead of doing any films, Diamond chose to do more live performing. He decided to play Los Angeles for the first time since the 1976 comeback Greek dates. He had promised to return by 1978 and had actually been booked into the Greek prior to his medical problems. After he recovered from his surgery, *The Jazz Singer* took precedence. And after that, Neil figured the time was right to play other cities.

Diamond wanted to play the Greek, but he realized he'd have to play the facility for about three weeks to give all of his local fans a chance to see him. Weintraub finally persuaded him that he could do more for his audiences and himself by agreeing to play at the Inglewood Forum, which seats more than 17,000. At first, only four nights were tentatively scheduled. But when the tickets went on sale, pandemonium broke loose. Weintraub reportedly canceled his appointments the day the box office opened and watched in amazement as the tickets almost flew out the window within hours. The Forum was temporarily expanded to 18,600 seats by including behind-the-stage seating. Seven nights had to be booked, and at least two more could easily have been sold out.

Neil could still be surprised by his success, as he told Robert Hilburn of the *Los Angeles Times*: "Surprised? *Stunned* was more like it. When Jerry [Weintraub] said we could do that many nights, I didn't believe him. I still find it hard to believe because the only thing I can relate it to is when Elton did a series of nights at the Forum, and he was sizzling at the time. The surprising thing for me is I don't feel like I'm anywhere near that point right now. I don't even feel like I'm particularly warm. It's just like a normal period or something."

Diamond's June 1983 seven-night stand at the Forum set all-time attendance and revenue records for the facility, which had presented Elvis Presley, Elton John, and Led Zeppelin, among others, in the past: 126,131 people saw the shows, which grossed over $1.8 million.

Opening night, June 13, 1985, was proclaimed "Neil Diamond Day" by Los Angeles Mayor Tom Bradley. Front-row tickets for the show reportedly ran anywhere from $300 to $500 each. Unannounced, Diamond and Columbia were taping each show for another live record to be called *Live at the Forum*. Originally designed as a three-record set to be the ultimate Neil Diamond concert testament, it was cut down to a two-record package before being scrapped altogether.

Columbia reportedly had it set for a Christmas 1983 release, but Diamond was said to be annoyed at the sound quality of the tapes. The collection of performances, culled from the best of the seven nights, were to focus on the post-*Love at the Greek* catalog, including *The Jazz Singer* highlights, the "Forever in Blue Jeans" and "Dancing in the Streets" marathons, and Neil's salute to American popular music that was then in most of his shows. This segment began with "The American Popular Song" and led into his talk about the heritage of the genre before going into his covers of "Teach Me Tonight," "Dedicated to the One I Love," and Ben E. King's "Spanish Harlem." He then explained how he felt the Beatles had been influenced by these types of songs and sang their own "Golden Slumbers/Carry That Weight/ The End." The album also included new live versions of his all-time biggest hits like "Cherry Cherry," "Song Sung Blue," and the final encore of "Brother Love's Travelling Salvation Show."

Except for the sound quality on some songs, the album would have been a good sampling of Neil Diamond in the 1980s. The Forum dates showed a relaxed Diamond kibitzing with his audience and asking them to sing and dance along with him, especially on the two triple (at least) encore numbers—"Forever in Blue Jeans" and "Dancing in the Streets." Again, Diamond's major fault was his over-dramatization of "America," which he more than made up for as soon as he segued into "I'm Alive." His best songs were those in which he played the guitar and sang, and allowed his music to do the talking. His concert selections are usually interesting enough without the high glamour. The ambience he tries to create in some segments, especially the *Jonathan Livingston Seagull* medley, is just not his style. A record would have been proof of this.

Neil may believe that it would represent a step backwards if he only played his guitar and sang with some talk between numbers. But this is precisely what made *Hot August Night* exceptional. Another such album would not be repetitive. Stripping down a performance to its bare essentials is not reactionary—it just makes sense. The crowds do not come to see his sequined tuxedo pants, flashy shirt, and a guitar that glows in the dark. They're not here to see a laser diamond or bird or giant American flag or fireworks. They've come to see and to hear and to feel with Neil Diamond.

In September 1983, Neil sang "Heartlight" at Los Angeles' Shrine Auditorium for television. The occasion was a performance of the song during one of three pilot episodes of an NBC variety series which was to be called "Live . . . and in Person." He was coaxed into this unfamiliar situation by old friend Sandy Gallin, who organized the shows and hosted them à la Ed Sullivan. Gallin had enlisted the aid of Neil, Kenny Rogers, Dolly Parton, Linda Ronstadt, and bands ranging from Culture Club to Menudo, in an attempt to revive the variety show concept on network television.

Neil sang "Heartlight" with some style but obvious stage fright. It was his first performance on an American variety show since appearing with the Everly Brothers in 1970. The Shrine crowd was politely enthusiastic, but most of them, expecially in the balcony, happened to be thirteen-year-old girls who had come to scream for Menudo.

Diamond spent the remainder of 1983 recording tracks for his upcoming *Primitive* album and finishing his tour of California and the Pacific Northwest. This included stops in San Diego, where he put on three very good shows while facing a ticket availability controversy; and in Seattle, where a fire in his hotel forced him out of his room in the middle of the night.

San Diego's legitimate ticket brokers had been voluntarily restricting themselves to buying only six tickets through each person they paid to wait in line. But Weintraub, perhaps hoping to see Diamond book seven nights in San Diego, set no limit on the amount of tickets customers could purchase. Only three nights were scheduled in the San Diego Sports Arena, a total of 43,500 seats, and *Billboard* reported that as many as 30,000 wound up with scalpers. Diamond sold out, but a check of the arena each night showed an alarming amount of empty seats in all areas. It was as if the fans had called a strike. It was a shame, since Diamond put on better shows than he had a few months earlier at the Forum. In noticing the amount of vacant seats, Neil said something to the effect that when he first started performing and saw people leaving in the middle of the set, it meant they were gone for good. Now, they just get up to get a hot dog or use the restroom, but it still worries him. He later found out about the problem and decided to set ticket limits in the future.

United Press International reported that when Diamond played Seattle the next week, arsonists tried to burn down the hotel where he was staying. The Seattle Fire Department said that the fire began in a storage area and the smoke quickly spread up to Neil's suite as well as to his band's rooms. No one was hurt. As firefighters put out the blaze, Diamond and NDRRT ate an early breakfast in the hotel restaurant.

The rest of the tour went well, with Diamond selling out every venue. It seemed that wherever he played, he found new fans and set new attendance records. He was also testing reaction to new material, asking his fans what they thought of new songs like "Primitive," "Fire on the Tracks," and "Positive Vibes."

The holiday season had come, and Columbia had hoped to release the live set—it could have been a present under many, many Christmas trees. Columbia expected something, but *Primitive* was still in the recording studio, so a compromise was reached. What they got instead of *Live at the Forum* was *Classics—the Early Years*, an altered reissue of a 1977 Columbia Record Club package. The album answered the pleas of long-suffering Diamond fans who had clamored for a Bang set for two years.

Classics—the Early Years is interesting in that Neil had charge of the Bang masters for the first time and chose versions of the songs he wanted people to remember, not necessarily the takes that appeared on the hit singles of the late 1960s.

The album fared well, but certainly was not the smash the live album could have been. Though never publicly admitting it, Columbia would not forget this.

It's almost as if he is somewhat forgotten by the mass pop audience and essentially in a place where he may need to prove himself all over. He may have to come up with a work that is undeniably attractive, catchy, and inviting, a work that will pull in more than just the proven audience he's had.

—Mikal Gilmore
Los Angeles Examiner

12
Headed for the Future (1984–1986)

Diamond faced nearly seven months of struggle to get *Primitive* released. Columbia, having its own reasons, deemed the effort insufficiently commercial. Claims of this nature are not unusual in cases of new artists, but for someone of Diamond's calibre to be accused of "uncommerciality" was a slap in the face. It is reasonable to suspect that bad blood had been stirred when Neil used his contractual privilege to cancel the release of *Live at the Forum*. Diamond, in any event, was angered enough to file a lawsuit which claimed that Columbia had to release any new album he delivered to them within forty-five days. This stipulation was part of his 1981 contract.

Diamond said that he became angry enough with Columbia to file a lawsuit because nobody at the company told him what the problem was. "Mainly, I liked the album and I was angry because I didn't get a response when the album was delivered to Columbia. I waited and waited. So I was pretty angry by the time they did call back."

Bob Altshuler of Columbia's press and publications department in New York said that the label saw its differences with Diamond as relatively minor.

"We've had a long, and for the most part, a cordial relationship with Neil Diamond. We're working with a strong artist who writes strong material and who reaches many, many people with [his music]. But we don't always agree on everything," Altshuler said. "But [this disagreement] is minor when compared to all the successes. I think our relationship is evident when looking at the sales figures and the quality of the product Mr. Diamond has produced."

Diamond told *USA Today* what he thought of Columbia's action: "People feel a need to compartmentalize their tastes, and there's a snobbery that comes along with it."

Diamond and Columbia settled out of court. Most of *Primitive*'s original line-up stayed intact, but four recorded songs—"Hit Man," "Act Like a Man," "What Was It Like For You, Marlene," and the very good "Positive Vibes"—were shelved indefinitely.

By 1986, Diamond had not cooled off sufficiently to discuss the lawsuit, but he said "both sides had their point and the album could have been better."

Primitive marked the second time that Diamond and NDRRT had tried to do their album with little outside help. But Diamond did try working with producer Richard Perry, who had done such great work with Ringo Starr and continues to have hits with the Pointer Sisters. Perry's techniques seemed to match Neil's style well; the sessions resulted in two Diamond/Bacharach/Bayer Sager compositions, "Sleep with Me Tonight" and "Crazy." Aside from those two tracks, the rest of the original *Primitive* was Neil and his band at work.

In return for the four songs dropped from the album, Neil was allowed to include two songs written by his band and a member of his office staff—"My Time with You" and "Love's Own Song." But he had to agree to include "Turn Around," a third Diamond/Bacharach/ Bayer Sager collaboration, and to accept the assistance of Columbia in-house producer Denny Diante on the three new songs.

"Turn Around" and "Sleep with Me Tonight" were issued on singles to startlingly small response. "Turn Around" could only get to number sixty-two, while "Sleep with Me Tonight" did not chart at all. Both were slow ballads, which partly explained their poor showing; but even Diamond didn't seem to care enough about them to sing them in concert more than a few times. The third single, "You Make It Feel Like Christmas," also failed to chart. The album only reached number thirty-five. Columbia might have legitimately warned Diamond that his mainstream pop sound would no longer easily find a home on Top Forty radio. All pop artists, including Streisand and Manilow, were facing the same problem. It would even happen to Kenny Rogers by the end of 1985.

Top Forty now consisted mostly of synthesizer-based dance music. It wasn't called disco, but honest people would be hard pressed to deny that it *was* disco. Hard rock even found difficulty in the format unless the artist was a teen idol. As good as Bruce Springsteen has been since the middle 1970s, he didn't fit the Top Forty format until he was discovered by the youth of America.

As explained earlier, Diamond had begun to lose his mass appeal to teens by *Serenade*. He continued to hang on until "You Don't Bring Me Flowers," which was so unique it couldn't fail. *The Jazz Singer* score was boosted by a movie and tremendous publicity, and this carried over to "Heartlight," which, like "You Don't Bring Me Flowers," was special: E.T., although fictional, had a youth following. There was nothing between "Heartlight" and "Turn Around" to keep most teenagers interested in Diamond.

Diamond's popularity was as strong as ever with young adults exposed to his music and the core of his fans being adults aged twenty-five and older, especially women. This is the age group of adult contemporary radio, and not surprisingly, this format embraced pop performers like Streisand, Manilow, Rogers, and Diamond. "Turn Around" made Top Five on the adult contemporary charts, and the two follow-up singles also did well. Moving to adult contemporary audiences was not a disgrace; it just marked the passing of time. This is not to say Diamond could never have another Top Forty hit, but it had to be special enough to catch the ear of the Top Forty listener.

There was such a song on *Primitive,* "Fire on the Tracks," which is the best song Diamond has done since "America." "Fire on the Tracks" was a show-stopper in pre-release concerts despite the fact it was new and unrecorded.

Although *Primitive* was his best Columbia album since *Beautiful Noise,* few reviews informed the public of this. Thus, *Primitive* did not sell well at the outset, but eventually sold 500,000 copies to keep Diamond's Gold Record streak intact. Diamond did not help the album by refusing to make a music video for any song from it. He was still uncomfortable with the idea of such an activity and probably would never have made a video if the adult-contemporary VH-1 cable channel had not come into being. The song he chose was not one of his *Primitive* numbers, but a live rendition of "Heartlight" done in 1985. He simply stood there and sang.

Diamond seemed disappointed in the whole album. Soon, he stopped performing *Primitive* songs altogether. But he told Robert Hilburn in May 1986, that he really didn't hate the album. "I still love the album, but I think all the talk in the industry hurt it . . . [it] made people skeptical about it from the beginning."

Diamond toured Europe in 1984. When he visited England in late June and early July, he learned that he was one of Princess Diana's favorite singers, and he was invited to meet the Prince and Princess of Wales. News magazines got plenty of mileage from footage showing

Neil, accompanied by Marcia and Jesse, greeting Prince
Charles and Princess Diana and presenting the princess
with a big stuffed Garfield toy. A portion of his July 5
benefit performance for the Prince's Trust at Earl's Court
was shown as part of ABC's 1984 Olympic gala variety
special. The truly memorable part of the evening occurred when Neil began the "Forever in Blue Jeans"
ritual dance. When he asked the audience to dance, a
pregnant Princess Diana joined in.

When Charles and Diana visted America in November,
1985, Diamond crossed his political boundaries for an
evening and accepted President Reagan's invitation on
behalf of the royal couple to the official state dinner in
their honor.

Diamond said that his "knees were shaking" when
Princess Diana asked him to dance. During the dance,
they talked of the royal couple's itinerary, and when they
were finished, Neil next danced with Marcia.

"I danced with my wife or I would have been in major
trouble," he said.

He sang Princess Diana's two favorite Diamond tracks,
"September Morn' " and a solo version of "You Don't
Bring Me Flowers."

In 1985 Neil was interviewed by Barbara Walters for
one of her television specials. He had refused her requests
for interviews many, many times over the years. But now
he was telling reporters that he was a "changed" man and
not as introverted as he had been. She reportedly challenged him with this claim at a dinner party, and he
finally relented.

Unfortunately, the interview shed almost no new light
on Diamond. Walters did get the "Eice Cherry" story out
of him—a story that had been in some 1960s teen magazines that were hardly reliable. Like many other reporters,
she tried to get at the root of the man; but, true to form,
he recited song lyrics in his answers. His most famous
statement about himself is that one can tell who Neil
Diamond is by listening to the songs. Although the

statement was over fifteen years old, the Barbara Walters interview proved that Neil Diamond still believed it.

While on tour in the Pacific Northwest and British Columbia, Neil received the bad news that his father had suffered a heart attack in Florida. He flew his parents to Los Angeles, where Akeeba was admitted to Cedars-Sinai Medical Center. He reportedly showed signs of improvement, but on March 25, 1985, he passed away following another attack.

Neil had been finishing his tour commitments after he had been assured that Akeeba would survive. He found comfort in the fact that Jesse was on the road with him. Neil told *People* in 1986 that he needed Jesse to get through the performance the night his father died. "[Jesse] was very concerned that I would be able to handle doing the show the next day. I told him, 'If I turn to you while I'm onstage and you give me a big smile, I'll get through it.' I turned to him at least once a song, he'd flash me a smile . . . and we made it through that show."

Diamond elaborated: "There was a show the day after [my father] died and going through with it was one of the most difficult things I have ever done. I was numb . . . in shock, really. In my mind, I told myself I was doing the show for him. My son was playing conga drums on that tour, so we made a deal before the show. . . . We did that show, then got a plane the next day and went to the funeral."

Neil postponed a few dates, but he decided he needed his audiences to get him through the rough time. He brought his entire family with him on tour and absolutely no visitors or reporters were allowed backstage. Neil found the concerts therapeutic, and the Diamonds found strength together.

When the tour commitments were finished, Neil went home to Los Angeles and took some time off. Thinking of his late father soon inspired him to write some new material.

But all too soon, Marcia's mother died.

"Between my dad passing away and Marcia's mom passing away, we had one hell of a year," Diamond said. "I had always been close to my dad and it came as a shock because he was such a vital guy . . . in great shape. His death helped change me a lot. I began to feel that I couldn't hold back any more. I have to go out there and enjoy myself, enjoy my life, try to live it to the fullest. I never had that attitude before. I was always very tunnel visioned. My life rose and fell on the basis of whether I was writing a good lyric or a bad one. I spent a lot of time thinking about things like that. Finally, I realized I had to take a deep breath and get back to work."

Diamond spent the next few months composing an introspective album called *The Story of My Life*. The ten-song record dwelled on Diamond's reactions and thoughts after Akeeba's death. The songs, besides the title track, are believed to be: "Falling," "I'm Sayin' I'm Sorry," "Angel Above my Head," "Dancing to the Party Next Door," "It Don't Seem Likely," "I'm Your Man," "Long Nights," "Moonlight Rider," and "Headed for the Future." It was completed in November 1985, but when Neil delivered it to Columbia, a repeat of the *Primitive* commerciality hassles ensued. Syndicated columnist Marilyn Beck reported in early December that CBS Records President Walter Yetnikoff had turned down the disc, unsatisfied with Neil's production work. Other reports stated that the lack of potential singles deeply concerned Columbia's sales staff. It was clear that Diamond had more to do on the project.

When Columbia expressed its doubts about the album, Diamond told Stephen Holden of the *New York Times* in 1986 that he understood. "The songs on *The Story of My Life* were written after the death of my father and were very personal and dark."

In attempts to redesign the album, which was subsequently titled *Headed for the Future* after a new upbeat song Neil had written to help him out of his doldrums, Diamond decided to work with several different producers. He first enlisted the help of longtime friend Maurice White, leader of Earth, Wind, and Fire.

While working on *Headed for the Future*, White told Dennis Hunt of the *Los Angeles Times* what his role would be in the completion of the disc. "[Neil] had finished four or five of the songs and wanted another sound to go with what he already had. He wanted to bring in songs with some energy, songs with a certain impact. Neil does a certain kind of music. He does it very well. He doesn't need me to do that kind of middle-of-the-road music. He brought me in to give him something different."

Although White brought in jazz guitarist Bobby Caldwell ("What You Won't Do For Love" was his big hit in 1978) and Greg Phillinganes (a frequent collaborator with Michael Jackson), White did not attempt to make his portion of the album overly soul-sounding. "It's not R&B," he told Hunt. "I'm not going to turn Neil into James Brown. There's a little R&B feel on the songs I did with him, as much as he can handle and not sound like a fish out of water." White's songs all listed Phillinganes as co-producer and included "Stand Up For Love," which featured Toto guitarist Steven Lukather, "Angel," and the closing track, "Love Doesn't Live Here Anymore."

Neil then called on David Foster ("Love Theme from *St. Elmo's Fire*"), with whom he had co-written "I'm Alive." One of the resulting tracks was another Diamond-Foster tune called "The Man You Need." The other was "It Should Have Been Me," written by Canadian rocker Bryan Adams and his writing partner Jim Vallance. Foster had worked with Adams on the Northern Lights ("Canada for Africa") project and knew of his abilities. Adams had just enjoyed six Top Fifteen hits from his quadruple-platinum album *Reckless* and had written two songs for Who vocalist Roger Daltrey. "It Should Have Been Me" turned out to be the best song on *Headed for the Future*.

By November 1985, Diamond's stop-start method of planning tours and his presumed cancellation of *Beautiful Noise* and *Brother Love* led to disagreements with Weintraub, who was to have produced both films. Neil left Management III after ten years to sign with Sandy Gallin. The Gallin/Addis/Morrey firm handles acts like Dolly Parton, the Pointer Sisters, and Patti LaBelle.

Neil had also reorganized his concert repertoire. He premiered his new show on December 9 in Ames, Iowa, and took it through a two-week, six-city run. He opened the show with "Headed for the Future," and mixed the song selection so the laser fireworks of "America" now joined the other *Jazz Singer* tracks in the middle of his performance. Besides the new song, the only post-1980 songs he sang were "Heartlight" and a slightly rearranged "I'm Alive." He also did new arrangements of "Girl, You'll Be a Woman Soon," "Cherry, Cherry," "Jungletime," and "Brooklyn Roads." Diamond steadfastly refused to do anything from *Primitive*; he didn't even include his own "You Make It Feel Like Christmas" with the secular Christmas carols.

Already noticeably nervous about the changes, Neil was teary-eyed by the time he chose to sing "Brooklyn Roads" in memory of his father. This was the first time he had sung this song live in several years.

Neil came home and with Bacharach and Bayer Sager finished up two songs for his next album, "I'll See You on the Radio (Laura)" and "Me Beside You." The background singers on these songs included members of the Waters family, who had been in *The Jazz Singer*.

In January 1986, Neil appeared on the televised tribute to Dr. Martin Luther King, Jr. The show was hosted by Stevie Wonder and featured Bill Cosby and Eddie Murphy, among many others. Diamond sang "America" from the Radio City Music Hall stage and really looked excited.

Plans were underway for a Neil Diamond CBS television special with Stevie Wonder and Carol Burnett as

guests. Dwight Hemion and Gary Smith, who had produced both of Diamond's 1977 NBC specials, signed to
organize the new show, and Kenny Solms, a veteran of
"The Carol Burnett Show" became the head writer.
Although Neil repeatedly swore he would never do a
variety special, he simply changed his mind. Gallin's love
of the genre may have been an influence, but Diamond
told Jeff Yarbrough of *People* in May that the special was
his own idea. "I've had this secret yearning," he said.
"Maybe CBS will give me a shot. My manager will have
a stroke if he hears I'm even thinking about this."

Diamond told *USA Today* that he specifically wanted
Wonder and Burnett as his guests. "Working with Carol,
she'd make me seem funny, and Stevie would make my
music sound better. Performing with two geniuses is
good insurance for any performer."

He told Hilburn, "I wanted this show to be a stretch for
me . . . to try new things, to have fun. And everything was
fun. It was great working with Carol and Stevie. I had
never done any comedy before and we came here the first
day to read the script and . . . Carol was hysterical. She is
one of those talents who can make you laugh whenever
she wants to. She was very easy to work with, the same
with Stevie."

The special, originally entitled "Neil Diamond . . . A
Special Day" was described in the trade papers as "a
light-hearted look at a day in the life of the singer-
songwriter," who would meet Burnett and Wonder along
the way. The idea was reminiscent of Paul McCartney's
Give My Regards to Broad Street movie; unfortunately, a
lot of the comic bits in retitled "Hello Again" special
were equally panned by critics.

Half of the jokes poked fun at the many people who
peddle songs to successful singers like Diamond. They
included Neil's mailman, gas station attendant, and a
guard at CBS. Diamond told "Entertainment This Week"
that these situations really happen regularly and that the
most audacious song peddler was the nurse who quickly

jotted down a song in the X-ray room where Neil had taken one of his sons who had broken his arm.

The other half of the jokes involved showing how Diamond, Wonder, and even Lionel Richie (in a cameo) get ideas for song titles from regular folks. Diamond was shown thinking of "Play Me" at a playground and Wonder getting the idea for "I Just Called to Say I Love You" from overhearing a guy at an adjoining pay phone.

In another scene, Diamond and Wonder met at the Aquarius Theater where the two were working on the same TV show. Wonder did a fine performance of his then-current hit "Overjoyed." But then the show hit its absolute peak of absurdity when Wonder and Diamond sang a rendition of Stevie's "Sir Duke." The soulful tribute to Duke Ellington and other music pioneers sounded like a Vegas lounge act completely devoid of any real emotion.

The show picked up again with Neil and Carol on the old soundstage of her television show. Diamond sat in Burnett's old chair and daydreamed about hosting a show like Burnett's with her as the guest. Burnett portrayed a few of her more memorable characters and joined Neil in a duet of Diamond songs. Their rapport during the medley was the best part of the show next to Diamond's live performance segment.

Just as the "Love at the Greek" special showcased Diamond's stage presence, "Hello Again" reinforced it. Diamond sang about ten more songs during the audience tapings at the Aquarius Theatre on his forty-fifth birthday, but the six that made the special—"I'm Alive," "Cherry, Cherry," "September Morn'," "Sweet Caroline," "America," and "Hello Again"—were among the best. Not included in the television special were versions of "Jungletime" and "Brother Love's Travelling Salvation Show" that brought down the house.

The Diamond special resulted in a fairly strong finish in the weekly ratings—number twenty-one—as well as a song for *Headed for the Future*. Wonder brought a piece of music to Diamond backstage at the Aquarius, and Neil immediately liked it; he wrote lyrics for it and quickly recorded "Lost in Hollywood." The song replaced a track called "We're Doin' It," but "Lost In Hollywood" added little to the album's weak songwriting.

A modified version of "Headed for the Future" performed at the Aquarius audience taping became Diamond's first current video. Diamond maintained that he still disliked videos because he wanted his audience to picture their own images to his songs, but that he finally relented on son Jesse's advice. He also said that Jesse keeps him up-to-date on the music scene, although he admitted that he listens to the radio while cleaning the house. "I can tell if a song's going to be a big hit on the radio if it's easy to clean to." He added that part of his own writing criteria remained a song's stage potential. "If I can imagine performing a song on stage when I write it, I know it's good."

In April, Diamond appeared at a birthday tribute to Carol Burnett. The event was a fundraiser for the UCLA Foundation, which raises money to aid development of the performing arts at the Westwood campus. Other guests included Burnett's old castmates, Elizabeth Taylor, James Stewart, Jim Nabors, and Beverly Sills. Diamond sang several songs before introducing Burnett and leading a sold-out Pauley Pavilion crowd in singing "Happy Birthday."

The announcement of Diamond's miniconcert at UCLA caused quite a stir in Los Angeles. Ticket brokers were getting $500 a piece for the $75 seats—the best tickets available to the general public—because it was believed Diamond would not play Los Angeles again for some time. But Diamond's summer 1986 tour plans in support of *Headed for the Future* included not only Detroit and Chicago, and the July 3 to 6 Statue of Liberty extravaganza but also a whopping fourteen-night stand at the Greek Theater. Originally, only seven shows were scheduled; but when all the tickets sold out within two hours, three more dates were announced just to accommodate the thousands of people still waiting in line outside of the Greek. A total of 61,000 seats were sold by the afternoon for a pre-concert gross of $1.64 million. This more than doubled Barry Manilow's record at the Greek—$633,682 over four dates.

But this was the house that Neil built. This was also the tenth anniversary of *Love at the Greek*. Four more shows, for a total of fifteen, were eventually added the next week after horror stories about ticket scalpers began circulating. Outside of the theater, but out of range of police, scalpers offered ticket buyers at least $100 for a single ticket. The scalpers also hired migrant farm workers to buy tickets for them.

Diamond told Hilburn that he had wanted to play the Greek many times in the recent past, but that his fear of not living up to expectations and old memories kept him back. "But I feel like I'm ready for it this year. I've been preparing for it . . . thinking about it every day. What can I do? What kind of sound system can we build? It's a challenge to go back and make it work. It's probably the biggest challenge of the year for me . . . more than the TV special, more even than the album."

Not content with the intensity of the Greek booking, Diamond signed for several shows at New York's Madison Square Garden—a venue he hadn't played in 10 years. When the tickets were counted, Diamond had broken all house attendance and gross receipt records (160,000 people, $3.2 million) by a solo performer during his eight-night stand.

By the time Diamond reached the Greek Theater on August 14, the gross there had topped $2.3 million, and a celebration of sorts was warranted. Although receiving lukewarm reviews at best, *Headed for the Future* soon earned Diamond another gold record, and it has spawned at least the one national hit—the title track. Diamond had pushed this album, granting more interviews than usual, and even Columbia was pleased with the results. They too supported the album by launching a major promotional campaign. And the television special had introduced the entire country to the new song and reminded them about the older hits.

Although not confirmed at press time, the rumors of Diamond returning to the Greek to record another live album did not seem preposterous.

During the last three shows, he introduced a new up-tempo rock song called "Back in L.A.," which would be an obvious single and the showcase of such a live set. The song is one of Diamond's best of the past twelve years. The crowd loved it, and Diamond loved back.

Neil got what he wanted after all.

There seem to be two categories of singers who are has-beens. One is made up of singers who never reached their potential, and the other, singers who overshot their potential. It causes a lot of frustration. I'm wondering which group I'll end up in."

—Neil Diamond
Hit Parader
December 1967

13
Dry Your Eyes (June 1986)

Into his twenty-first year as a popular performer, Neil Diamond has become part of the popular psyche. Show-business types refer to him as one of their own, and his name is dropped irregularly in one-liners on television situation comedies, newspaper comic strips, and *MAD* magazine. Even during his recent decline in status on the Top Forty singles chart, he became one of the most-heard artists on adult contemporary radio. If he never again achieves consistent Top Forty success, he will still maintain a healthy following that will prevent any of his periodic hits from being labelled as comebacks.

There are, and may always be, the massive ticket-buying crowds. They provide him with several "he's-immortal-and-everybody-loves-him" news feature stories wherever he goes. In spite of the occasional heartaches, there seems to be no reason why he can't go on until he's eighty, as he told an Indianapolis audience. Except that he has already had cancer, yet is apparently still unable to quit smoking.

He has also achieved the normal, everyday family life that he felt had eluded him until the mid-1970s concert sabbatical. By choosing to continue with his minitour scheduling, he finds time for Marcia and his children and all the cities along the way. It may take a while before some fans see him, especially those in New York and Los Angeles. But he consistently plays the Midwest, the Southwest, and the Pacific Northwest. Although he may need to play the Deep South and his dual hometowns a bit more often, he really owes Australia another visit.

His touring technique only allows him to balance his time among his family, his songwriting, and his business commitments. He allows himself little time for rest. As he told David Hartman of ABC's "Good Morning America" in 1980: "I don't [find the time to relax]. I'm not really good at that. I really relax when I'm working with my band, when I'm working in music. It's the most freeing experience that I have. It just relieves me of all kinds of tensions and pressures and I think of nothing else when I'm doing that. So, I think the music does it for me."

He explained this further to Robert Hilburn in 1983: "If the songwriting stops, everything will stop for me. It's really the flame that keeps the pot boiling, so to speak. It's where all my ideas, and I think, a lot of my inspiration comes from. That's one area in which you can never really relax. There's always the constant fear: the day the writing stops."

Over the years, Diamond has come to regard Hilburn as the one reporter he can rely on to ask intelligent questions and get the story straight. For a time in the early 1980s, Hilburn was a commentator on the syndicated television concert show "The Midnight Special." His interview with Diamond for the show, conducted in Neil's award room following the release of *The Jazz Singer*, is the best televised interview Diamond has given.

Diamond talked about living up to his past success: "I see these things [his gold and platinum records and other awards] and I know it's passed. It doesn't pertain to what

I do now. I still have to concern myself with the song I'm writing today—and with the record that I'm making, with the performance that I'm doing tonight. These are the things that you really think about. This is passed, and it's wonderful, and you know, I couldn't be happier about it."

What kept him changing? "I suppose it's a certain restlessness involved in that, and also, I spent a good number of years trying to just get accepted on a very basic level. . . . When you finally get a chance to do things, the tendency is that you're willing to take the chances and to do them. . . . [And] there's so many things I haven't done yet."

How had he learned from the experiences of others? "Well, first of all, Stephen Foster died in the [New York] Bowery of tuberculosis. He was penniless. . . . You want to be able to live your life out and create your work and end it all with some kind of dignity. I've read books about all kinds of writers and performers because I'm part of that. I want a sense of what it was like, and how these people lived, and how their lives turned out. I'd like to learn from that, but you just never know. It could end tomorrow. If it does, I've had a nice long tremendous run. I couldn't ask for anything more than that, but I'm going to keep plugging away. I love writing. It's part of what I do, and I love performing now, too. As long as there's an audience out there that appreciates what I do, I'll be out there and working.

"I have made a lot of wrong moves and I think everybody has those tendencies to be self-destructive, to be fearful, to be insecure, especially when you're a public figure. I've resisted them only because basically I'm a writer. I don't need anything but a pad and a pencil and a guitar. I don't need anything [else]. That's what I need. I did it for a long time before anyone accepted it, and I'll continue to do it even if people don't accept it anymore. Because it's what I do. It's what I love doing.

"I listen to the radio. I listen to records. I have all kinds of albums, interesting new releases. People that I haven't heard before and I want to hear what they're doing. But mostly the music I'm involved with is my own. So the music that I would listen to today would probably be songs that I'm working on now. . . . When I'm finished with my music, it's difficult for me to go and listen to other people's music. I tend to be very self-focused, very highly focused on what I'm doing."

Diamond told the *Orange County Register* how he measured his success: "By quantum non-leaps. No one wants to make a fool of himself. The key, I feel, is to stay excited about what you're doing. By that, I mean there must be a little bit of fear to keep you honest and give you an edge. Without it, performing is no longer personal, it's mass production."

"I think my problem has always been that I suffer from self-doubt," he told *Us* in 1981. "The fear factor is crucial to my work. I'm scared all the time."

"I'm incredibly moody and I don't know how my family puts up with me," Diamond told the British press the same year. "I get incredible highs of elation and sometimes I sink to the depths. Maybe that's why I always try to do things that are scary. That's what gives me a kick in life—being scared."

Neil explained to Australia's *TV Week* how Marcia has helped him through the rough times. "When I'm at the studio, whether I've been filming or recording, I'm the boss. When I come home, I'm the baby. I need looking after. I like it. I need a family to balance my other life. And, of course, the work I do is so up and down it's impossible not to carry some of these moods home with you, not to become either depressed or very elated. Those are the two options. She's had to learn to deal with that. It was very difficult for her at first, even though she knew what she was getting into when she married me.

"The key is that she is in love with me so she is willing to put up with things that most people might not put up with. It's worked out well. She's helped me. She gives me the freedom to do my work and yet she gives me a family. I need to be married."

In *People*, Neil credited Marcia with literally keeping him alive: "When you are a star, you get used to being taken care of. I remember one time Marcia had to go somewhere and I wanted to eat but didn't know what to do in the kitchen. I was helpless, so I stayed hungry until she returned. I'm like Ozzie in 'Ozzie and Harriet.' I come to the office to keep out of my wife's hair."

He gave his highest tribute to Marcia in April 1986 to *USA Today*: "Make believe I'm just a little boat in an ocean very big. She's my harbor. She's my island. She's my safe place. She's kept me together for a long time. . . . I'm more in love with my wife now than when I got married. Marcia and I have a history together. . . . I'd give up all my success if I had to in order to maintain my marriage. . . . Everything I would want from a woman—the love, the friendship, the stability—I have with Marcia. . . . The only problem we have is when I don't bring her home any flowers. When you write a song like 'You Don't Bring Me Flowers,' you can't tell your wife any excuses why you didn't bring her some."

He talked some more about his personal life in the *Washington Post*. "It's more difficult to live your own private life—to be a husband, a father, or a friend—than to be a performer. I have never really gone public, except under special circumstances. I've kept myself very much protected. It's not very easy to go out with [Micah] and somebody asks me for my autograph and I have to explain to him why they want me to sign my name.

"I try to keep all of my creative strength and preserve it for those moments of writing and recording. You can't be a star twenty-four hours a day. You can be a star for two hours, and that's fine.

"It's much more difficult for me to deal with real life than being that guy on stage. He's just a fantasy that I had and you can't live that fantasy twenty-four hours a day. So I just lived it [again by doing this concert], and now I'm here [backstage] and my throat hurts.''

He has said repeatedly that he doesn't care if he is remembered when he is gone. But he is either being polite or showing false modesty. He advises most people to listen to his songs in order to know Neil Diamond. He told Pat Collins of the "CBS Morning News" in 1984: "I think parts of my life are in every song I've written. People that I've known, experiences that I've had. I never realized that until eight or ten years ago; that, in fact, I was talking about myself, and it's a nice feeling. It's a legacy, if only for my kids. . . .''

Despite the fears and insecurities, and his sometimes eager attempts to analyze himself, Diamond confessed to Barbara Walters in the 1985 interview: "Well, in a sense, I have made it, and I've felt that from the moment that I was able to earn a living as a writer. That I had made it, and not only that, but people—lots of people—like my songs. A lot of people come to hear me sing, and people respect my work. I don't think I could ask for more. I never dreamed that it would happen. It's everything that I could imagine wanting.''

It is interesting to note that an unofficial straw poll at a mid-1980s Elvis Presley convention named Diamond as second favorite among the dedicated fans of the King. In spite of several years of very inconsistent recordings, Diamond's strong presence and charisma have carried him past the hundreds of singers who have had only a few years of chart life apiece. Like Presley, he has become—in spite of his claim to privacy, for better or worse—a superstar, an institution larger than life, able to have even his direst moments acclaimed.

"I've succeeded beyond my wildest expectations. My goal was to exist as a musician, and when your songs work, it tells you that you, too, are worthwhile. Once you've established that, you just have to meet your own standards.''

Compositions List

This is a record of all songs Neil Diamond has registered with the Library of Congress for copyright control as of mid-1986— following the release of *Headed for the Future*. Publishing companies and dates of registration accompany the titles; [r] indicates renewal of registration.

Many songs, particularly in the early Tin Pan Alley period, were never recorded by Diamond. Several are not known to have been recorded by any artist. Diamond's luck in getting such popular CBS artists as Bobby Vinton, Andy Williams, and Cliff Richard to test out his songs was facilitated by his association with Columbia's songwriting arm, Blackwood Music—note that his term there coincides with "Clown Town."

A few technical mysteries appear in the song log as well. How Sunbeam managed to land a 1967 copyright is anybody's guess, as is why the date for *Jonathan Livingston Seagull*'s medley, "The Odyssey," comes more than half a year after its release.

The tracks dating from January 1986 form the basis of the rejected *The Story of My Life* album, which was supplanted by *Headed for the Future*.

In addition to the split copyrights listed, Gilbert Becaud's collaborations were co-licensed by EMA-Suisse; Michael Masser's by Prince Street Music; Carole Bayer Sager's by Unichappel Music and Begonia Melodies; and the Diamond-Bacharach-Sager team-ups by New Hidden Valley Music and Carole Bayer Sager Music.

7-22-60	What Will I Do	Neil Leslie Diamond
8-1-60	'Till You've Tried Love	Neil Leslie Diamond
3-13-62	'Till You've Tried Love	[r] Saxon Music
8-15-60	Gone Is My Love	Neil Leslie Diamond
8-15-60	Time Will Tell	Neil Leslie Diamond
8-15-60	You Keep Me Wondering	Neil Leslie Diamond
8-15-60	You Keep Me Wondering	[r] Blackwood Music
12-6-60	It's You, It's You	Neil Leslie Diamond
10-12-61	Every Minute, Every Hour	Saxon Music
1-15-62	You are My Love at Last	Saxon Music
1-15-62	I'm Afraid	Saxon Music
4-18-62	Blue Destiny	Neil Leslie Diamond
4-18-62	Make Believe	Neil Leslie Diamond
6-6-62	Make Believe	[r] Sunbeam Music
4-18-62	Runnin' Free	Neil Leslie Diamond
6-6-62	Runnin' Free	[r] Sunbeam Music
4-18-62	But Only in Name	Neil Leslie Diamond
6-6-62	A Fool All Over Again	Sunbeam Music
6-6-62	I'm Nobody's Fool	Sunbeam Music
6-6-62	Recipe for Happiness	Sunbeam Music
6-6-62	All I Have Is Me	Sunbeam Music
8-20-62	Handle with Care	Sunbeam Music
8-20-62	A Million Miles Away	Sunbeam Music
8-20-62	I'll Be Back Someday	Sunbeam Music
8-20-62	Miss Lonely Hearts	Sunbeam Music
8-20-62	It Don't Seem Right	Sunbeam Music
8-20-62	On the Outside Looking In	Sunbeam Music
8-20-62	Things Have Changed	Sunbeam Music
8-20-62	But That Was Yesterday	Sunbeam Music
12-5-62	Santa Santa	White Castle Music
6-7-63	We Got Love	Blackwood Music
6-7-63	Lightnin' Hand	Blackwood Music
6-7-63	Indian Giver	Blackwood Music
6-7-63	Mortal Man	Blackwood Music
6-7-63	I've Never Been the Same	Blackwood Music
6-7-63	Clown Town	Blackwood Music
6-25-63	At Night [with Al Kasha]	Blackwood Music

8-15-63   I'm Not All That Bad...............Blackwood Music
8-15-63   On My Side of the Street [with Barry
           Richards].......................Blackwood Music
9-30-63   I'm a Man........................Blackwood Music
12-23-63   I Just Need You [with Carl D'Errico]..Blackwood Music
12-23-63   Say No [with Carl D'Errico]..........Blackwood Music
12-23-63   Believe It [with Carl D'Errico].......Blackwood Music
2-2-64   Just Smile.......................Blackwood Music
2-19-64   Good Time Sue....................Blackwood Music
2-27-64   If You Need Me [with Carl D'Errico]...Blackwood Music
2-27-64   Blue Donna [with Carl D'Errico]......Blackwood Music
3-12-64   Fool That I Am...................Roosevelt Music
3-22-64   I Care Enough to Give the Very Best
           [with Carl D'Errico]..............Roosevelt Music
4-1-64   I Don't Want to Love Linda [with
           Carl D'Errico]...................Blackwood Music
4-9-64   Little Doll Baby [with Larry Kusick]..Blackwood Music
4-19-64   Mama Cried.......................Jimskip Music
7-1-64   This Time Last Year [with Carl
           E'Errico].......................Melody Trails
7-4-64   Mister Moon......................Blackwood Music
7-24-64   Farewell, So Long, Goodbye [with
           Carl D'Errico]...................Blackwood Music
9-1-64   Bobby Did [with Carl D'Errico].......American Metropolitan
                                           Enterprises of N.Y.
11-23-64   Act Like a Lady [with Denny Randell]Painted Desert Music
1-4-65   Nathaniel B. Jackson [with Carl
           D'Errico].......................Daffodil Music
1-4-65   You'll Never Be Anything But Mine
           [with Carl D'Errico]..............Daffodil Music
2-3-65   That New Boy in Town [a.k.a. That
           New Girl in Town] [with Carl
           D'Errico].......................Suffolk Music
2-9-65   Measles..........................Painted Desert Music
2-10-65   Just Another Guy.................The Shadows Music
5-3-65   Don't Go Away Mad................Gil Music
5-3-65   It Comes and Goes................Gil Music
5-5-65   Sticks and Stones................Trio Music
5-5-65   Black and Blue (From Kicking Myself) Trio Music
5-21-65   Straw in the Wind................Trio Music
5-21-65   A Hundred Times Before I Go to
           Sleep...........................Trio Music
6-14-65   It's So Strange (The Way Love Works)
           [with Jeff Barry and Ellie
           Greenwich]......................Trio Music

6-28-65	Baby, Be Good	Trio Music
6-28-65	Love to Love	Trio Music
9-24-65	Where Do You Run? [with Jaye Posner]	Suffolk Music
10-27-65	Sunday and Me	Tallyrand Music
3-1-66	Solitary Man	Tallyrand Music
3-1-66	Do It	Tallyrand Music
5-23-66	Comin' Apart	Tallyrand Music
5-23-66	A Taste of Roses	Tallyrand Music
5-23-66	I Got Love for You	Tallyrand Music
5-23-66	I'll Come Runnin', Babe [different version of I'll Come Running]	Tallyrand Music
5-23-66	I Got the Feeling [a.k.a. Oh No No]	Tallyrand Music
5-23-66	Raisin' Cane	Tallyrand Music
5-23-66	The Non-Conformist Marching Song	Tallyrand Music
7-8-66	Cherry, Cherry	Tallyrand Music
7-8-66	Someday Baby	Tallyrand Music
7-8-66	I'll Come Running	Tallyrand Music
8-26-66	The Time Is Now	Tallyrand Music
8-29-66	Shout It	Tallyrand Music
9-23-66	The Long Way Home	Tallyrand Music
9-23-66	Red Red Wine	Tallyrand Music
7-8-66	I'll Come Running	Tallyrand Music
10-12-66	The Boat That I Row	Tallyrand Music
12-12-66	Look Out (Here Comes Tomorrow)	Screen Gems–Columbia
12-16-66	I'm a Believer	Screen Gems–Columbia
1-9-67	You Got to Me	Tallyrand Music
1-24-67	You Played the Field, I Played the Fool	Sunbeam Music
2-6-67	Hello, Goodbye	Regent Music
2-17-67	A Little Bit Me, A Little Bit You	Screen Gems–Columbia
3-14-67	Girl, You'll Be a Woman Soon	Tallyrand Music
3-24-67	You'll Forget	Tallyrand Music
4-5-67	My Babe	Tallyrand Music
4-5-67	Put My Mind at Ease	Tallyrand Music
6-28-77	Thank the Lord for the Nighttime	Tallyrand Music
7-25-67	Back from Baltimore	Tallyrand Music
7-25-67	Shilo	Tallyrand Music
9-27-67	Kentucky Woman	Tallyrand Music
11-27-67	Crooked Street	Tallyrand Music
12-27-67	Shot Down	Tallyrand Music
2-13-68	Flame	Screen Gems–Columbia
6-14-68	Brooklyn Roads	Stonebridge Music
6-14-68	Two-Bit Manchild	Stonebridge Music
6-17-68	Holiday Inn Blues	Stonebridge Music
6-17-68	Merry-Go-Round	Stonebridge Music
6-19-68	Broad Old Woman (6. A.M. Insanity)	Stonebridge Music

8-29-68	Honey-Drippin' Times	Stonebridge Music
8-29-68	Sunday Sun	Stonebridge Music
8-29-68	A Modern-Day Version of Love	Stonebridge Music
8-29-68	And the Grass Won't Pay No Mind	Stonebridge Music
8-29-68	The Pot-Smoker's Song	Stonebridge Music
8-29-68	Practically Newborn	Stonebridge Music
8-29-68	Knackelflerg	Stonebridge Music
2-4-69	The Boy (Girl) with Green Eyes	Monday Morning Music
2-3-69	Brother Love's Travelling Salvation Show	Stonebridge Music
2-8-69	Glory Road	Stonebridge Music
3-14-69	River Runs, Newgrown Plums [a.k.a. River Runs on Down]	Stonebridge Music
3-17-69	I've Been Living Lies	Suffolk Music
4-7-69	Deep in the Morning	Stonebridge Music
4-7-69	Dig In	Stonebridge Music
4-7-69	Long Gone	Stonebridge Music
4-7-69	If I Never Knew Your Name	Stonebridge Music
4-7-69	You're So Sweet, Horseflies Keep Hangin' 'Round Your Face	Stonebridge Music
4-7-69	Hurtin' You Don't Come Easy	Stonebridge Music
4-7-69	Juliet	Stonebridge Music
4-7-69	Memphis Streets	Stonebridge Music
7-19-69	Sweet Caroline (Good Times Never Seemed So Good)	Stonebridge Music
10-20-69	Holly Holy	Prophet Music
11-12-69	Smokey Lady	Prophet Music
11-12-69	New York Boy	Prophet Music
11-12-69	Ain't No Way	Prophet Music
11-12-69	And the Singer Sings His Song	Prophet Music
4-1-70	Soolaimon	Prophet Music
4-15-70	Lordy	Prophet Music
8-20-70	Childsong	Prophet Music
10-19-70	Free Life	Prophet Music
10-19-70	Coldwater Morning	Prophet Music
10-19-70	Done Too Soon	Prophet Music
10-19-70	I Am the Lion	Prophet Music
2-1-71	Cracklin' Rosie	Prophet Music
2-1-71	The African Suite	Prophet Music
2-1-71	Madrigal	Prophet Music
2-1-71	Missa	Prophet Music
3-10-71	I Am . . . I Said	Prophet Music
10-26-71	Stones	Prophet Music
10-26-71	Crunchy Granola Suite	Prophet Music
4-11-72	Song Sung Blue	Prophet Music

4-11-72	Gitchy Goomy	Prophet Music
6-28-72	Porcupine Pie	Prophet Music
6-28-72	High Rolling Man	Prophet Music
6-28-72	Canta Libre	Prophet Music
6-28-72	Captain Sunshine	Prophet Music
6-28-72	Play Me	Prophet Music
6-28-72	Walk on Water	Prophet Music
6-28-72	Theme [Orchestral]	Prophet Music
6-28-72	Prelude in E Minor	Prophet Music
6-28-72	Morningside (For My Children)	Prophet Music
6-29-73	Entiendeme [Spanish version of A Little Bit You, A Little Bit Me; with Augustin Villego]	Screen Gems–Columbia
9-7-73	Be	Stonebridge Music
9-7-73	Flight of the Gull	Stonebridge Music
9-7-73	Lonely Looking Sky	Stonebridge Music
9-7-73	Skybird	Stonebridge Music
9-7-73	Dear Father	Stonebridge Music
10-15-73	Anthem	Stonebridge Music
10-17-73	Prologue [for *Jonathan Livingston Seagull*]	Stonebridge Music
4-26-74	The Odyssey (Be/Lonely Looking Sky/Dear Father)	Stonebridge Music
9-27-74	Longfellow Serenade	Stonebridge Music
9-27-74	Rosemary's Wine	Stonebridge Music
10-7-74	I've Been This Way Before	Stonebridge Music
10-7-74	Lady Magdelene	Stonebridge Music
10-7-74	Yes I Will	Stonebridge Music
10-7-74	Reggae Strut	Stonebridge Music
10-7-74	The Gift of Song	Stonebridge Music
10-17-74	The Last Picasso	Stonebridge Music
6-1-76	Beautiful Noise	Stonebridge Music
6-1-76	Stargazer	Stonebridge Music
6-25-76	Lady-Oh	Stonebridge Music
6-25-76	Surviving the Life	Stonebridge Music
6-25-76	Street Life	Stonebridge Music
6-25-76	Home Is a Wounded Heart	Stonebridge Music
6-25-76	Signs	Stonebridge Music
6-28-76	Don't Think . . . Feel	Stonebridge Music
6-28-76	Dry Your Eyes [with Jaime "Robbie" Robertson]	Stonebridge Music
10-12-76	Sunflower	Stonebridge Music
3-21-77	Let the Little Boy Sing [with Bob Gaudio]	Stonebridge Music/ Four Seasons Music

3-21-77	Let Me Take You in My Arms Again...Stonebridge Music
3-21-77	You Don't Bring Me Flowers [with
	Alan and Marilyn Bergman].......Stonebridge Music/
	Threesome Music

3-21-77 Let Me Take You in My Arms Again...Stonebridge Music
3-21-77 You Don't Bring Me Flowers [with
         Alan and Marilyn Bergman].......Stonebridge Music/
                                         Threesome Music
5-6-77   Listen...........................Stonebridge Music
11-27-77 Dance of the Sabres................Stonebridge Music
11-28-77 Once in a While...................Stonebridge Music
11-28-77 As If............................Stonebridge Music
11-28-77 Desiree..........................Stonebridge Music
5-8-78   Heaven Can Wait..................Stonebridge Music
7-24-78 Remember Me.....................Stonebridge Music
7-24-78 Faithful Man.....................Stonebridge Music
7-24-78 I Seek the Night..................Stonebridge Music
7-24-78 You Baby (Ooh, Baby, Baby).........Stonebridge Music
7-24-78 C'est La Vie [with Gilbert Becaud]....Stonebridge Music
7-24-78 September Morn' [with Gilbert
         Becaud].........................Stonebridge Music
7-28-78 Memphis Flyer....................Stonebridge Music
11-29-78 Forever in Blue Jeans.............Stonebridge Music
11-29-78 Say Maybe........................Stonebridge Music
11-29-78 Diamond Girls....................Stonebridge Music
12-5-78 The Dancing Bumble Bee..........Stonebridge Music
12-14-79 Mama Don't Know [with Gilbert
         Becaud].........................Stonebridge Music
12-14-79 Jazz Time........................Stonebridge Music
12-31-79 That Kind........................Stonebridge Music
4-25-80 Amazed and Confused [with Richard
         Bennett].........................Stonebridge Music
4-25-80 America..........................Stonebridge Music
4-25-80 Love on the Rocks [with Burt
         Bacharach and Carole Bayer Sager]..Stonebridge Music
4-25-80 Summerlove [with Gilbert Becaud]....Stonebridge Music
4-25-80 Hello Again [with Alan Lindgren]....Stonebridge Music
4-25-80 Hey Louise [with Gilbert Becaud].....Stonebridge Music
4-25-80 Songs of Life [with Gilbert Becaud]...Stonebridge Music
4-25-80 Rainy Day Song [with Gilbert
         Becaud].........................Stonebridge Music
4-25-80 Only You [with Tom Hensley and
         Alan Lindgren]..................Stonebridge Music
5-5-80   Jerusalem........................Stonebridge Music
5-6-80   On the Robert E. Lee [with Gilbert
         Becaud].........................Stonebridge Music
11-17-80 Acapulco [with Doug Rhone]........Stonebridge Music
4-13-81 On the Way to the Sky [with Carole
         Bayer Sager]....................Stonebridge Music

10-15-81	Yesterday's Songs.....................Stonebridge Music
10-15-81	Guitar Heaven.......................Stonebridge Music
11-2-81	Right by You [with Richard Bennett and Doug Rhone].................Stonebridge Music
11-2-81	Save Me...........................Stonebridge Music
11-2-81	Be Mine Tonight....................Stonebridge Music
11-2-81	The Drifter........................Stonebridge Music
11-2-81	Fear of the Marketplace..............Stonebridge Music
8-26-82	Heartlight [with Burt Bacharach and Carole Bayer Sager]...............Stonebridge Music
8-26-82	You Don't Know Me [with Burt Bacharach and Carole Bayer Sager]..Stonebridge Music
9-23-82	I'm Alive [with David Foster]........Stonebridge Music Foster Frees Music
9-23-82	Hurricane [with Burt Bacharach and Carole Bayer Sager]...............Stonebridge Music
9-23-82	I'm Guilty [with Burt Bacharach and Carole Bayer Sager]...............Stonebridge Music
9-23-82	Lost Among the Stars [with Burt Bacharach and Carole Bayer Sager]..Stonebridge Music
9-23-82	In Ensenada [with Burt Bacharach and Carole Bayer Sager]...........Stonebridge Music
9-23-82	Front Page Story [with Burt Bacharach and Carole Bayer Sager]...........Stonebridge Music
9-23-82	Comin' Home......................Stonebridge Music
9-23-82	First You Have to Say You Love Me [with Michael Masser].............Stonebridge Music
11-25-83	Positive Vibes......................Stonebridge Music
11-25-83	Primitive..........................Stonebridge Music
11-25-83	It's a Trip (Go for the Moon).........Stonebridge Music
11-25-83	You Make It Feel Like Christmas......Stonebridge Music
11-25-83	Fire on the Tracks..................Stonebridge Music
11-25-83	Act Like a Man....................Stonebridge Music
3-13-84	You Are the Girl That I Dreamed Of [with Michael Masser].............Stonebridge Music
3-13-84	I'll Never Ask Again [with Michael Masser].........................Stonebridge Music
3-13-84	Do It for Yourself [with Michael Masser].........................Stonebridge Music
3-13-84	Brooklyn on a Saturday Night........Stonebridge Music
3-13-84	One by One.......................Stonebridge Music
3-13-84	What Was It Like for You, Marlene?...Stonebridge Music
3-13-84	Hit Man...........................Stonebridge Music
7-13-84	Turn Around [with Burt Bacharach and Carole Bayer Sager]...........Stonebridge Music

7-13-84	Sleep with Me Tonight [with Burt Bacharach and Carole Bayer Sager]..Stonebridge Music
7-13-84	Crazy [with Burt Bacharach and Carole Bayer Sager]...............Stonebridge Music
1-23-86	The Story of My Life...............Stonebridge Music
1-23-86	Falling..........................Stonebridge Music
1-23-86	I'm Saying I'm Sorry..............Stonebridge Music
1-23-86	Angel Above My Head..............Stonebridge Music
1-28-86	Dancing to the Party Next Door......Stonebridge Music
1-28-86	It Don't Seem Likely................Stonebridge Music
1-28-86	I'm Your Man....................Stonebridge Music
1-28-86	Long Nights, Hold On..............Stonebridge Music
1-28-86	Moonlight Rider...................Stonebridge Music
4-21-86	Headed for the Future [with Tom Hensley and Alan Lindgren].......Stonebridge Music
4-21-86	The Man You Need [with David Foster].........................Stonebridge Music/ Air Bear Music
4-21-86	I'll See You on the Radio (Laura) [with Burt Bacharach and Carole Bayer Sager]....................Stonebridge Music
4-21-86	Me Beside You [with Burt Bacharach and Carole Bayer Sager]...........Stonebridge Music
4-21-86	Lost in Hollywood [with Stevie Wonder].......................Stonebridge Music/ Jobete Music

No information is available regarding: four tracks left off of the *On the Way to the Sky* album ("It's All Right," "It's Gonna Be a Good Night," "The Revolutionary," "Another Sad Lament"); one track left off of *Headed for the Future* ("We're Doing It"); or his early country novelty "Ballad of the Super Stud (I Ain't Got No Trouble Getting It On)," which was featured in some of his pre-*Hot August Night* concerts. His first-ever composition, "Hear Them Bells," apparently exists only in his personal notes.

In addition, the following tracks are known to have been recorded in early 1983, and are thought to be part of an abortive album that was to have followed *Heartlight*:

"Motown Days" [duet with Diana Ross; recorded 2-1-83]
"No Expectation" [recorded 2-2-83]

"Back to California" [2-3-83]
"Maybe" [2-24-83]
"Marry Me" [3-3-83]
"Best of Intention" [3-7-83]
"Sing Out Tonight" [3-17-83]
"My Bouquet" [3-22-83]
"Either Way" [3-24-83]

Other songs known to exist: "Be Good to My Baby," "Christmas in Virginia," "He'll Make Her Mine," "I'll Deliver," and "Last Train to St. Tropez."

American Discography

SINGLE RELEASES

As Neil and Jack (Parker)

1962   You Are My Love at Last/What Will I Do [Duel 508]
1962   I'm Afraid/'Till You've Tried Love [Duel 512]

As Neil Diamond

1963   Clown Town/At Night [Columbia 4-42809]
1966   Solitary Man/Do It [Bang B-519]
1966   Cherry, Cherry/I'll Come Running [Bang B-528]
1966   I Got the Feeling (Oh No No)/The Boat That I Row [Bang B-536]
1967   You Got To Me/Someday Baby [Bang B-540]
1967   Girl, You'll Be a Woman Soon/You'll Forget [Bang B-542]
1967   I Thank the Lord for the Night Time/The Long Way Home [Bang B-547]
1967   Kentucky Woman/The Time Is Now [Bang B-551]
1968   New Orleans/Hanky Panky [Bang B-554]
1968   Red Red Wine/Red Rubber Ball [Bang B-556]
1968   Brooklyn Roads/Holiday Inn Blues [Uni 55065]
1968   Two-Bit Manchild/Broad Old Woman (6 A.M. Insanity) [Uni 55075]

221

1968 Sunday Sun/Honey-Drippin' Times [Uni 55084]

1969 Shilo/La Bamba [Bang B-561]

1969 Brother Love's Travelling Salvation Show/A Modern Day Version
        Of Love [Uni 55109]

1969 Sweet Caroline (Good Times Never Seemed So Good)/Dig In
        [Uni 55136]

1969 Holly Holy/Hurtin' You Don't Come Easy [Uni 55175]

1970 Shilo/La Bamba [Bang B-575]

1970 Until It's Time for You to Go/And the Singer Sings His Song
        [Uni 55204]

1970 Soolaimon (African Trilogy II)/And the Grass Won't Pay No
        Mind [Uni 55224]

1970 Solitary Man/The Time Is Now [Bang B-578]

1970 Cracklin' Rosie/Lordy [Uni 55250]

1970 He Ain't Heavy . . . He's My Brother/Free Life [Uni 55264]

1970 Do It/Hanky Panky [Bang B-580]

1971 I Am . . . I Said/Done Too Soon [Uni 55278]

1971 I'm a Believer/Crooked Street [Bang B-586]

1971 Stones/Crunchy Granola Suite [Uni 55310]

1972 Song Sung Blue/Gitchy Goomy [Uni 55326]

1972 Play Me/Porcupine Pie [Uni 55346]

1972 Walk on Water/High Rolling Man [Uni 55352]

1973 Cherry, Cherry [From *Hot August Night*]/Morningside (For My
        Children) [MCA-40017]

1973 The Long Way Home/Monday, Monday [Bang B-703]

1973 The Last Thing on My Mind/Canta Libre [MCA 40092]

1973 Be/Flight of the Gull [Columbia 4-45942]

1974 Skybird/Lonely Looking Sky [Columbia 4-45998]

1974 Longfellow Serenade/Rosemary's Wine [Columbia 3-10043]

1975 I've Been This Way Before/Reggae Strut [Columbia 3-10084]

1975 The Last Picasso/The Gift of Song [Columbia 3-10138]

1976 If You Know What I Mean/Street Life [Columbia 3-10366]

1976 Don't Think . . . Feel/Home Is a Wounded Heart [Columbia
        3-10405]

1976 Beautiful Noise/Signs [Columbia 3-10452]

1977 Song Sung Blue [From *Love at the Greek*; stereo version/mono
        version; Columbia AE7-1115]
        This is a disc-jockey-only single used to promote the release
        of *Love at the Greek*.

1977 Desiree/Once in a While [Columbia 3-10657]

1977 I'm Glad You're Here with Me Tonight/Dance of the Sabres
        [Columbia 3-10720]
        Never released but was given a catalog number during the
        planning stages.

As Barbra (Streisand) and Neil

1978   You Don't Bring Me Flowers/Instrumental version by Alan
        Lindgren [Columbia 3-10840]

As Neil Diamond

1979   Forever in Blue Jeans/Remember Me [Columbia 3-10897]
1979   Say Maybe/Diamond Girls [Columbia 3-10945]
1979   September Morn'/I'm a Believer [1979 version; Columbia 1-11175]
1980   The Good Lord Loves You/Jazz Time [Columbia 1-11232]
1980   Love on the Rocks/Acapulco [Capitol 4939]
1981   Hello Again/Amazed and Confused [Capitol 4960]
1981   America/Songs of Life [Capitol 4994]
1981   Yesterday's Songs/Guitar Heaven [Columbia 18-02604]
1982   On the Way to the Sky/Save Me [Columbia 18-02712]
1982   Be Mine Tonight/Right by You [Columbia 18-02928]
1982   Heartlight/You Don't Know Me [Columbia 38-03219]
1982   Heartlight [special one-sided single; Columbia CNR-03345]
1983   I'm Alive/Lost Among the Stars [Columbia 38-03503]
1983   I'm Alive [special one-sided single; Columbia CNR-03572]
1983   Front Page Story/I'm Guilty [Columbia 38-03801]
1984   Turn Around/Brooklyn on a Saturday Night [Columbia
        38-04541]
1984   Sleep with Me Tonight/One by One [Columbia 38-04646]
1984   You Make It Feel Like Christmas/Crazy [Columbia 38-04719]
1986   Headed for the Future/Angel [Columbia 38-05889]
1986   The Story of My Life/Love Doesn't Live Here Anymore
        [Columbia 38-06136]

REISSUED SINGLES

1973   Cherry, Cherry/Girl, You'll Be a Woman Soon [Solid Gold/Bang
        SG-105]
1973   I Thank the Lord for the Night Time/Kentucky Woman [Solid
        Gold/Bang SG-106]
1973   Shilo/Red Red Wine [Solid Gold/Bang SG-107]
1973   Solitary Man/I'm a Believer [Solid Gold/Bang SG-108]
1973   I Got the Feeling (Oh No No)/Do It [Solid Gold/Bang SG-109]
1973   Holly Holy/Soolaimon (African Trilogy II) [MCA 60017; black/
        rainbow label]
1978   Holly Holy/Soolaimon (African Trilogy II) [MCA 60017; tan
        label]
1981   Holly Holy/Soolaimon (African Trilogy II) [MCA 60017; clouds/
        rainbow label]

1973   Cracklin' Rosie/He Ain't Heavy . . . He's My Brother [MCA
        60018; black/rainbow label]
1973   Cracklin' Rosie/He Ain't Heavy . . . He's My Brother [MCA
        60018; tan label]
1973   Cracklin' Rosie/He Ain't Heavy . . . He's My Brother [MCA
        60018; clouds/rainbow label]
1973   I Am . . . I Said/Done Too Soon [MCA 60019; black/rainbow
        label]
1978   I Am . . . I Said/Done Too Soon [MCA 60019; tan label]
1981   I Am . . . I Said/Done Too Soon [MCA 60019; clouds/rainbow
        label]
1973   Sweet Caroline (Good Times Never Seemed So Good)/Brother
        Love's Travelling Salvation Show [MCA 60032; black/
        rainbow label]
1978   Sweet Caroline (Good Times Never Seemed So Good)/Brother
        Love's Travelling Salvation Show [MCA 60032; tan label]
1981   Sweet Caroline (Good Times Never Seemed So Good)/Brother
        Love's Travelling Salvation Show [MCA 60032; clouds/
        rainbow label]
1973   Song Sung Blue/Gitchy Goomy [MCA 60116; black/rainbow
        label]
1978   Song Sung Blue/Gitchy Goomy [MCA 60116; tan label]
1981   Song Sung Blue/Gitchy Goomy [MCA 60116; clouds/rainbow
        label]
1975   Longfellow Serenade/Be [Columbia Hall of Fame 13-33265; red,
        white, and black label]
1985   Longfellow Serenade/Be [Columbia Hall of Fame 13-33265; silver
        and black label]
1978   Desiree/Beautiful Noise [Columbia Hall of Fame 13-33352; red,
        white, and black label]
1978   Desiree/Beautiful Noise [Columbia Hall of Fame 13-33352; silver
        and black label]
1979   You Don't Bring Me Flowers [by Barbra and Neil]/Forever in Blue
        Jeans [Columbia Hall of Fame 13-33382; red, white, and
        black label]
1985   You Don't Bring Me Flowers [by Barbra and Neil]/Forever in Blue
        Jeans [Columbia Hall of Fame 13-33382; silver and black
        label]
1980   September Morn'/Say Maybe [Columbia Hall of Fame 13-33391;
        white and black label]
1985   September Morn'/Say Maybe [Columbia Hall of Fame 13-33391;
        silver and black label]
1983   Love on the Rocks/Acapulco [Capitol 4939; purple label]
1985   Love on the Rocks/Acapulco [Capitol 4939; tri-color border
        label]

1983   Hello Again/Amazed and Confused [Capitol 4960; purple label]
1985   Hello Again/Amazed and Confused [Capitol 4960; tri-color
            border label]
1983   America/Songs of Life [Capitol 4994; purple label]
1985   America/Songs of Life [Capitol 4994; tri-color border label]
1985   Heartlight/Yesterday's Songs [Columbia Hall of Fame 13-05486;
            silver and black label; "hip-pocket record"]
1968   Girl, You'll Be a Woman Soon/Cherry, Cherry [HP-5]
1968   You Got to Me/Solitary Man [HP-17]
1968   Hip-Pocket Promotional Five-Pack [HP 5-Pack 120-1338 PX;
            includes the You Got To Me/Solitary Man disc, which is
            numbered the same as above]

ALBUM RELEASES

1966   *The Feel of Neil Diamond* [Bang BLP-214; mono; gun label]
1966   *The Feel of Neil Diamond* [Bang BLP-214; stereo; gun label]
            Side One: Solitary Man/Cherry, Cherry/I Got the Feeling (Oh
            No No)/La Bamba/Red Rubber Ball/Hanky Panky
            Side Two: I'll Come Running/Do It/Red Red Wine/Someday
            Baby/New Orleans/Crooked Street

1967   *Just for You* [Bang BLP-217; mono; gun label]
1967   *Just for You* [Bang BLPS-217; stereo; gun label]
            Side One: Girl, You'll Be a Woman Soon/The Long Way Home/
            Red Red Wine/You'll Forget/The Boat That I Row/Cherry,
            Cherry
            Side Two: I'm a Believer/Shilo/You Got to Me/Solitary Man/I
            Thank the Lord for the Night Time

1968   *Neil Diamond's Greatest Hits* [Bang BLP-219; mono]
1968   *Neil Diamond's Greatest Hits* [Bang BLPS-219; stereo; gun label]
1973   *Neil Diamond's Greatest Hits* [Bang BLPS-219; stereo; sky label]
            Side One: Cherry, Cherry/I Got the Feeling (Oh No No)/New
            Orleans/Girl, You'll Be a Woman Soon/Do It/You Got to
            Me
            Side Two: Solitary Man/Kentucky Woman/I Thank the Lord for
            the Night Time/Red Red Wine/Hanky Panky/The Boat
            That I Row

1968   *Shilo* [Bang BLPS-221; gun label]
1973   *Shilo* [Bang BLPS-221; sky label]
            Side One: Shilo/Kentucky Woman/Girl, You'll Be a Woman
            Soon/You Got to Me/Monday, Monday/Cherry, Cherry
            Side Two: Solitary Man/I'm a Believer/Red Red Wine/I Thank
            the Lord for the Night Time/I'll Come Running/I Got the
            Feeling (Oh No No)

1968 *Velvet Gloves and Spit* [Uni 73030; original portrait cover]
1968 *Velvet Gloves and Spit* [Uni 73030; artist's rendition cover]
1971 *Velvet Gloves and Spit* [Uni 93030; artist's rendition cover]
1973 *Velvet Gloves and Spit* [MCA 2010; artist's rendition cover; black/
         rainbow label]
1978 *Velvet Gloves and Spit* [MCA 2010; artist's rendition cover; tan
         label]
1981 *Velvet Gloves and Spit* [MCA 2010; artist's rendition cover;
         clouds/rainbow label]
1983 *Velvet Gloves and Spit* [MCA 37056; artist's rendition cover;
         clouds/rainbow label]
1985 *Velvet Gloves and Spit* [MCA 1603; artist's rendition cover;
         clouds/rainbow label]
         Side One: Two-Bit Manchild/A Modern Day Version of Love/
         Honey-Drippin' Times/The Pot Smoker's Song/Brooklyn
         Roads
         Side Two: Shilo [1968 version]/Sunday Sun/Holiday Inn Blues/
         Practically Newborn/Knackelflerg/Merry-Go-Round

1969 *Brother Love's Travelling Salvation Show* [UNI 73047; original
         medicine show wagon cover]
         Side One: Brother Love's Travelling Salvation Show/Dig In/River
         Runs, Newgrown Plums/Juliet/Long Gone/And the Grass
         Won't Pay No Mind
         Side Two: Glory Road/Deep in the Morning/If I Never Knew
         Your Name/Memphis Streets/You're So Sweet, Horseflies
         Keep Hangin' 'Round Your Face/Hurtin' You Don't Come
         Easy
1969 *Brother Love's Travelling Salvation Show/Sweet Caroline* [Uni
         73047; original medicine show wagon cover]
1969 *Brother Love's Travelling Salvation Show/Sweet Caroline* [Uni
         73047; portrait cover]
1971 *Brother Love's Travelling Salvation Show/Sweet Caroline* [Uni
         93047; portrait cover]
1973 *Brother Love's Travelling Salvation Show/Sweet Caroline* [MCA
         2011; portrait cover; black/rainbow label]
1978 *Brother Love's Travelling Salvation Show/Sweet Caroline* [MCA
         2011; portrait cover; tan label]
1981 *Brother Love's Travelling Salvation Show/Sweet Caroline* [MCA
         2011; portrait cover; clouds/rainbow label]
1983 *Brother Love's Travelling Salvation Show/Sweet Caroline* [MCA
         37057; portrait cover; clouds/rainbow label]
1985 *Brother Love's Travelling Salvation Show/Sweet Caroline* [MCA
         1604; portrait cover; clouds/rainbow label]
         Side One: [Same as original album]
         Side Two: [Sweet Caroline (Good Times Never Seemed So Good)
         added as last track]

1969 *Touching You, Touching Me* [Uni 73071]
1971 *Touching You, Touching Me* [Uni 93071]
1973 *Touching You, Touching Me* [MCA 2006; black/rainbow label]
1978 *Touching You, Touching Me* [MCA 2006; tan label]
1981 *Touching You, Touching Me* [MCA 2006; clouds/rainbow label]
1983 *Touching You, Touching Me* [MCA 37058; clouds/rainbow label]
1985 *Touching You, Touching Me* [MCA 1605; clouds/rainbow label]
Side One: Everybody's Talking/Mr. Bojangles/Smokey Lady/
Holly Holy
Side Two: Both Sides Now/And the Singer Sings His Song/Ain't
No Way/New York Boy/Until It's Time for You to Go

1970 *It's Happening!* [MCA Special Markets 734727]
Side One: [Tracks by Diana Ross and the Supremes]
Side Two: Brooklyn Roads/Long Gone/Glory Road/And the
Grass Won't Pay No Mind/If I Never Knew Your Name

1970 *Do It* [Bang BLPS-224; gun label]
1973 *Do It* [Bang BLPS-224; sky label]
Side One: Do It/Solitary Man/Red Red Wine/I'll Come
Running/Love to Love/Someday Baby
Side Two: Shot Down/Crooked Street/The Boat That I Row/I'm
a Believer/You'll Forget/Hanky Panky

1970 *Gold—Recorded Live at the Troubador* [Uni 73084]
1971 *Gold—Recorded Live at the Troubador* [Uni 93084]
1973 *Gold—Recorded Live at the Troubador* [MCA 2007; black/
rainbow label]
1978 *Gold—Recorded Live at the Troubador* [MCA 2007; tan label]
1981 *Gold—Recorded Live at the Troubador* [MCA 2007; clouds/
rainbow label]
1983 *Gold—Recorded Live at the Troubador* [MCA 37209; clouds/
rainbow label]
1985 *Gold—Recorded Live at the Troubador* [MCA 1683; clouds/
rainbow label]
Side One: Lordy/Both Sides Now/Solitary Man/Holly Holy/
Cherry, Cherry
Side Two: Kentucky Woman/Sweet Caroline/I Thank the Lord
for the Night Time/And the Singer Sings His Song/Brother
Love's Travelling Salvation Show

1970 *Tap Root Manuscript* [Uni 73092]
1971 *Tap Root Manuscript* [Uni 93092]
1973 *Tap Root Manuscript* [MCA 2013; black/rainbow label]
1978 *Tap Root Manuscript* [MCA 2013; tan label]
1981 *Tap Root Manuscript* [MCA 2013; clouds/rainbow label]
1983 *Tap Root Manuscript* [MCA 37196; clouds/rainbow label]
1985 *Tap Root Manuscript* [MCA 1671; clouds/rainbow label]

Side One: Cracklin' Rosie/Free Life/Coldwater Morning/Done
Too Soon/He Ain't Heavy . . . He's My Brother
Side Two: The African Trilogy/Childsong/I Am the Lion/
Madrigal/Soolaimon/Missa/The African Suite/Childsong
[reprise]

1985   *Tap Root Manuscript* [MCA D-37196 DIDX-273; compact disc]

1971   *Neil Diamond Disc Jockey Sampler* [UNI ND-11]
[Presented to participants of the thirteenth annual National
Association of Record Merchandisers (NARM) Convention in
Los Angeles from February 26–March 3, 1971.]
Side One: Sweet Caroline (Good Times Never Seemed So Good)/
Brother Love's Travelling Salvation Show/Brooklyn Roads/
Mr. Bojangles/Both Sides Now/Shilo
Side Two: Until It's Time For You to Go/Cracklin' Rosie/New
York Boy/Solitary Man [from *Gold*]/Cherry, Cherry [from
Gold]/I Thank the Lord for the Night Time [from *Gold*]

1971   *Stones* [UNI 93106]
1973   *Stones* [MCA 2008; black/rainbow label]
1978   *Stones* [MCA 2008; tan label]
1981   *Stones* [MCA 2008; clouds/rainbow label]
1983   *Stones* [MCA 37195; clouds/rainbow label]
1985   *Stones* [MCA 1670; clouds/rainbow label]
Side One: I Am . . . I Said/The Last Thing on My Mind/
Husbands and Wives/Chelsea Morning/Crunchy Granola
Suite
Side Two: Stones/If You Go Away/Suzanne/I Think It's Gonna
Rain Today/I Am . . . I Said [reprise]

1971   *Stones Open-End Interview Album* [UNI U-7-1913]
[Diamond introduces tracks from the *Stones* album, telling
of their significance to him, and briefly discusses his career.]
Side One: [Diamond talks]/I Am . . . I Said/[Diamond talks]/
The Last Thing on My Mind/[Diamond talks]/Chelsea
Morning/[Diamond talks]/Stones
Side Two: [Diamond talks]/I Think It's Gonna Rain Today/
[Diamond talks]/I Am . . . I Said [reprise]

1972   *Moods* [UNI 93136]
1973   *Moods* [MCA 2005; black/rainbow label]
1978   *Moods* [MCA 2005; tan label]
1981   *Moods* [MCA 2005; clouds/rainbow label]
1983   *Moods* [MCA 37194; clouds/rainbow label]
1985   *Moods* [MCA 1669; clouds/rainbow label]
Side One: Song Sung Blue/Porcupine Pie/High Rolling Man/
Canta Libre/Captain Sunshine

       Side Two: Play Me/Gitchy Goomy/Walk on Water/Theme
       [orchestral]/Prelude in E Minor/Morningside (For My
       Children)

1985   *Moods* [MCA D-37194 DIDX-272; compact disc]

1972   *Double Gold* [Bang BDS-2-227; gun label]
1973   *Double Gold* [Bang BDS-2-227; sky label]
       Side One: I'm a Believer/Monday, Monday/The Long Way
       Home/I'll Come Running/Red Red Wine
       Side Two: Solitary Man/New Orleans/Cherry, Cherry/Someday
       Baby/Girl, You'll Be a Woman Soon
       Side Three: Shilo/Do It/I Got the Feeling (Oh No No)/Love to
       Love/I Thank the Lord for the Night Time
       Side Four: Kentucky Woman/The Boat That I Row/You Got to
       Me/You'll Forget/Crooked Street/Shot Down

1973   *Hot August Night* [MCA 2-8000; black/rainbow label]
1978   *Hot August Night* [MCA 2-8000; tan label]
1980   *Hot August Night* [Mobile Fidelity MFSL-2-024; half-speed
       mastered audiophile disc]
1981   *Hot August Night* [MCA 2-8000; clouds/rainbow label]
1983   *Hot August Night* [MCA 2-10013; clouds/rainbow label]
1985   *Hot August Night* [MCA 2-6896; clouds/rainbow label]
       Side One: Prologue/Crunchy Granola Suite/Done Too Soon/
       Solitary Man/Cherry, Cherry/Sweet Caroline (Good Times
       Never Seemed So Good)
       Side Two: Porcupine Pie/You're So Sweet, Horseflies Keep
       Hangin' 'Round Your Face/Red Red Wine/Soggy Pretzels/
       And the Grass Won't Pay No Mind/Shilo/Girl, You'll Be a
       Woman Soon
       Side Three: Play Me/Canta Libre/Morningside (For My
       Children)/Song Sung Blue/Cracklin' Rosie
       Side Four: Holly Holy/I Am . . . I Said/Soolaimon/Brother
       Love's Travelling Salvation Show

1985   *Hot August Night* [MCA D2-6896 DIDX-274-275; compact disc]

1973   *Rainbow* [MCA 2103; original artist's rendition cover; black/
       rainbow label]
1973   *Rainbow* [MCA 2103; portrait cover; black/rainbow label]
1978   *Rainbow* [MCA 2103; portrait cover; tan label]
1981   *Rainbow* [MCA 2103; portrait cover; clouds/rainbow label]
1983   *Rainbow* [MCA 37059; portrait cover; clouds/rainbow label]
1985   *Rainbow* [MCA 1606; portrait cover; clouds/rainbow label]
       Side One: Everybody's Talking/Both Sides Now/Husbands and
       Wives/Chelsea Morning/Until It's Time for You to Go/The
       Last Thing on My Mind

1973   *Jonathan Livingston Seagull* [Columbia KS 32550]
1981   *Jonathan Livingston Seagull* [Columbia HC 42550; half-speed
            mastered audiophile disc]
1985   *Jonathan Livingston Seagull* [Columbia JS 32550]
        Side One: Prologue [overture]/Be/Flight of the Gull/Dear
            Father/Skybird [instrumental]/Lonely Looking Sky
        Side Two: The Odyssey (Be/Lonely Looking Sky/Dear Father)/
            Anthem/Be [instrumental]/Skybird/Dear Father
            [instrumental]/Be [finale]
1985   *Jonathan Livingston Seagull* [Columbia CK 32550; compact
            disc]

1974   *His Twelve Greatest Hits* [MCA 2106; black/rainbow cover]
1978   *His Twelve Greatest Hits* [MCA 2106; tan label]
1980   *His Twelve Greatest Hits* [Direct Disk Labs SD-11612; audiophile
            disc]
1981   *His Twelve Greatest Hits* [MCA 5219; clouds/rainbow label]
1983   *His Twelve Greatest Hits* [MCA 37252; clouds/rainbow label]
1985   *His Twelve Greatest Hits* [MCA 1489; clouds/rainbow label]
        Side One: Sweet Caroline (Good Times Never Seemed So Good)/
            Brother Love's Travelling Salvation Show/Shilo/Holly Holy/
            Brooklyn Roads/Cracklin' Rosie
        Side Two: Play Me/Done Too Soon/Stones/Song Sung Blue/
            Soolaimon (African Trilogy II)/I Am . . . I Said
1985   *His Twelve Greatest Hits* [MCA D-37252 DIDX-271; compact
            disc]

1974   *Serenade* [Columbia PC 32919]
        Side One: I've Been This Way Before/Rosemary's Wine/Lady
            Magdelene/The Last Picasso
        Side Two: Longfellow Serenade/Yes I Will/Reggae Strut/The
            Gift of Song
1986   *Serenade* [Columbia CK 32919; compact disc]

1976   *Beautiful Noise* [Columbia PC 33965]
1985   *Beautiful Noise* [Columbia JC 33965]
        Side One: Beautiful Noise/Stargazer/Lady-Oh/Don't Think . . .
            Feel/Surviving the Life/If You Know What I Mean
        Side Two: Street Life/Home Is a Wounded Heart/Jungletime/
            Signs/Dry Your Eyes
1986   *Beautiful Noise* [Columbia CK 33965; compact disc]

1976   *And the Singer Sings His Song* [MCA 2227; black/rainbow label]
1978   *And the Singer Sings His Song* [MCA 2227; tan label]
1981   *And the Singer Sings His Song* [MCA 2227; clouds/rainbow label]
1983   *And the Singer Sings His Song* [MCA 37060; clouds/rainbow
            label]

1985   *And the Singer Sings His Song* [MCA 1607; clouds/rainbow
        label]
        Side One: Captain Sunshine/Free Life/Hurtin' You Don't Come
        Easy/Coldwater Morning/Walk on Water/Stones
        Side Two: And the Grass Won't Pay No Mind/If I Never Knew
        Your Name/Merry-Go-Round/Brooklyn Roads/And the
        Singer Sings His Song

1976   *Love at the Greek* [Columbia KG2 34404]
1985   *Love at the Greek* [Columbia KC2 34404]
        Side One: Street Life/Kentucky Woman/Sweet Caroline (Good
        Times Never Seemed So Good)/The Last Picasso/
        Longfellow Serenade
        Side Two: Beautiful Noise/Lady-Oh/Stargazer/If You Know
        What I Mean/Surviving the Life
        Side Three: Glory Road/Song Sung Blue/Holly Holy/Brother
        Love's Travelling Salvation Show
        Side Four: *Jonathan Livingston Seagull* (Be/Dear Father/Lonely
        Looking Sky/Sanctus/Skybird/Be [encore])/I've Been This
        Way Before
1987   *Love at the Greek* [Columbia CGK 34404; compact disc]

1977   *I'm Glad You're Here with Me Tonight* [Columbia JC 34990]
        Side One: God Only Knows/Let Me Take You in My Arms
        Again/Once in a While/Let the Little Boy Sing/I'm Glad
        You're Here with Me Tonight
        Side Two: Lament in D Minor/Dance of the Sabres/Desiree/As
        If/You Don't Bring Me Flowers [solo version]/Free Man in
        Paris
1986   *I'm Glad You're Here with Me Tonight* [Columbia Ck 34990;
        compact disc]

1978   *You Don't Bring Me Flowers* [Columbia FC 35625]
1981   *You Don't Bring Me Flowers* [Columbia HC 45625; half-speed
        mastered audiophile disc]
        Side One: The American Popular Song/Forever in Blue Jeans/
        Remember Me/You've Got Your Troubles (I've Got Mine)/
        You Don't Bring Me Flowers [duet version]
        Side Two: The Dancing Bumble Bee (Bumble Boogie)/Mothers
        and Daughters, Fathers and Sons/Memphis Flyer/Say Maybe/
        Diamond Girls
1986   *You Don't Bring Me Flowers* [Columbia CK 35625; compact disc]

1978   *Early Classics* [Frogking/CBS H 30023]
        [Columbia House Record Club package for its membership.
        Forerunner to later 1960s reissue album.]

232 DIAMOND

Side One: Cherry, Cherry/I Got the Feeling [Oh No No]/Shilo/
Girl, You'll Be a Woman Soon/Do It/You Got to Me
Side Two: Solitary Man/Kentucky Woman/I Thank the Lord for
the Night Time/Red Red Wine/The Boat That I Row/I'm a
Believer

1979 *September Morn'* [Columbia FC 36121]
1985 *September Morn'* [Columbia PC 36121]
Side One: September Morn'/Mama Don't Know/That Kind/Jazz
Time/The Good Lord Loves You
Side Two: Dancing in the Streets/The Shelter of Your Arms/I'm
a Believer [1979 version]/The Sun Ain't Gonna Shine
Anymore/Stagger Lee
1986 *September Morn'* [Columbia CK 36121; compact disc]

1980 *The Jazz Singer* [Capitol SWAV-12120; original raised-lettering
cover; custom *Jazz Singer* label]
1981 *The Jazz Singer* [Mobile Fidelity MFSL-1-071; half-speed
mastered audiophile disc]
1983 *The Jazz Singer* [Capitol SWAV-12120; flat cover; purple label]
1985 *The Jazz Singer* [Capitol SWAV-12120; flat cover; tri-color border
label]
Side One: America/Adon Olam/You Baby/Love on the Rocks/
Amazed and Confused/On the Robert E. Lee/Summerlove
Side Two: Hello Again/Acapulco/Hey Louise/Songs of Life/
Jerusalem/Kol Nidre/My Name Is Yussel [theme]/America
[reprise]
1985 *The Jazz Singer* [Capitol CDP-7-460262; compact disc]

1981 *On the Way to the Sky* [Columbia TC 37628]
1981 *On the Way to the Sky* [Columbia HC 47628; half-speed mastered
audiophile disc]
Side One: Yesterday's Songs/On the Way to the Sky/Right by
You/Only You/Save Me/Be Mine Tonight
Side Two: The Drifter/Fear of the Marketplace/Rainy Day Song/
Guitar Heaven/Love Burns
1986 *On the Way to the Sky* [Columbia CK 37628; compact disc]

1981 *Love Songs* [MCA 5239; clouds/rainbow label]
1983 *Love Songs* [MCA 37253; clouds/rainbow label]
1985 *Love Songs* [MCA 1490; clouds/rainbow label]
Side One: Theme [orchestral]/Stones/If You Go Away/The Last
Thing on My Mind/Coldwater Morning/Juliet/Both Sides
Now
Side Two: Play Me/Hurtin' You Don't Come Easy/Husbands and
Wives/Until It's Time for You to Go/And the Grass Won't
Pay No Mind/A Modern Day Version of Love/Suzanne

1982 *Heartlight* [Columbia TC 38359]

1982 *Heartlight* [Columbia HC 48359; half-speed mastered audiophile disc]

1985 *Heartlight* [Columbia QC 38359]
Side One: Heartlight/I'm Alive/I'm Guilty/Hurricane/Lost Among the Stars
Side Two: In Ensenada/A Fool for You/Star Flight/Front Page Story/Coming Home/First You Have to Say You Love Me

1986 *Heartlight* [Columbia CK 38359; compact disc]

1985 *Heartlight* [Columbia AS 99-1586]
[Special one-sided picture disc (12") presented to disc jockeys in gratitude for the song's success. Side A has the *Heartlight* LP cover shot and the song; side B has a plain brown background which states "Thank You For Your Fantastic Support Of *Heartlight*. Happy Holidays and Best Wishes for 1983—Neil Diamond."]

1983 *His Twelve Greatest Hits Volume Two* [Columbia TC 38068]
Side One: Beautiful Noise/Hello Again/Forever in Blue Jeans/ September Morn'/Desiree/You Don't Bring Me Flowers
Side Two: America/Be/Longfellow Serenade/If You Know What I Mean/Yesterday's Songs/Love on the Rocks

1985 *His Twelve Greatest Hits Volume Two* [Columbia HC 48068; half-speed mastered audiophile disc]

1985 *His Twelve Greatest Hits Volume Two* [Columbia CK 38068; compact disc]

1983 *Classics—The Early Years* [Columbia PC 38792]
Side One: Kentucky Woman/Cherry, Cherry/Solitary Man/You Got to Me/I Got the Feeling (Oh No No)/I Thank the Lord for the Night Time
Side Two: I'm a Believer/Girl, You'll Be a Woman Soon/Shilo/ Do It/Red Red Wine/The Boat That I Row

1986 *Classics—The Early Years* [Columbia CK 38792; compact disc]

1984 *Primitive* [Columbia QC 39199]

1984 *Primitive* [Columbia 9C9-39915 S1; picture disc]
Side One: Turn Around/Primitive/Fire on the Tracks/Brooklyn on a Saturday Night/Sleep with Me Tonight/Crazy
Side Two: My Time with You/Love's Own Song/It's a Trip (Go for the Moon)/You Make It Feel Like Christmas/One By One

1986 *Primitive* [Columbia CK 39199; compact disc]

1986 *Headed for the Future* [Columbia OC 40368]
Side One: Headed for the Future/The Man You Need/I'll See You on the Radio (Laura)/Stand Up for Love/It Should Have Been Me
Side Two: Lost in Hollywood/The Story of My Life/Angel/Me Beside You/Love Doesn't Live Here Anymore

1986 *Headed for the Future* [Columbia CK 40368; compact disc]

VARIOUS ARTIST COMPILATIONS

Any performer who began his career in the 1960s and has enjoyed the longevity Neil Diamond has is a safe bet to be on as many different various artist albums as Diamond is. Because there are so many, many more than space or time allows, we feature here only those which were either record company samplers or TV-advertised discs. Others do exist; especially from radio stations in the late 1960s and early 1970s, when a station having its own greatest hits album was the goal of any competitive program director. As such, "Solitary Man," "Cherry, Cherry," "Kentucky Woman," or "I Thank the Lord for the Night Time" made their way onto literally hundreds of these types of albums. There are several military records which include those four tracks and existed as radio shows over the Armed Forces Radio Network.

1967   *Golden Hits From the Gang at Bang* [Bang LP-215]
        Includes "Solitary Man," "Cherry, Cherry," "Monday, Monday," and "Red Rubber Ball"

1967   *The "In" Sound—November 13, 1967* [U.S. Army USA—1S69]
        Includes "Kentucky Woman"

1967   *KHJ 30 Boss Goldens 30* [Pacer 93]
        Includes "Girl, You'll Be a Woman Soon"

1968   *Chartbusters* [Harmony/CBS H 30023]
        A *must* find—it contains a third 1963 Columbia song, "I've Never Been the Same," which was previously unreleased; also includes "Clown Town"

1968   *Bang and Shout Super Hits* [Bang LPS-220]
        Includes "Cherry, Cherry"

1968   *SUPERstars—superHITS Volume Two* [Columbia Musical Treasuries DS-400]
        Includes "Kentucky Woman"

1969   *Do It Now* [First Vibration 1001]

1970   *Do It Now* [Ronco LP 1001]
        Anti-drug abuse benefit album includes "Mr. Bojangles"

1970   *24 Solid Hits* [Crystal LP-506]
        Includes "I Got the Feeling [Oh No No]"

1970   *24 Happening Hits* [Crystal LP-900]
        Includes "Cherry, Cherry"

1970   *72 Top Original Hits by the Original Stars* [Columbia Special Products C4-10567]
        Four-album boxed set includes "Cherry, Cherry"

1972   *20 Dynamic Hits Volume Two* [K-Tel TU-223]
        Refugee benefit album includes "Until It's Time for You to Go"

1978   *The Last Waltz* sampler album [Warner Brothers PRO-A-737]
        Special record released only to disc jockeys features the
        performances of "Dry Your Eyes" and Diamond joining in
        on "I Shall Be Released"
1979   *Columbia's 21 Top 20* [Columbia A2S-700]
        Year-end sampler album includes "Forever in Blue Jeans"
        and Barbra and Neil's "You Don't Bring Me Flowers"
1980   *Hitline '80!* [Columbia A2S-890]
        Year-end sampler album includes "September Morn' "
1981   *The Elite* [K-Tel TU-3000]
        Includes "Longfellow Serenade"
1982   *Columbia's 24 Hits in the Top 20 for 1982!*
        Year-end sampler includes "Yesterday's Songs" and
        "Heartlight"